The State, Democracy and Globalization

The State, Democracy and Globalization

Roger King
and
Gavin Kendall

First published 2004 by
PALGRAVE MACMILLAN
Houndmills, Basingstoke, Hampshire RG21 6XS and
175 Fifth Avenue, New York, N.Y. 10010
Companies and representatives throughout the world

PALGRAVE MACMILLAN is the global academic imprint of the Palgrave Macmillan division of St. Martin's Press, LLC and of Palgrave Macmillan Ltd. Macmillan® is a registered trademark in the United States, United Kingdom and other countries. Palgrave is a registered trademark in the European Union and other countries.

ISBN 0–333–96911–1 hardback
ISBN 0–333–96912–X paperback

This book is printed on paper suitable for recycling and made from fully managed and sustained forest sources.

A catalogue record for this book is available from the British Library.

Library of Congress Cataloging-in-Publication Data
King, Roger, 1945–
    The state, democracy and globalization/Roger King and Gavin Kendall.
      p. cm.
    Includes bibliographical references and index.
     ISBN 0–333–96911–1   ISBN 0–333–96912–X (pbk.)
      1. Democracy. 2. Liberalism. 3. Decentralization in government
   4. Supranationalism. 5. Globalization. 6. Sovereignty. I. Kendall, Gavin. II. Title.

JC423.K47 2003
320.1—dc22   2003060864

10 9 8 7 6 5 4 3 2 1
13 12 11 10 09 08 07 06 05 04

Printed and bound in Great Britain by
Creative Print & Design (Wales), Ebbw Vale

Contents

List of Boxes

Acknowledgements

We are very grateful to Mark Bahnisch, Clive Bean, Jeremy Kendall, Kate Kendall, Trischa Kendall, Steven Kennedy, Mike Michael, Michael Moran, Katherine Sheehan, Zlatko Skrbis, Gary Whickam and Ian Woodward for reading early parts of the draft.

We are also grateful to Queensland University of Technology (QUT), and the University of the Sunshine Coast, in Queensland, Australia, for the periods that Roger King spent as Visiting Professor at the two universities in 2001 and 2002, and which provided the basis for the collaboration for this book. Stuart Cunningham, in the Faculty of Creative Industries at QUT, is thanked particularly for facilitating the involvement of Gavin Kendall as a joint author.

Battle, East Sussex, England   Roger King
Brisbane, Australia   Gavin Kendall

Chapter 1

Why Study the State?

Challenges to the nation state
The market and the state
Some key terms
Legitimacy
The following chapters

The notion of 'the state' is associated with the most authoritative and dominant institutional concentrations of power found within nations. The coupling of the term 'nation' to 'state' – thus 'nation state' – recognizes that state agencies are for the most part located within clearly delineated territories that exhibit popular signs and sentiments of national identity (such as flags, money, armies, and sporting teams). Yet, rather like the iceberg, we suspect that there is more to the state than meets the eye. It conjures up an image of a slightly mysterious and, at times, a rather fearsome entity. There is, if you like, a secretive side to it, one that perhaps most people recognize as inevitable for maintaining the security and protection of its citizens.

The institutions that make up the state in one of the predominant forms of rule worldwide – the liberal democratic one – comprise many that are quite visible, such as parliamentary and similar assemblies whose members have been elected by popular vote, and governments and ministers drawn from these representatives (although some liberal democracies, including the US, do not have governments drawn from assemblies). They include also the offices of formal heads of state, such as presidents or monarchs, who often undertake 'dignified' responsibilities, such as opening new sessions of parliament and other ceremonies, and who may or may not have real or substantive political power. But they also contain institutions that are purposefully not, for the most part, elected or representative, such as the police, governmental administrative structures, the intelligence services, and, in most countries, the judiciary. Most of the positions in such agencies are filled on an appointed basis, in some cases appointed directly by the head of government. But state authority can extend further than this, and include a range of bodies, such as occupational or sector associations, who may be said to function with powers (such as determining the qualifications that need to be obtained in order

1

to practice a profession, as with medicine) that have been delegated by more official state bodies, such as governmental departments. All these institutions function 'legally', within rules and practices found in formal constitutions, or as contained in varieties of statutes and precedents.

However, increasingly in many countries, even the non-elected and non-dignified parts of the state are becoming more visible, in the sense of being open to public scrutiny. In part this stems from the democratic idea that all those who seek to exercise power in the name of public authority or the state should be held to be accountable for it, usually to governments or to parliamentary assemblies. We live no longer, if we ever did truly, in age of deference when we trusted politicians, state bureaucrats, or professionals such as doctors or architects, to act for us honestly and disinterestedly on the basis of strongly held values. Too many scandals have occurred, and too many risks for individuals are involved, for people to trust any longer in the altruistic motivations of such professionals and in the secretive methods of the associations that represent them.

The factors underlying the steady movement of the modern state into the spotlight are several. One is the remorseless rise of electoral or majoritarian forms of democratic representation, accountability, and legitimacy. Even the secret state has to justify itself more than ever to the people and to its representatives. Another reason is the increased influence of what is often termed 'the mass media', which includes newspapers (such as 'tabloids' selling daily copies in many millions), television (with an explosion in the number of channels available, including many devoted to 24-hours-a-day news coverage), and radio. Driven by both the commercial consideration to steal a headline march on rivals, and the feeling that 'investigative reporting' is a means of democratic holding-to-account in an era when executive governments have powerful and self-serving forms of communication and control ('spin') available to them, the media constantly searches out scandal, and employs often hostile ways of interrogating political figures and their actions. A third reason why the state is often in the limelight is that its power and authority matter to people. Governments possess the means to make lives riskier than ever with their possession of highly destructive modern armaments; and yet they are also the potential recourse for citizens to minimize the dangers of, say, environmental catastrophe or pharmaceutical risk.

These are good reasons for studying the state. It is powerful, it is a means for protecting individuals from dangers, it matters to people, symbolically and as an object of popular representation, and virtually every country has one. But it is also increasingly challenged, at least in its national territorial form. There are some who are even prepared to contemplate 'the end of the nation state', after around 300 years of dominance of this political form in the world. And yet the numbers of independent nation states continues to grow – it is now over 200 – and groups without one, such as the Palestinians or the Kurds, press forcefully for their own. What explains this apparent paradox?

Challenges to the nation state

For the purposes of classification we can identify four reasons why the nation state faces some of its sternest challenges since the Treaties of Westphalia in 1648. (This established a world system of nation states among the major European nations, and legitimized the efforts of rulers to consolidate their territories under new, secular forms of national administration and symbols.) We can describe these four challenges as those of: globalization; supranational governance; national territorial fragmentation and political apathy; and 'lifestyle'.

First, globalization generally refers to the processes of worldwide economic integration made possible by communication and information technologies that conduce almost instantaneous flows of finance, and goods and services, around the globe. At the heart of these processes are the large multinational corporations, whose operations span many countries and who, it is often argued, make investment location decisions according to their own corporate interests, and on the basis of how these are advanced (or not) by the 'friendly' (or otherwise) policies of nation states. And because nation states are dependent on these corporations for the economic prosperity of their populations, it is felt by some that governments are compelled to adopt policies such as those of low corporate and direct personal taxation, and minimal trade union rights, that attract inward funds from these organizations. One result, in this view, is that the state loses its sovereignty and the independence to make policies on the basis of electoral support and its view of domestic wellbeing. It becomes, to use an expression, 'hollowed out' (Camilleri and Falk, 1992).

We examine these claims in more detail in later chapters. The supporting evidence, however, is not overwhelming. Multinational corporations are not in a position to keep switching their operations according to variations in national policies, and are very aware of the benefits that they obtain from, for example, locating their research and development facilities close to their manufacturing ones, irrespective of tax breaks from governments. They prefer stable systems of political rule, including those in which governments apparently pursue apparently 'anti-business' policies. On closer inspection, too, many social welfare and high taxation approaches can be welcomed by the corporations, especially if these involve higher expenditure on education, or on transport, which potentially also advantage their interests as well as meeting social democratic political aspirations. State policies between different countries have not all converged and national governments retain considerable flexibility in their policy outlooks. Unlike economic corporations, too, they have a popular legitimacy not available to the former. It is doubtful, therefore, if globalization is withering the state – at least in its ability to pursue distinctive programmes – as much as is claimed.

Second, nation states may be losing more of their sovereign powers to other tiers of government. 'Supranational' forms of governance are found at both the regional (an area of several countries) and at the global levels. The strongest model of economic, legal and political integration at the regional level is the European Union (EU). Although the EU is not a state, its regulations and directives in a number of competences take legal precedence over those of national governments. In pursuit of the economic advantages of a common market for goods and services, and other benefits, governments have 'pooled' a number of their powers. The EU's 'civil service' – the European Commission – has considerable authority and strong 'supranational' characteristics. Yet the EU is predominantly an inter-governmental arrangement and its continued development is dependent upon the agreement of nation states.

At the global level, inter-state and more private bodies often have considerable economic and political clout that is deployed against nation states, in requiring that financial aid, for example, is reciprocated by market and political reforms. The International Monetary Fund (IMF), the World Bank (WB), and the World Trade Organization (WTO) are examples of such regimes. Moreover, a range of global social or civil associations – such as Greenpeace or Christian Aid – are increasingly involved in seeking to influence the policies of such organizations, often to the consternation of the less powerful or developing states. The major developed countries, such as the USA, have less difficulty, however, in exerting their national interests in these global bodies. On military or collective security issues, too, nation states are increasingly part of 'blocs' (such as NATO, which has enlarged since the ending of the Cold War between East and West in the late 1980s) that make the traditional idea of a national state engaging independently in war with another most unlikely. Even for the world's only current superpower, the US, there remain strong political and moral constraints on unilateral military action, as the recent conflict in Iraq testifies. In this sense, therefore, the sovereignty of nation states has declined, although their continued domestic and rising inter-state influences hardly suggest that the study of nation states has become correspondingly unimportant.

Third, although the issues of globalization and supranational governance raise questions about whether the sovereignty and capabilities of nation states are considerably weakened by external processes, nation states also face challenges within their territories, usually based on claims of remoteness and lack of sensitivity to local issues. This may be founded on longstanding feelings of nationalism or other strong senses of regional identity, such as articulated by some in Wales, Scotland and Northern Ireland, or in Slovakia; or as resurfaced in the recent Yugoslavian regime and which lay behind the eruption of inter-communal violence in the 1990s. Devolution and decentralization, particularly in strongly unitary states such as the UK, have been among the central policy responses to such claims. But the creation of independent states has also been a response where lack of legitimacy exacerbated by misrule has drained a state of its ability to continue as constituted. Despite the era of globalization, local community identities and desires for forms of 'self-rule' appear stronger than ever. But at least such decentralist challenges often express a form of engagement with conventional political processes. Governments virtually everywhere face another form of challenge to their legitimacy by the increased unwillingness in many countries for populations to participate at all in the political process. Young people especially appear particularly 'turned-off' by conventional politics.

It is not clear why participation in democratic politics is declining and why governments are held in low regard. Some have blamed politicians and the continual revelations of corruption and 'sleaze' for this condition, although politicians and officials are more inclined to blame the rise of an aggressive and often contemptuous mass media. It is also possible that the state and its preoccupations have become too boring for most people – political language and parliamentary rituals are exposed more than ever through regular television coverage, and look arcane. Expanding opportunities for leisure pursuits of many kinds can appear more enticing. State legitimacy is in danger of being seriously eroded if such trends continue.

Box 1.1 Low trust in politicians

The poor opinion that people have of politicians is evidenced in a MORI poll published in the *Financial Times* (London) on 18 February 2003. Its findings are likely to be replicated in countries other than the UK. The question asked was: 'Who do we trust to tell the truth?'

Top five	%	Bottom five	%
Doctors	91	Trade union officials	33
Teachers	87	Business leaders	28
Professors	74	Government ministers	20
Judges	72	Politicians generally	18
Clergy	71	Journalists	18

This brings us to a fourth and final challenge for the state. Not only do people have many more forms of leisure entertainment than that provided by state politics with which to preoccupy themselves, but the concerns that matter most to them do not appear 'public' but 'individual'. Lifestyle issues, such as those of morality, fitness and health, and sex and gender are regarded as requiring personal not collective choice, and are considered as more important than parliamentary debates on, for example, the condition of the roads. Moreover, when lifestyle issues are politicized as, say, on the environment or poverty, these are increasingly regarded as matters transcending the competency of the nation state, and as constituting problems for humankind that are resolvable only at a worldwide level.

These cultural changes have helped to stimulate a view in political sociology that the study of political power should not be confined to state institutions or to examinations of conventional organizations such as traditional political parties. Rather the operation of power can be found all around us and in groups and institutions of all kinds. In some interpretations, such as those of Foucault, the state reflects and makes use of cultural and symbolic artefacts for power purposes, rather than being a dominant instigator. Later in this volume we examine these 'cultural turns' in analyses of power and the state.

Again, however, it is as well not to overestimate the unconcern with the state. Environmental groups may find, for example, that the remedies for many of their concerns do lie with the nation state. They may regard the state as often part of the problem, but without its influence on their behalf they may be powerless. Moreover, for every person concerned with private lifestyle rather than public issues, there is somebody else calling for state intervention to regulate a social problem or to reduce consumer risk. The modern state may own and directly provide less than it did, before the political ascendancy in recent decades in a number of countries of market solutions for many of our contemporary ills, but it shows little sign of not wishing to regulate the activities of its citizens. The regulatory state looms larger than ever, and, perhaps benign in intent, its consequences may often appear perverse.

The market and the state

A further reason why the state may be viewed as less important than before is the belief that it is less important than the market as a source of national prosperity. In our reference to globalization (above) we note the proposition that increasingly worldwide market forces have debilitated national sovereignties, although we are dubious about how far this view is sustainable. Ideologically and programmatically, however, we have witnessed in recent decades a turn to the market as a means for securing both greater economic prosperity and more efficiency in public services. The state appears in these modes to be an enabler (of more effective economies and services) rather than a direct provider, the aim being to help individuals and businesses to help themselves, freed from state bureaucratic red tape, and provided with more corporate and personal financial incentives. Whereas at the height of the 'welfare state' in the thirty years or so after the ending of the Second World War in 1945, the state was seen as a defence against and a corrector of generally perverse market tendencies, these days the positions have been reversed. The market is seen as the defence against perverse state tendencies.

Yet we have to be careful not to overplay these developments. The state, as mentioned above, has generally increased its regulatory role while shedding some others, including its shift of ownership of state assets to private investors, as in so-called 'privatizations' of government-owned utilities and other services. In these instances independent regulatory agencies have usually been established to protect the consumer from possible predatory pricing and other policies of organizations that although they have been restored to the private sector may still enjoy dominant and often monopoly positions – a legacy from their state-ownership days.

Markets, however, should not be seen as always in antagonistic or in mutually incompatible relationships with the state. They are also in large part constituted by the state and by a variety of legal and other public institutions. Markets generally require legal institutions and processes – such as contract, or property, or trade law – in order to have the stability and protection to grow. We have seen, in eastern Europe after the fall of communism, that the introduction of market reforms has been hampered by the lack of state-backed legal frameworks and instruments – such as for the protection of private ownership and for business agreements.

Although the state and the market are generally counterpoised to each other in political and journalistic rhetoric, this is frequently mistaken. Companies are not averse to seeking state protection for the dominance of their market positions by eliciting governmental regulations to help reduce market entry opportunities for new competitors, or through seeking the provision of public subsidies for domestic companies in the face of more efficient foreign providers, or even in helping to quell social unrest at times of sector decline and readjustment (as happened in the case of the coalmining industry in the UK and elsewhere). The 'freer' the market, the stronger or more coercive may need to be the state in having the authority to intervene in the economy to help with its restructuring. This rests on the proposition that marketization is likely to produce increased social dislocation as the continuous process of capitalist destruction and innovation threatens existing interests, thus requiring state action, either to ensure compensation for the dispossessed, or to use police and military means to quell resistance. It is by no means the case that a fully *laissez-faire* economy goes hand-in-hand with a weak state.

State and market are not simply the two ends of a see-saw, with strength at one end being reflected in weakness or decline at the other, but often are closely entwined. Centralizing monarchs and states historically have looked upon the market, and particularly the traders and other business interests in the towns and cities, to provide them with funds to finance armies and expeditions, and also to support the expanding administrative institutions of government. Major economic interests consequently are not like other group interests. They are privileged (Lindblom, 1977). States rely upon them to provide the economic conditions and wealth for the prosecution of a range of social and political objectives. The examination of the economic role of the state in capitalist and democratic societies is more a question of looking at the relationships, mostly symbiotic, between it and the market, rather than as a gladiatorial contest between two totally opposed principles and processes.

Some key terms

Already we have started to employ notions – such as 'sovereignty', 'the state', and 'nation' – without being too concerned about their precise meanings, although we have tried to provide some sense of that to which they refer. For those dealing with the state from a more formal or constitutional (or even a 'drier') perspective, such descriptions would feature much more prominently and at length than they do here. We are more concerned with the relationships between state institutions and actors, and the powers that they possess or deploy, and the wider society. And by 'society' we mean more than the national formations to which the term traditionally has been applied in the social sciences, but to wider forces, both transnational (those being somehow 'above' territories, by virtue of instantaneous electronic communication) and international (as in the case of intergovernmental relationships). Yet, without becoming lost down the byways of constitutional or conceptual exegesis, it is important that we take a little space to outline the key terms generally used in state analyses and to provide some readily usable interpretations. Without these it would be that much harder to understand what is happening to the contemporary state and to identify where we might look to discover whether it is changing its form and its powers in the face of challenges from all sides.

Sovereignty

This term, in its straightforward sense, refers to supreme power or authority, including the authority of a state to govern itself. As can be guessed, the notion derives from the position of a monarch or sovereign as possessing ultimate power as a ruler. Here the sense is personal – sovereign power derives from royal power and status. Throughout sixteenth- and seventeenth-century Europe, monarchs in England, France, Spain and elsewhere used the notion of sovereignty to consolidate power within national boundaries, and to rebut alternative claims to such authority from non-national bodies, such as the Catholic Church. These days, however, the notion of sovereignty is applied more to a nation and to its state institutions than to a king, and refers to a nation state's ability to act independently (free from the constraint of other states, or without interference from private or economic organizations, such as multinational corporations). A sovereign state in this sense is capable of governing itself – it is self-governing.

Of course, such purist interpretations are rarely realized in practice. Even the most powerful and independent-minded rulers and nations take account of the intentions and influences of others, recognizing their ability to resist and to make trouble, which adds, at least, to costs of time and resources. These costs also are bound to increase if other rulers or peoples have legitimate interests or values in the eyes of third parties that are being overridden (perhaps as expressed by 'world opinion' through, say, the United Nations). None the less, levels of sovereignty, or the capability to act independently by states, do vary, not only between countries but also historically, and may be open to some form of measurement.

Within states, however, supreme power is reflected in the ability by state rulers to enjoy popular compliance with their decisions and policies, if necessary by exercising a legal or justified monopoly over the deployment of the police and the military. In some cases this supreme authority is formally located in one part of the state, such as a parliament and, as such, cannot be challenged easily by, say, recourse to other parts of the state, through, for example, legal action. In others, however, particularly where 'sovereignty' is dispersed or 'separated' among several levels or institutions, as in devolved or federal constitutions (such as in the US, Australia or Germany), governments are more likely to have their decisions subject to legal or institutional challenge where social groups may involve other state institutions. Of course, popular compliance with state policies is not the same as full-throated acclamation or willing support, but generally it is sufficient to sustain sovereignty.

We shall see in later chapters, when we look at theories of the state, that some philosophers, such as Hobbes, have tended to place priority in security and order, rather than in individual freedom and democratic consent to rule, as the basis for state legitimacy. The state, to achieve these outcomes and to avoid anarchy, consequently needs to be the single focus of allegiance and the supreme source of law. We find echoes of this thinking more contemporarily in times of war or perceived terrorist and other threats to national security, when, for example, controls over immigration, or over travel, or the introduction of government-issued personal identity cards, may be accepted by citizens as essential to minimize danger and risk, even though individual liberties may be curbed. Others commentators, however, are more concerned to ensure that individual rights are not trampled upon by actions designed to protect the citizens from bombs and other outrages.

Generally these days the notion of sovereignty is regarded as based on a nation state's legal autonomy. Sovereign states are so-called because no higher body has the right to authoritatively direct them. Yet increasingly nation states are not in this position. The development of 'supranational' bodies such as the EU and the European Court of Justice, and the related establishment of international law (and the International Criminal Justice Court), have reduced the legal independence and thus the sovereignty of many states. EU legal directives are superordinate to national law, even if procedurally they have to be incorporated and implemented by formal national – sovereign – procedures, as by parliamentary decision. Moreover, state rulers operating outside the bounds of accepted behaviour worldwide, as in the cases of Saddam Hussein or Slobodan Milosovic, face internationally coordinated military and legal action against them. In such cases, norms of sovereignty for nation states are regarded as secondary to broader humankind values of civilized conduct.

The state

The concept of the state clearly follows on from that of sovereignty. It is comprised of those permanent institutions within a country through which supreme authority is exercised. Its scope – its jurisdiction – is defined and limited by territorial borders. Part of the 'mystery' and 'fearsomeness' of the state to which we referred in the opening paragraph of this chapter stems from its impersonality. It is not that the state lacks individuals – in fact it has quite a lot of them and is often one of a country's largest employers – but that they are required to operate rather dispassionately – without a great deal of concern for individual circumstances. Although this picture is not strictly accurate at the level of many individual interactions by state functionaries with the general public, their authority is construed as legal–bureaucratic, as applying to everybody uniformly and according to laid-down rules promulgated by government departments and parliament. Treating everybody the same through formal regulation may be regarded as avoiding arbitrariness and self-interested or even corrupt behaviour, which tended to occur with pre-modern forms of rule when officials owed allegiances to nobles and other 'private' interests.

Modern state officials generally are recruited openly and formally – on the basis of qualifications and competitive entry – and are expected to be politically neutral and supportive of the elected government. In this sense they act with technical expertise on behalf of the common good or for the benefit of the 'public', as contrasted with the partisan behaviour and ideological commitments of politicians. Both state politicians and officials, however, serve a population oriented to the state's authority through a shared and subjective sense that they 'belong' to a national community (Anderson, 1983). Flags, emblems, uniforms, and rituals are some of the means by which such belonging is represented at the national level, and all the nation's citizens are regarded as possessing common rights and obligations. The history of nation-state building is of populations being gradually pacified and 'civilized' through the extension of manners and courtly customs, inculcated increasingly in families and schools (Elias, 1978).

In comparison, traditional imperial empires prior to the modern state had considerable difficulty in extending rule from the centre outward to heterogeneous and tribally distinct populations. Moreover, they lacked effective monopoly control over the means of force and surveillance and were constantly battling with warlords and bandits. Most of their subjects, except for the payment of taxes, had little awareness of state officials, and the boundaries of the empire state were rarely settled or fixed, but moved with periodic conquests and defeats in battle.

The modern state, however, is part of a world system of states, with its borders and national jurisdictions generally recognized by other states and sustained through diplomatic and other protocols. Unlike the position of the state within national territories, the world system of states cannot be said to possess a single or centralized authority to control and coordinate the actions of states. Although international bodies, such as those associated with the United Nations, or the World Trade Organization, for example, do exercise constraints and impose sanctions on countries, they still serve predominantly as forums for the interplay of interests and values between national governments.

Within International Relations theory there is considerable debate as to whether states operate on the world stage according to their perception of national interests (that is, that they are oriented solely to obtain comparative advantage against other countries) or whether they are capable of acting according to shared norms and values, including at times when these are at variance with their territorial interests. In the so-called 'neorealist' school, the international order is explicitly conceptualized as the outcome of nations pursuing their self-interest, not least to survive militarily and economically (Waltz, 1979). Other theorists, however, argue that inter-state behaviour is predominantly normative and not constituted simply by naked self-interest (Keohane, 1989; Bull, 1995). That is, countries can do 'the right thing' in terms of accepted worldwide and current values, even if this means that their material position may be damaged. Occasionally a hegemonic (dominant) country is seen as being able to impose some form of world order which other countries feel able to accept, such as occurred with the dominance of Britain and its empire in the nineteenth century, and the United States in the twentieth. Periodically, too, there have been calls for forms of world government to establish greater peace and prosperity, although to no avail.

Nation states are regarded generally as the site of the rule of law and democratic decision-making, although there have been attempts in recent years to 'stretch' notions of democracy to include wider international bodies. Particularly the idea of worldwide 'cosmopolitan' democracy has been articulated as a response to the challenge of globalization at the turn of the twenty-first century (Held, 1996, 2002; Linklater, 1998). In this view, the starting-point is what human beings have in common, such as basic individual rights and ecosystems, and then a consideration of how worldwide democratic institutions and common frameworks of standards can be promulgated. However, a global framework of cosmopolitan democratic law would still appear to require strong nation states to implement it, although admittedly such states would also be constrained by such law. It is not clear why states would necessarily wish to go far in introducing global forms of democratic governance if this compromised their existing and remaining sovereignties too much. This is one reason why some proponents of global democracy prefer to focus less on nation states than on the potential of non-state or civil associations at the worldwide level to achieve their goals.

Nation

Although we have suggested that the idea of the state in the minds of many is rather enigmatic and even a source of anxiety or dread, in political theory the picture is more complex. In much continental philosophy, for example, particularly in Germany from the nineteenth century, the state has been viewed much more as a positive moral force. In part this stems from the point we make above, namely that the modern state is a nation state. And the nation in this European view is a natural community. A nation and its people are defined in terms of common and longstanding sentiments, habits and language. It is comfortable and at ease with itself through centuries of customary association.

It is only a short step from this notion of the nation to the view that the territorial state embodies or represents the nation and that this provides the basis for its political authority. State power then is to be exercised on behalf of the people. It is the 'national interest' that should drive state actions, not personal honour or dynastic ambitions, as generally occurred in monarchical and pre-modern forms. Of course, the idea of 'the national interest' is not unproblematic and can be interpreted in a variety of ways. Initially it was conceived, rather as promulgated by Hobbes, as collective security, not least in times of war. In the twentieth century this gave way to a more social characterization, centred on the people's welfare and wellbeing. It was a notion that helped fuel the rise of the welfare state and the idea that popular support for the nation state required not only individual rights (such as voting, freedom of speech, and so on) but also reciprocal social care and protection as well. In turn, however, throughout the twentieth century the notion of national or popular interest as expressed through the state was interpreted variously by non-liberal democratic regimes. These included views that it required a ruling political party with exclusive knowledge of the people's 'objective interest' (as in Marxism-Leninism and the Soviet socialist state), or that state control by, say, a fundamentalist religious grouping was needed (as found in theocracies, and contemporarily in the Muslim clerical rule in Iran), or that the national interest could be found through an authoritarian leader with charismatic claims to popular support, such as Hitler in the inter-war years of the mid-twentieth century (Beetham, 2001).

The view of the nation as a group of people who see themselves as a natural political community, and as the basis of state authority, has proved remarkably durable. For two centuries or more the nation has generally been regarded as the most appropriate unit for state rule. The result is that the world is divided largely into nation states. International law is predominantly based on the assumption that nations, like individuals, have rights, notably the right to political independence and self-determination.

For some, the nation state is a natural arrangement, as state formation helps to 'reveal' and to represent an underlying and well-established cohesive community. Others, however, regard the nation as a more contrived and artificial affair. Rather than a pre-existing nation finding expression through state-building, the state finds expression through nation-building. Nations, in this view, are created by territorial leaders as part of their consolidation of, and justification for, power. Among the instruments for achieving these purposes can be listed such artefacts as books, art, flags, a uniformed military, a national currency, national secularized education systems, and also the 'licensing' of universities and intellectuals to help promulgate senses of national culture and identity. These are some of the means by which populations come to 'imagine' themselves as belonging to a national community.

Legitimacy

We have suggested that states find it difficult and costly to rule without a fairly widespread belief that they do so legitimately, particularly if they have recourse to the use of force and violence to defend national interests. All rulers face the problem of justifying their power and authority, not only to those who are expected to comply, but also to themselves and their supporters, in order to infuse their rule with moral certitude and elite solidarity. Moreover, rule by force is hazardous and, with the growth of larger and more dispersed populations, prone to ineffectiveness. Far better (and cheaper) to utilize principles that justify rule (other than simply that 'might is right', of course) and which others accept.

Loyalty by a population to a nation and its symbols, the sense of 'belonging' and not simply compliance or cowering in the face of violence and threat, needs to be accompanied by acceptance that the nature of the political regime is both morally right, protective and broadly efficient. Historically, and particularly with the spread of liberal democracy, the idea has eventuated that this legitimation of rule comes from the people, not least as the state represents them at home and abroad.

State and society

We stated at the outset that our analysis of the state was less a dry constitutional or administrative approach than one that examines state relationships with the wider society and how these are changing. Of course, such an approach assumes that we are able to distinguish satisfactorily the border between the state and society. In many countries this is not always easy. We have referred already to the rise of the 'regulatory state' in a number of developed nations in recent decades, although it has a longer history in the US. In the regulatory state, private, independent and self-governing interests become increasingly subject to state jurisdiction, codification and supervision in the name of democracy and public protection (Moran, 1991, 1999, 2003; Jessop, 2002). The experience of privatization in the UK and elsewhere has also redrawn the boundaries between the state and the private economy, shifting ownership of certain key industries away from the state and into the market, but yet also imposing wider state regulation for the protection of consumers on these privatized organizations than traditionally has been found within the confines of company law, which generally has emphasized the autonomy of firms (Moran, 2003).

These changes indicate that the 'market' (as a component of society) is generally contrasted with the state as a separate sphere, and that this comparison is the more striking in capitalist economies in which major productive assets are privately owned. This differs in socialist or even social democratic societies, where significant parts of the economy are in the hands of the state. But even in liberal democracies the distinction has become clouded – not necessarily through greater state ownership of the means of production, as tended to occur in the aftermath of the Second World War years, but through political efforts to have the state act more like the market, by introducing such policies as competitive tenders for suppliers, and performance-related individual rewards for employees, and also by stripping down the functions of the state and devolving many operational matters to separate or distinctive agencies. Policy or strategic decision-making remains in the hands of politicians and officials at the centre (at least in theory, as it has often proved difficult to distinguish between policy and operational matters, especially in times of political crisis or heightened media sensitivity). A further basis for distinguishing between the state and the economy may be found at the level of social action, by seeing what it is that primarily motivates actors in these different realms. For Crouch (2001) state actors are propelled by the desire to maximize power, while businesspeople have the pursuit of private wealth as their main ambition.

Box 1.2 The market

The term 'market' tends to be used for a number of rather different phenomena. These include:

- competition
- the means for conveying choice (consumerism) and the allocation of resources in a way that differs from electoral or wider political decision-making
- capitalism and the private ownership of productive property
- a minimally-regulated economic system

See Moran and Wright (1991) for a fuller outline.

The approach to examining state–society contrasts based on social action is quite common in sociology, and tends to follow in the classical tradition associated with Weber (1925) and his work at the turn into the twentieth century. It rests in part on the analytical separation of two ideal-typical (simplified) forms of social relations. The state typically is held to entail relations of command and obedience in which individual actions are guided by a belief in the existence of a legitimate order of authority. Identifiable persons, such as political leaders and officials, maintain order through the exercise of authority, and this order endures as long as the legitimacy of the arrangement is shared both by those who exercise authority and those who are subject to it.

In the more informal groups in society, however, relations typically are based on sentiments of shared ideas, as in some religious groups, or of emotional warmth, as in families. They tend to be based often on custom and to be maintained voluntarily. But societal arrangements may also be centred on interests. Markets, for example, are generally based on individual considerations or calculations of material advantage, rather than on authority. In the work sphere, professional or ideological solidarity with other occupational practitioners (doctors or lawyers, for example) may be the prevailing sentiment – even though undoubtedly in such cases elements of material advantage are involved too. These calculative and affective forms of social action differ typically from action oriented to state authority, which is based on authoritative command.

Although public authority and voluntary relations are relatively autonomous and distinctive spheres of action in virtually all societies, the separation has been greatest in modern western societies. Access to positions of state authority has gradually become disconnected from kinship ties, property interests and inherited privileges, at least in a formal sense. Decision-making at the legislative, judicial and administrative levels has become subject to impersonal rules and has attained a degree of freedom from the constellations of social interests.

It must be remembered that we are focusing here on analytical distinctions rather than describing exact empirical developments. State administrations are never entirely free from social power. As late as the First World War (1914–18) in Britain, aristocratic class power and influence was strongly influential in the development of foreign policy. Indeed the 'social embeddedness' of state administrations – their closeness rather than distance or autonomy from wider social interests – is often regarded as more of a source of political power than a rather stiff-necked independence (Mann, 1993: 749–57); that is, as a strength rather than as a weakness. Feminists, too, have been disinclined to accept a sharp disjunction between the public and the private realms, arguing that the personal is the political. The state–society distinction is seen to hide conveniently from view the oppression of women that takes place away from public scrutiny in patriarchal institutions such as the traditional family. Moreover, developments in the private sphere can have radical implications for the public domain. Hart (1989), for example, has pointed to the modern decline in gender inequality as helping to explain the ebbing of class politics, through particularly a reduction in the masculine work and pub cultures that traditionally reinforced working-class consciousness and activity in labour parties and trade unions.

An additional point that needs to be considered in discussing the distinction between state and society is that made by Foucault (1979) and which we discuss further in Chapter 8. The emergence of the modern state is accompanied by the concept of the people or a population as a demographic entity. It becomes the object of what Foucault terms 'bio-politics', which is the attempt to govern the key components of life itself, including birth and death. This made it possible for the state to target various social groups, such as criminals, or the young. Ruling a territory gradually became conceived as less ruling a land or property than governing different social groups within it, and with regard for the general environmental and social conditions in which they lived, reproduced, became ill, or maintained health. In this the state was supported by a range of information on the general population that steadily emerged from surveys and other sampling techniques. The nation state has therefore from the very beginning regarded 'society' as a body with its own specific dynamics and as a legitimate object of its attentions. This too has contributed both to the separation of the state from 'civil society' analytically, and to their mutual interconnectivity empirically.

Civil society

A further development of the state–society distinction may be found in the notion of 'civil society', which refers to the organizational characteristics of the society realm, such as voluntary groups, which are autonomous of the state and are essentially 'private'. For many, the strength of such associations is a critical factor in the formation and the maintenance of a healthy democracy, as it allows for choice and the freedom to pursue individual concerns, and to have these clearly articulated at the political level. Participation in community activity is also seen as developing a sense of moral responsibility and efficacy in individuals that is helpful in conducing a socially concerned and democratic culture. By contrast, dictatorships or 'totalitarian' regimes (where everything is totally controlled by the state) generally abolish or severely curtail such groups (Etzioni, 1993; Putnam, 1993).

As well as the democratic need for voluntary associations, centralizing state formation over the last couple of centuries or more has led to repeated concerns that, to avoid despotism and to maintain civil protection, more extensive forms of 'local state' or local democratic government are also necessary, to advance and to be sensitive to local interests in the face of strangers from outside that are bent on imposing uniformity throughout the land and are not sensitive to the particular needs of local communities. Both these 'localisms' (voluntary and state) are seen as helping to inculcate norms of tolerance and political learning essential for liberal democracy (de Tocqueville, 1835; Siedentop, 2001).

The following chapters

So far we have examined why the nation state is an important object of study. It matters to people and it helps to protect them, it possesses a representative legitimacy not available to other large organizations, and it is playing an increasingly vital part in the development of worldwide and regional governing arrangements. Much recent attention has focused on its alleged diminished role in the face of powerful and globally integrated markets and supranational governing entities, and on its less direct power as a consequence of the 'stripping down' of some its key functions in managing a welfare society and securing macroeconomic stability (such as with privatizations, and with the reorientation of governments towards procuring or contracting for the delivery of state services, and away from providing them directly). The argument is that it has become more of an 'enabling state', in which increasingly it is required to work with a range of non-state organizations in a variety of policy-making networks. We suggest, however, that the state is no less ambitious and often more encroaching than ever before. The growth of a regulatory state covering a wide swathe of previously autonomous business and professional occupational sectors underlines this point. The modalities of state influence may have changed – from ownership to regulation, and including the global as well as the national stage – but its forecast demise is exaggerated.

We have outlined at least four key challenges to the modern nation state: globalization, supranationality, 'localism', and 'lifestyle'. Yet we do not find convincing evidence to suggest that the state is holed below the waterline as a consequence. Rather it is adapting and changing and is likely to retain considerable powers and authority even though it is losing some of its sovereignty. A number of terms associated with the study of the state have also been examined – not simply because a glossary is helpful and expected, but because at least some elemental understanding of these notions supports a wider understanding of the state story and its future.

In the following chapters we examine the state and the challenges to it in greater detail. Understanding the historical evolution of the modern state as outlined in the next chapter highlights the variability of its development not only within the core European countries where it originated, but also in other parts of the world. But this evolution needs explaining theoretically, and in Chapter 3 we examine state theories as found in a variety of perspectives, including some that are 'classical' and well-established. These theories, of course, contain views on what constitutes the good political society, and particularly what is meant by democracy. In Chapter 4 we examine whether the long 'waves' of liberal democratic state development to include most parts of the world are to be regarded as heralding the final triumph of such forms and the 'end of history', as some would have it.

Chapter 5 looks at the state in what might be termed its most ascendant forms – as interventionist, corporatist and regulatory – in support of welfare distribution, macroeconomic stability and competitive market enhancement. Again, despite claims to the contrary, it is clear that liberal economic forms have not prevailed everywhere, despite the compelling pressures of globalization, and some countries, especially in northern and eastern parts of Europe, retain quite strong social democratic and corporatist forms of state policy-making.

In Chapter 6 we examine what is meant by the increasingly used term 'globalization' and whether, as some argue, it heralds the end of the nation state and the rise of worldwide forms of rule. We follow this in Chapter 7 with an account of another form of challenge to the nation state – the growth of supranational levels of government 'above' it. A key question is whether supranational regulatory bodies particularly should be regarded as severely constraining national governments, or whether they are best viewed as forums for intergovernmental bargaining.

By Chapter 8 we feel that a fuller account is needed of liberalism and the liberal state. Underlying much of what we say to that point has been a tacit consideration of liberalism as the main form of 'governmentality', at least in the West. Yet it is necessary to seek to understand what liberalism means and particularly to examine whether apparently non-liberal forms, as found in socialism, fascism and Confucianism, for example, are truly quite different or whether they display what might be considered surprising affinities with liberalism. This leads us on to a consideration of power and its relationship to the state in Chapter 9. We look here at what has been termed 'the new political sociology', and especially at a more cultural turn in the social sciences, to examine issues of dominance and control in more everyday social settings, and which do not necessarily fall within the direct purview of the state.

We then conclude with some observations on the future of the state and, given that it has one, in what form.

Chapter 2

The Development of the Modern Nation State

Historical origins
The beginnings of modern forms of rule
The sources of the modern state
Inter-state relations
War, revolution, ideas and administration
The origins of liberalism and capitalism
The development of liberalism and capitalism
The state outside west Europe
Conclusion

This chapter examines the development of the modern nation state. Specifically it looks at the emergence of a more impersonal and public system of rule over increasingly territorially delineated societies than the largely localized and dynastic forms of power that preceded it. This rule is exercised through more complex and formal sets of institutional arrangements and offices than existed hitherto. The general structural contours of the emergent modern state will be outlined, while recognizing that this may hide considerable diversity in practices and historical trajectories at the level of particular societies.

The aim of the chapter is to utilize an analytical interpretation of historical developments over many centuries, focusing particularly, but not exclusively, on western Europe during the recently concluded second millennium. This will show that the formation of the modern nation state is of relatively recent origin and that, despite the current tally of over 200 such states, it cannot be assumed to be a universal or timeless phenomenon. A further feature of the chapter will be the emphasis on the plurality of causal agents and interpretations that underlie the construction of the modern state. This is not simply a device for ensuring that readers are presented with the materials to make up their own minds on these matters, but reflects a belief that no single set of factors – economic, military, politico-administrative or social – is sufficient to account for the rich complexity of state-society pathways over the centuries and around the world.

20

Historical origins

The distinction between a realm of private interests and a public realm based on 'civic' and other virtues is not simply a modern invention, but was exemplified in the ancient city state of Greece. Political power in these regimes was seen to be quite separate from family and clan allegiances and to be exercised for the good of the community. Officials commanded compliance, not because of their personal standing or virtues, but because of the offices that they held. Moreover, Roman concepts of public, civil and criminal law, when they were 'rediscovered' in eleventh-century Europe, supported a sense of a rational, hierarchical, almost bureaucratic form of state administration, which helped the historical and legal claims of the centralizing absolutist monarchs in their early shaping of the modern territorial state. It was a lineage that gave particular force to efforts from around the twelfth century onwards to overcome the centrifugal and fragmentary consequences of the Germanic tribes and kingdoms that had followed the collapse of the Roman Empire (Opello and Rosow, 1999). The myriad Germanic kingdoms, in which developed the notion of the kingly realm as almost personal property, had no formal political and administrative apparatus or standing army, unlike the Romans. So Roman law provided a rich conceptual storehouse for the legal institutions that were necessary for the rational development of both the state and capitalism (Braithwaite and Drahos, 2000), and for overcoming the personal and divided fiefdoms of Germanic medievalism.

The potentialities and beginnings of national state formation in west Europe are discernible in the competing structures of patrimonialism and feudalism, as found within the Germanic and Roman traditions of rule respectively. In effect, it refers to the struggles and the determination of the balance of forces between kings and landed nobles over the kind and extent of limitations to be placed on the monarch's powers. On the one hand, patrimonialism describes the organization of the royal household and its domains, which is in the hands of the king's personal servants, as the dominant structure of authority that occurs with the territorial expansion of royal jurisdiction. With feudalism, however, power is more widely and locally distributed. Feudalism is characterized by the system of fiefs and landholdings in the possession of nobles and aristocrats, and by levels of rights and 'immunities' (as well as obligations) generally associated with such possession. As such, patrimonialism and feudalism came to be regarded as constituting two types of governing system, and regimes could be described to the extent that their political arrangements reflected either closeness to central and monarchical, or alternatively to more local and lordly, forms of power. In actuality, however, the relationships between the two were more complex, with feudalism, for example, based on notions of the kingly possession of land (patrimonial), which was exchanged as part of personal vassalage obligation (feudal).

The king's authority in medievalism was constrained in a more spiritual way, of course, by religious norms and institutions, especially as these were promulgated and interpreted by the transnational and authoritative Catholic Church. The king's capriciousness in ruling his subjects was tempered by the recognition that such rule was exercised under God, a matter made manifest in the consecration of his succession to the throne, and which required him to protect his subjects and their welfare. To flout these divine limitations would be to raise doubts about the king's own position (not to mention his secular wisdom).

Nor are these simply moral bounds. A distinguishing characteristic of western European kingship from other types of patrimonial rule is that it had to face considerable organizational resources possessed by the Catholic Church, which would be used against the absolute claims of secular rulers by submitting them to stringent legal, canonical enquiry. Consequently, 'democratic' notions of the 'consent of the people', of a reciprocal obligation between ruler and ruled, are at least nascent in medieval political practice and provide the foundations for their later, more formally legalistic, consolidation.

Box 2.1 Feudalism

Feudalism is a term that was only conjured up in the sixteenth century to explain how different such a system was to the patrimonial arrangements that were then beginning to flower. People in feudalism were personally loyal to local lords (directly) and the king (remotely), not to a state, and any translocal identity was generally located within the authority and beliefs of the Catholic Church. Vassalage held things together in feudalism as a hierarchy of homage, loyalty, reciprocity, and duty, expressed with appropriate ceremony, from top to bottom. Localism, exemptions and personal relations provided cohesion for the country, rather than obedience to a sovereign territorial state. In virtually all countries centralizing and state-building rulers, seeking to consolidate power within a defined territory and thus jurisdiction, ensured that feudal localism was largely debilitated. However, it is generally agreed that feudal ideas and practices persisted for longer in Britain. These days, of course, local forms of self-administration, representation and self-regulation are often regarded as providing systems with the flexibility and adaptability that are generally not found in more state authoritarian or totalitarian arrangements.

It was the determination of later English kings that their writ should run supreme throughout England, especially given the shifts to royal courts of justice and away from baronial courts, that led to collisions with the Church. The Church never accepted the supreme and absolute sovereignty of the king in matters religious, including appointments to positions such as bishoprics that clearly had important secular and political consequences. And while the monarch had armies, the Church had the threat of excommunication, at least until others came forward to establish spiritual services deliverable by a more compliant and local Church of England.

Where feudalism was the stronger in west Europe it became characterized by an explicit ideology of 'rights'. The relations between a ruler and his vassals were consecrated through an affirmation of rights and duties under oath and before God that reinforced the autonomy of feudal jurisdictions. Where patrimonialism was the stronger influence, the fiefdoms enjoyed by local notables were much more firmly embedded within the royal jurisdiction, and less subject to 'subcontracting', the devolving or parcelling out of parts of the fief, or the establishment in them of proprietorial or familial rights. In effect, however, patrimonial and feudal domains competed and existed within particular societies and empires. In medieval polities the tugs and pulls between the patrimonial and feudal principles of authority resulted in a system of divided and overlapping jurisdictions competing for power and influence (Anderson, 1974; Poggi, 1978; Giddens, 1985). Almost inevitably, the king lacked a monopoly of legitimate physical coercion, relying for order and the redress of grievances on the self-interested duals and conflicts of the landed nobles (Mann, 1988).

As a result, medieval states possessed minimal power, with consequently little impact on the development of class relations, and only a little more over the outcome of warfare, which could be described as occurring largely between amalgamations of autonomous feudal groups funded by levies (Mann, 1986). The relations between such states were predominantly based upon the pursuit of territory as part of dynastic acquisitions of hazily defined clusters of provinces (Giddens, 1985). From an analysis of state finances in England/Britain it would appear that the functions of the state were overwhelmingly military and mainly international rather than domestic, and this situation generally remained until the seventeenth and eighteenth centuries. Somewhere between 75 and 90 per cent of the state's financial resources were almost continuously expended on acquiring and using military force, predominantly for the prosecution of international wars rather than for domestic repression (Mann, 1988).

Generally, however, over time patterns of fragmentary rule in the Germanic style were replaced in the fifteenth, sixteenth and seventeenth centuries by systems of rule continuously influenced, particularly in

continental Europe, by rediscovered Roman law. There was a displace-
ment of political legal coercion upwards towards a centralized, militarized
apparatus of royal power. Steadily states acquired the powers of warfare
from local and autonomous bodies as they began to offer national organization and geopolitical diplomacy which became increasingly useful for
dominant groups, both in the execution of war and in the organization of
trade (Mann, 1986). Yet the state continued to grow only spasmodically
and incrementally, generally as the outcome of war. Its financial strength
remained small in relation to the resources of the economy and its activities had little impact on the lives of most of its inhabitants (Mann, 1988).

The beginnings of modern forms of rule

The modern period of state formation and other characteristics of modernity may be said to have their origins in Europe in around 1450
(Wallerstein, 1974/1980/1989; Skocpol, 1979), although this is contested
by some (Frank, 1967). As we shall see, other parts of the world, notably
China, had many if not more of these features at this time, too, but did
not go on to develop the nation state and capitalist forms that followed
in Europe. The world prior to around 1450 had often been characterized
by empires and transnational religions, which enabled ancient societies to
be linked in significant ways. This 'proto-globalization' (Cohen and
Kennedy, 2000: 42) enabled the civilizations of the Middle East, China,
Greece and Rome to unify large areas. In the five centuries or more prior
to the fifteenth century, the fragmented regimes in Europe also were
cohered in relative stability by the extended reach and impact of the
Catholic Church. It acted as a powerful continental unifier and pacifier,
through its cultural universalism, its use of Latin and liturgy as a
common language, the political influence and standing of the papacy, and
the trans-state character of its organizational structure.

   Cohen and Kennedy also point to the multiple relations between
Europe and other civilizations at this time, notably Islam, whose territorial expansion as far as southern Spain by the late fifteenth century
was to provoke its eventual expulsion. The formation of the Holy
Roman Empire as a coalition between Christian states in the tenth century had aimed to protect Christianity from external attack (Cohen and
Kennedy, 2000: 43; also Smith, 1992). During its period of ascendancy
in southern Europe, Islam contributed significantly to developments in
the arts and sciences, the creation of centralized governmental structures, and innovations in agriculture. Moreover, gold and other bullion
helped to establish trade links (and eventual colonization) between
Europe, and Africa and South America (especially by Portugal and

Spain), while China, Persia and India were the source of advanced ideas in areas such as mathematics and technology.

Prior to the fifteenth century, and the formation of a European world economy, empires, where a common political structure and power governed many territories, were a characteristic form of political jurisdiction in many parts of the world for several millennia (Wallerstein, 1974). Empires, although also characterized by long-distance movement and trade, unlike more modern forms of world economy were socioeconomic systems that were also single political units, albeit often less integrated than both modern states and imperialisms. Trade occurred within the same political structure. Often a number of empires existed in various parts of the world at any given time, and were characterized by strong forms of political centralization. Although this tended to ensure economic flows, in the form of taxation, tribute and monopolistic control of trade, from the peripheries to the centre, its concomitant bureaucratization tended to be costly to maintain and to generate revolt that often required military action for it to be suppressed. As such,

> political empires are a primitive means of economic domination. It is the social achievement of the modern world, if you will, to have invented the technology that makes it possible to increase the flow of the surplus from the lower strata to the upper strata, from the periphery to the centre, from the majority to the minority, by eliminating the 'waste' of too cumbersome a political superstructure. (Wallerstein, 1974: 15–16)

Box 2.2 World systems theory

Wallerstein, articulating what has come to be known as 'world systems theory', defines 'world' in social rather than geographical terms (Brown, 2001: 149). A world is characterized as an extended social system, with regular social interaction, whose size is determined by the level of existing transport technology. Only in the twentieth century does the world in both the social and geographical sense become the same. That is, the capitalist market effectively is a global or world market in a territorial sense and is not simply a 'world system' as a consequence of a dense set of socio-economic relationships predominating in a particular world region. However, throughout the ages 'world systems' are characterized by inequalities between countries in terms of their incorporation into the core or periphery of such systems. A criticism is that such positioning by countries is not as permanent or as fixed as world systems theory suggests, and that countries have the policy ability to develop (or regress) in world core-periphery terms.

Although world economies (conceived as regional trading areas) had existed prior to the European one, such as those established by China, Persia and Rome, they had generally transmuted into empires. They lacked that happy conjunction of early capitalism and scientific and technological advance that enabled the market to generate surplus and the state to tax and use that surplus to ensure the market's further development, thus avoiding more politically direct forms of extraction. Thus, while China became a vast empire, with many of the factors in place, including overseas trading, an extensive state bureaucracy, and a monetary economy, that might have led to capitalist take-off, its Imperial structure was to turn it away from expansion abroad and towards an emphasis internally on its agrarian economy and on centralized authority and administrative rule. This reduced the capacity for autonomous and independent initiatives and innovations that might have supported new distributions of economic and political power. The Chinese empire's maintenance requirements proved too costly and diverting to allow for investment in capitalist development (Miller, 2000).

Europe at this time, however, was comprised of small empires, nation states, and city states, with feudal characteristics more likely to dismantle imperial structures than to strengthen them. A number of competing and strong nation states emerged as key economic actors in the European world economy, being reinforced by the financial benefits of a new international division of labour, which, as a consequence of the economic benefits of national specialization and inter-country trade, increased their own capacity to promote the market. This generated a virtuous cycle of wealth creation–taxation–enhanced state capability – market development – wealth creation. These states began to monopolize force, generate legitimacy, extend bureaucratization and start the process of creating national identities amongst their subject populations. For Wallerstein, the outcome, as capitalism developed across national borders, was a 'world system' that developed in the sixteenth century with a structured, unequal, if not unchangeable set of relations between three types of country, belonging respectively to the dominant core, the semiperiphery, or the dependent periphery of the overall system.

Unlike empires, capitalism was able to flourish over the succeeding centuries because it had within its bounds not one but a multiplicity of political systems, with varying strengths, which allowed it flexibility and competitveness in an economic arena that could not be controlled by any one political unit. Exchanges took place between territories under different political control, which ruled out tribute, and took the form of trade, as there was no overarching central authority with the ability to extract payment from far-flung peripheries, which facilitated the desire of merchants to territorially roam in search of a profit and under largely customary laws. Capitalists were able to move freely between states, which meant that gradually the rulers had to deliver capitalist requirements, not least because rulers were increasingly dependent on capitalist revenues to finance their wars. States learnt not to hinder capitalist development but to encourage it by respecting the needs of the merchant classes.

The key to this comprising the start of a capitalist world economy for Wallerstein is that it involved the distribution of goods for profit in a world market. Essentially the core states are able to use their market power to economically subordinate the non-core states, a view that recently has found further expression in the 1960s and 1970s theories of 'third world underdevelopment' and regional economic disparities (Frank, 1967). Both old and new versions, however, have difficulty in explaining how so-called 'dependent' or 'peripheral' states are able quite successfully to overcome their supposedly permanent positions in the world economy, as has happened in the case of the rapid industrialization and economic take-off of a number of east Asia countries in recent years.

Wallerstein tends to locate the emergence of a continental European political structure of competing states, in which no one imperial state was dominant, as particularly dependent on economic factors. States necessarily seek to enhance the power of their dominant classes, and indeed are forced to by the increasing competitiveness of the capitalist world economy and their own requirements for military and other funds, and they have little if any independent impact on this economic structure (Hobson, 2000: 136). The capitalist world economy, therefore, is the international force that holds sway over states that have little or no capability to resist it.

However, it is equally plausible to argue that the military and other strengths of individual states were not solely explicable in terms of their economic positions. By the end of the medieval period it is increasingly possible to point to other factors, such as administrative efficiency, political capacities for military mobilization, and geographical position (Skocpol, 1979; Mann, 1986, 1988). Moreover, there is a potential circularity in Wallerstein's line of argument in that the multistate system is seen as crucial for the emergence of a capitalist world economy but, at the same time, it is also explained by this emergence

This developing system of European states began to territorially constrain early capitalism in ways that continue to endure today. These 'ready-for-war', competing geopolitical states preceded capitalist development and helped direct it, rather than being functionally reflective of it as a mode of production that was essentially transnational. As Mann

(1988: 119–20) has noted:

> Merchant and landlord capitalist entered a world of warring states.
> This need for state regulation both internally and externally, and the
> state's need for finances, pushed classes toward a national form of
> organization. ... These geopolitical parameters imply warfare
> between rivals in a way that the capitalist mode of production, as a
> 'pure type' does not. ... Thus, in the development of capitalism, the
> state has exercised a major role which cannot be reduced to its rela-
> tion to pre-existing classes or to civil society as a whole. Nothing in
> the capitalist mode of production ... leads of itself to the emergence
> of many capitalist systems of production, divided and at war, and of
> an overall class structure which is nationally segmental. It is an
> extraordinary paradox that the puny, marginalized state of the late
> feudal and early modern period had such a decisive role in system-
> integrating the world in which we live today.

Battles and wars, growing in intensity, helped forge the territorial
boundaries of both the absolutist states and the emerging European
nation states. This geopolitical environment was not simply a backcloth
to the development of absolutist and nation states, but the prime source
of them. The planning and operation of armed conflict provided the
major impulse for the centralization of administrative resources and fiscal reorganization that was a feature of the rise of the early modern state
(Giddens, 1985: 103 and 112).

The sources of the modern state

A key factor in the overcoming of medievalism by the centralizing of the
monarch's power and a growing state apparatus was the resurgent
influence of the towns, which, in a quite novel manner, became areas of
independent and collective political action. Here we find one of the earliest examples of expanding economic activity running up against the
administrative restrictions and legal–political fetters of the medieval system. The towns sought greater political freedom as a means of reducing
restrictions on trade, while the increasing translocal nature of such trade
also inclined the towns to welcome the wider system of rule provided by
the territorial rulers.

The towns also generated new political and administrative
arrangements that strongly influenced wider territorial rule, including
elected representative bodies that governed by enacting statutes, and by
establishing systems of differentiated offices or roles, conceived as

separate from the person, and which were gradually filled by a new type of political-administrative personnel, such as secular-educated lawyers and literati. Such personnel were in increasing demand by state-expanding rulers, who looked particularly to the growing universities to supply them in greater quantities. Political life also became more discursive, civilized and businesslike, in which the process and style of law sustained the notion of an increasingly 'public' domain. Gradually the ruler exercised authority as a public figure rather than as a feudal lord or property-owner, with a household that became the basis of an increased administrative system that was staffed by individuals in a more directly dependent relationship to the king than was the case with feudal vassalage (where there was a stronger sense of reciprocity of rights and obligations). The result was a significant step towards the modern nation state leading to absolutist systems of rule in a number of European states.

The fifteenth and sixteenth centuries saw the arrival of the great restorers of internal order in western Europe, who were given a strong impetus by the various crises of the late fourteenth century – war, disease, and economic stagnation – which considerably weakened the lords of the manor. It was crisis and instability in international affairs that, alongside dynastic ambition, encouraged the territorial consolidation and central-izing pressures that reinforced the patrimonial impulse. As we have seen, key factors which led to the creation of relatively strong state machiner-ies were located as much within the system of states that was emerging in Europe, as in the internal changes within each separate state.

Both economic and political competition generated power struggles between states respectively defining themselves as territorially sovereign. External challenges and forays made it imperative for territorial rulers to centralize and organize power internally. Most importantly, the ruler could count on at least the tacit support of urban commercial interests, as a strong state provided not only opportunities for the opening up of foreign trade, but also protected the domestic market and provided a general framework of order and stability necessary for entrepreneurial enterprise. Corporative medieval restrictions on trade and on the alien-ability of labour in the towns had hampered the entrepreneurial inter-ests of the commercial classes, and they were happier to accept the compelling opportunity to pursue profit through more centralized and wider territorial systems of political rule under a strong monarch.

Paralleling these developments, the economic and political position of the landed aristocracy, outside the special case of England, was gradually gnawed away by the commercialization of the economy. The influx of bullion, as a result of exploration, and regular debasements of the coinage, had inflationary consequences that debilitated the fixed revenues of the landed classes. Almost perpetual warfare in the fifteenth and sixteenth

---

Box 2.3 The 'bourgeoisie'

The bourgeoisie (literally, 'town dwellers' or burghers), predominantly merchants and artisans, formed one of the three main 'estates' (the other estates being the clergy and the nobility) by the fifteenth and sixteenth centuries, with the onset of both wider commercial markets and the growing territorial state. It was the estates as corporate groups that exercised rights and fulfilled responsibilities, not their individual members. As centralizing monarchs struggled to tame the status and power of the other two estates – with greater or lesser degrees of success – the bourgeoisie were able to lend their support for the introduction of laws governing commerce that overcame the local customary variability that so debilitated the standardization and enforceability of contracts and thus the expansion of trade. Their interest in regulation more widely was found also in their practice of organizing themselves into guilds to license and train those who practised the various trades, which also helped to moderate competition. Over the centuries, as we shall see, and not least in current times, the commercial classes have sought to balance the economic benefits that flow from competitive markets with the contrary impulse to use the state and other self-governing regulatory devices to protect their profits through a reduction in competitive market conditions. Their 'bargain' with the early rulers of the nascent modern state, in return for legal and military protection for their growing markets, including against unwarranted interference from the non-commercially minded clergy and landed and other nobles, who still had considerable status and politico-administrative clout, was that they would furnish the economic growth and taxation revenues that would help sustain a growing military and administrative state.

---

centuries, within the system of emerging states, resulted in increased taxation, heavy feudal dues, liquidity crises and stagnation, all of which weakened the landed estates while strengthening the monarchy. As Wallerstein (1974: 29–30) notes, taxation was the key issue. Territorial rulers were seeking to become part of an upward cycle in which increases in state administration, rather than becoming a drag on liquidity, were more than paid for from increased revenue drawn from an expanding economy. Accomplishing this 'take-off', however, harmed the financial and political strength of the nobility. Furthermore, the feudal element largely lost its military significance and one of its original political tasks as the evolution of military technology made obsolete the medieval knight and strengthened the hand of central authorities increasingly requiring large standing armies. By the sixteenth century, therefore,

> a number of important elements of territorial states would be in place: large standing armies, hierarchies of governmental functionaries loyal

to territorially-based rulers, and new ideas about human beings and their bodies as objects, about which secular knowledge was possible (Opello and Rosow, 1999: 47).

With new military technology, such as gunpowder, the introduction of uniforms, and armies drawn from the subject population rather than unreliable mercenaries, and better training and organization, wars became symbols of states and their power, not just battles between monarchs, and helped create the sense of state authority internally as well. Territory-wide law courts and financial institutions helped develop laws that were general and impersonal, too, and governed by 'natural' and non-religious rights. Women were regarded as confined to a 'private' and familial realm, where preparation and support for male performance and successes in the public sphere were regarded as essential functions. In comparison, males learnt to be individuals in the private sphere, the better able to perform their public duties as soldiers, administrators or, increasingly, commercial entrepreneurs.

As a result, the territorial ruler grew stronger with the acquisition of a body of permanent and dependable officials, although unlike modern state bureaucracies, monarchs also still had to rely on the practice of selling offices ('venality of office') to achieve both loyal executives and much needed revenue. While this practice helped meet the high costs of state-building and created a 'fourth' estate of office-holders whose interests were allied to the ruler, it could where it was extensively practised contain the seeds of its own destruction by proving to be not only very expensive, but, by creating a new hierarchy of offices, pose a threat to the status of traditionally powerful families. On the other hand, particularly in France, venality of office allowed the state to incorporate both landed and newly urban classes within its machinery, thus making possible the relative supremacy of the state system. Nevertheless, as Dyson (1980) points out, the sale of offices in France encouraged an exploitation of office for personal gain, in terms of both clientalism and profit, which contrasts with modern bureaucracy.

We can see in the formation of the modern state at least three key processes, or 'forms of power' (Poggi, 2001). One is the 'top-down' process of the building of managerial capacity to politically administer a large territory, impersonally and authoritatively through institutions staffed by well-educated, professional, and increasingly experienced 'civil' servants. Often routine and low-key practices were developed, initially at the margins, to persuade local populations of the benefits of national and central authority and administration, and to recognize themselves as subject to that authority, and to identify themselves as members of this new 'community'. In this, the exemplar of the Catholic Church in its model of a local component (such as a parish) being part of a wider collectivity was important, as was the significance of law as predictable and applicable to individuals within growing territorial jurisdictions. This transformed law into an instrument rather than a framework for rule. It was general law, which applied directly to all within a territorially delimited area (that is, unlike previous periods, law did not follow persons, which produced a variety of jurisdictions depending on the domestic geographical location of the individual), thus helping to separate state authority from that of the ruler, and providing the basis for abstract rights and duties conceived separately from historically accumulated, distinct prerogatives and rights (as found in feudalism particularly).

A second process is the military one. Theorists such as Mann and Giddens have demonstrated the criticality of war-making as an independent variable and source of power in the construction of the modern state, although its particular causal role varied from country to country (Tilly, 1990). Moreover, military requirements influenced state structures more generally, including the development of institutions to extract taxation effectively and efficiently without drawing popular discontent, as well as, in the nineteenth century, the introduction of welfare schemes to ensure that the conscripted infantry were up to the bodily rigours of their calling. Subsequently military forms of discipline and organization played an important part in capitalist work discipline and general corporate planning.

Finally, economic processes have been regarded by some (notably Marx) as explaining the development of the modern state as a key instrument in maintaining (but also ameliorating and masking) the growing class inequalities in capitalist societies. In this view, the growth of a powerful central state accompanies the extrusion of industrial and other workers from their means of production (and the means to defend themselves) and their subsequent exploitation by industrialists and other commercial interests, who organize factories and other more collective sites of capitalist production. Thus, a key source of state formation, and of the legal consolidation of jurisdictions, is its widening territorial span that helps to standardize and rationalize exchange relationships across ever-wider spaces. The state similarly sustains property and contract relationships, including its application to the employer/employee relationship. (These are issues to which we will return in Chapter 3.)

In addition to these three modes of power in the development of the state, we could also point to the influence of Italian humanism and the Reformation, which strengthened the power of the secular authority against that of the Church. The religious unity of the Christian community became fragmented, and the idea of the charitable role of the secular authorities was established. Religious upheaval in the sixteenth and seventeenth centuries sustained state power and encouraged the notion of a neutral political authority that gave priority to the secular purpose of protecting life and maintaining order rather than the imposition of one religious truth. Secularization, not just a rising bourgeoisie, played its part in the development of a public, state authority (Dyson, 1980: 30).

Inter-state relations

European absolutism also generated a new set of relationships between states (Held *et al.*, 1999). The centralization of authority kick-started several historically significant processes for nation state formation, such as the alignment of a standard system of rule within territorial boundaries, a more orderly management of public finances, administrative centralization, a growing monopoly of military power by the state through the initiation of standing armies, new arrangements for law enforcement, and the regularization of exchanges among states through the creation of more formal diplomatic relationships. As Held *et al.* (1999:36) point out:

> Absolutism helped initiate a process of state-making which began to reduce the social, economic and cultural differences within states and expand the differences among them, that is, it helped to forge political communities with a clearer and growing sense of identity – national identity.

Held *et al.* describe this as an evolving 'society of states' in which the principles of sovereignty and territoriality became paramount. The internal consolidation of power assisted the general creation of inter-state formation:

> The development of state sovereignty was central to the process of mutual recognition whereby states granted each other rights of jurisdiction in their respective territories and communities ... in the world of relations among states, the principle that all states had equal rights to self-determination became paramount in the formal conduct of states towards one another. (1999: 37)

A new concept of international law and normative obligation reflected this new inter-state order after the peace treaties of Westphalia of 1648. Although not fully articulated until the turn of the nineteenth century, the treaties promoted notions of non-intervention in the domestic affairs of other recognized states, and state consent as the basis of international obligation.

Box 2.4 The peace treaties of Westphalia 1648

The key principles were the following:

- the world consists of, and is divided into, sovereign territorial states that recognize no superior authority;
- the processes of law-making, the settlement of disputes and law enforcement are largely in the hands of individual states;
- international law is oriented to the establishment of minimal rules of coexistence.

In conclusion, however, within nations Roman law conferred on the continental European states the distinction between public and private (civil) affairs. A separate domain of public law, which pertained to the impersonal abstract character of the state, emerged with its own principles to guide legislation and administration, and with a distinct system of administrative courts, distinguishable from the civil law, which applied to relations of private individuals. This distinctively legal basis to the identification of the state was, however, absent in England. There, a relatively cohesive political community had already developed, through its feudal institutions, the idea of making law through statute, while Roman law's association with autocratic government appeared incompatible with the tradition of a limited monarchy.

War, revolution, ideas and administration

Absolutism provided a radical force for change in the sixteenth and seventeenth centuries and it was the absolutism of France that served as the main point of reference, particularly under Louis XIV, whose reign (1643–1715) was the longest in European history. However, the *ancien régime* created by Louis was to end in the disaster of the 1789 Revolution, which, 'while turning France into the apostle of Republicanism, brought French supremacy to a close' (Davies, 1997:580).

As Davies (1997: 713) observes, the French Revolution and its aftermath gave strong impetus to ideas of republicanism, revolutionary possibility and the concept of universal human rights, while 'the concept of the modern state, in the sense of a centralized administration applying common laws uniformly to all citizens over the whole territory, received an enormous boost'.

These ideas received considerable impetus from the increasingly accepted notion that politics was quite separate from religion, and had

Box 2.5 The French Revolution of 1789

The origins of the French Revolution lay in the inability of the royal household in the seventeenth century to eliminate medieval institutions, such as seigneurial domains and provincial estates. France remained predominantly an agricultural society in the seventeenth and eighteenth centuries, with an economy sluggishly characterized by a miasma of property interests that prevented any quick switch to capitalist agriculture or industrialism, and which retained a large peasant sector. A distinctive dominant class, neither feudal nor capitalist, appropriated surplus from this predominantly peasant-based agriculture through a complex pattern of rents and dues enforced in part by landlord-dominated juridical institutions, but with royal absolutism as the final back-up. This situation of dependence by propertied privilege on the state engendered a dominant class with a vested interest in opposing reform. When the system's economic foundations collapsed, the inability to secure reform against landed resistance led to the collapse of the royal administration and paved the way for social revolution (Skocpol, 1979: 64). As de Tocqueville observed, many aspects of government were actually improving under the old regime, but the most dangerous moment for bad governments is generally that in which it sets about reform.

The central parts in the Revolution were played both by peasants and sansculottes (proletarians). The former revolted against heavy rents and dues, which finally forced the deputies in the constituent assembly to sweep away feudal rights and the privileges of medievalism. The latter contained some fairly radical elements and generated several of the earliest doctrines of communism and socialism, and indeed may have had as much influence as the bourgeoisie who are usually regarded as the decisive agent.

its own principles. The writings of Machiavelli in the sixteenth century, on successful rulers mastering the stratagems of violence and the furtherance of state interests, as human not moral or religious matters, were especially influential. They led to increased focus on how states acted to increase their power, with politics and knowledge having secular outcomes and dynamics, not simply being routes to God. The treaties of Westphalia were crucial in this development by formulating the notion of secure and sovereign states with respected territorial borders that excluded incursions on religious and other grounds by other states (as had occurred in the Thirty Years War that preceded it). It was a secular solution that contained Christendom and its increasing 'reformation' fissures within political boundaries.

Between the sixteenth and eighteenth centuries in west Europe occurred a 'nexus of factors' known as modernity (Cohen and Kennedy,

2000: 44). Europe was composed of several independent states of sufficiently similar size to provide countervailing power, and situated closely together. The resultant balance of power and alliances allowed entrepreneurs and intellectuals to flourish, which stimulated the consequent challenge of rationalism and talent to inherited privilege.

During the eighteenth century these influences converged in a number of interlinked ideas that became known as the Enlightenment. Figures such as Hume, Kant and Voltaire offered science and rational knowledge as the basis for human progress through the power of reason, evidenced by a number of scientific discoveries over the previous two centuries (by such as Bacon and Newton). The free, rational and secular individual – full of infinite potential and tolerance – was regarded as the basic building-block for both progress and more universal (global) values, and found particular expression in the American Constitution of 1787, with its notion of fundamental human rights.

The origins of liberalism and capitalism

As Davies (1997) has noted, the major victory in influencing state-building finally went to British constitutionalism, not only because Britain was the dominant state of the nineteenth century but also, via the constitution of Britain's rebel colonies, because of its influence on the US, which was the major superpower of the twentieth century. What lay behind this eventual British ascendancy?

The north-west European states, as we have seen, became the heartland of the world economy when, towards the second half of the sixteenth century, an emergent capitalist sector began to be located in certain core states. The pacesetter was England. The reasons for this are complex, but may be classified as both political and economic. Politically, England had a number of plus points over other countries at this time – its unity was fairly well established, the machinery of government, expenditure and taxation was highly competent, it possessed stability and was not stretched by far-flung international dominions, while London – as the growing capital – was increasingly a cultural and economic source of cohesion and focus. England also had no large standing army that required resourcing through high taxation and an extended bureaucracy.

By the end of the eighteenth century, and in the context of the French Revolution and its Napoleonic aftermath (and English authoritarian reaction to them), military expenditure rose to around 40 per cent of available financial resources as intensifying geopolitical militarism ensured that the English state (like other states) grew on the back of warfare. It meant that for tax and manpower reasons the military state was becoming more intrusive for its citizens, which helped to underpin increasing interest in issues of both representation and nationality. As Michael Mann (1986) has evidenced, it was not until the second half of the nineteenth century that the overwhelming importance of military expenditure was overcome by civilian spending when states undertook major civilian functions, such as providing transport, communications and schools.

Box 2.6 England as colonial and capitalist pacesetter

Of particular importance was the development since the thirteenth century of the beginnings of representative government and institutional constraints on the power of the monarch. The result was sufficient royal efficiency and administrative and other capability to provide the basis for the development of a stable state framework, but operating increasingly within political restraints established by the balance of interests and forces found within the growing authority of parliament. Geographically, English stability and confidence were buttressed by being surrounded by the oceans as a defensive barrier against war-making continental states. With no standing army and little risk of maritime invasion, and in the context of the veto powers of the Commons, the English crown was unable to construct an effective administrative, financial and military base of its own from which to force its will on the country – which would have prevented the Civil War in the seventeenth century. The sale of confiscated monastery land by Henry VIII, which strengthened the position of the gentry, had lost for the monarchy its one great chance for absolutism by removing a firm economic base that was independent of parliamentary taxation. The Civil War was precipitated in the mid-seventeenth century by a crisis between the crown and the increasingly powerful gentry, who regarded royal monopolies and judicial protection of the peasants as barriers to commercial ambition.

The increase in parliamentary powers in contrast to those of the monarchy was reinforced by wars and the power of the Commons to vote the taxing measures to fund monarchical military ventures (Schama, 2001). However, the development of parliamentary processes was a close-run thing, indicating perhaps the essential contingency of historical trajectories. The anti-royal coalition of Puritan and military veered at times towards producing a military–theocratic dictatorship, with zealot soldiers enforcing not only a 'Rump Parliament' but also seeking to ban Christmas and its celebration. However, in confirmation of the view that the structures of society generate powerful constraints upon even the most ideological and the most determined, evangelical measures to ban enjoyment generally foundered on an inability to obtain compliance.

Davies (1997: 631) makes the important point that the constitutional revolutions of the mid-seventeenth century in the British Isles postulated a theory of sovereignty that differed fundamentally from those found in most other European countries or later in the US or revolutionary France. It postulated the absolute sovereignty of parliament, which, formally at least, had been transferred, supremacy intact, from the monarchy. It contrasted clearly from purer or more fundamentalist notions of the sovereignty of the people, and it also differed from those constitutional arrangements which 'checked and balanced' the power of parliament through formal divisions of powers with other branches, such as the judiciary or the president. In this sense, it could be claimed that Britain's parliamentary sovereignty was no less absolutist in its cast than continental forms (Opello and Rosow, 1999).

Through breaking the power of the king, the Civil War in England strengthened parliament as the locus of landlord power at the expense of the crown, and also removed the main barriers to the enclosing landlord and the demise of the peasantry. Moreover, it was a national single parliament with territorial representation that lacked the 'estates' divisions found elsewhere. The result was a flexible institution, which constituted both an arena into which new social elements could be drawn as their demands arose and an institutional mechanism for settling peacefully conflicts of interest among these groups. Although the landed classes may have kept political control until the twentieth century, the connection between the enclosing landlord and the commercial bourgeoisie was close, for both the capitalist principle and parliamentary democracy were directly opposed to religiously based authority in politics, and against production for use rather than for individual profit in the economy.

Consequently, from the seventeenth century onwards England's political development differed from the rest of Europe in that it remained remarkably well-nourished from its feudal roots. The political system was based on a complex process of negotiation between the monarch and the large landowners, while the crown's authority was limited, not least because the monarch was regarded as part of a wider community. The revolution of 1688 succeeded in protecting the traditional rights and privileges of parliament, the courts and local communities against the assertions of a centralizing crown. Public action became subject to parliamentary control, legitimated by the notion that sovereignty resided in crown-in-parliament, not by reference to the notion of an autonomous state acting to realize certain inherent purposes (Dyson, 1980: 117). There was a gradual movement to the view that executive power was an effusion of parliament, although parliament was not yet regarded as representative of 'the people', which would have been too radical a notion. Rather, constitutional arrangements, unlike continental absolutism and its aftermath, did not encourage an activist conception of the state.

In comparison, the French nobility achieved little independence from the king and continued to possess a more definite legal status than in England and an economic dependence on peasant dues. It lacked an economic base, such as that provided by the commercialized wool trade in England, and consequently relied upon royal absolutism to extract surplus from an increasingly unproductive and traditional system. As economic and military pressures intensified from more successfully commercializing states, the French agrarian economy could not produce a sufficient return to remunerate its office holders in a way that would ensure their real dependence on the king. 'Venality of office' was the alternative method for consolidating royal power, but it imparted feudal characteristics to a bourgeoisie that became rigid defenders of local privileges, especially in the parliaments, and tied an uncommercial nobility into a singularly unproductive style of conspicuous consumption, war, and general indolence within the royal household.

The value of Wallerstein's (1974/80/89) theoretical perspective of an emerging capitalist world economy is that it is possible to account for the variations in political and economic practice described above in terms of international constraints and opportunities, not simply as the consequence of discrete or domestically isolated factors internal to states. Wallerstein argues, for example, that it was England's position in the world economy that enabled it to become the first industrial nation, with a political accommodation between traditional and rising economic elements. It experienced the specific conjuncture of commercial opportunity (mainly textiles) and the absence of external threat or imperial obligations. The result was state machinery just strong enough to provide external security, but sufficiently weak not to favour either the landed nobility or the new state administrators, so that neither was able to totally consume the surplus of the most productive forces.

The combination of maritime strength and navigational and other advances with the accelerating potency of steam and machinery, gave the British a head start in the quest for colonial possessions in Asia, which gathered pace throughout the nineteenth century as it extended to Africa and elsewhere.

The development of liberalism and capitalism

The western state that emerged in the nineteenth century came to be understood in terms of two central ideas: a centralized power, which attempts to overawe all other powers in a given territory through the use of various agencies, including force; and a state founded on consent, in that the power must be legitimated and turned into authority. In respect of the former idea, as we have seen, the conception of the state which slowly develops is that of a public power that is purposefully created and distinct from other social powers and particular office-holders, including the king. It is characterized by authority, entailing relations of command and obedience, rather than utility and affinity ('state and society'), and involves at least some subordination of private to public interest, although in exchange for certain public rights. Clear territorial boundaries mark out the administrative province of the nation state, which previously had been indefinite and fluctuating, and become increasingly associated with the formation of national police forces. The determination of very precise administrative boundaries, not simply 'nationalism', integrates nation states, each of which operates in its own territory as the exclusive source of rule.

In contrast with the fragmentary power of medievalism, the nineteenth-century constitutional state is characterized by a unitary sovereignty which becomes manifest in a single currency, a unified legal system, and an expanding state educational system employing a single 'national' language. These processes in England can be traced back to the Protestant Reformation of the sixteenth century, particularly its emphasis on individual reflection and salvation rather than compliance with organized ecclesiastical authority and its personnel. Helped particularly by the revolution in printing, Protestantism introduced vernacular liturgies and emphasized the necessity – in order to avoid establishment dogma – for regular Bible reading by local communities:

> This meant that every new Protestant community sponsored a new translation of the Bible, that Protestant officialdom set special store on education and literacy, and that the general level of literacy in Protestant countries soon surpassed the level in Catholic countries. (Davies, 1999: 416)

It is unsurprising that observers have traced the origins of the 'first capitalist society' in no small part to the development of Protestantism. Most notably, Weber (1968) detected a close affinity between the 'spirit of capitalism' and the 'protestant ethic', particularly through shared notions of deferred gratification, the need for investment, and the values of unshowiness and hard work. However, although Protestantism clearly helped originate a wider diffusion of literacy in the nation-forming English language, the diffusion of English was rapidly secularized and spread downward from the dominant classes by the processes of commercial development and military state modernization. As in other countries, these took over much of the expansion of literacy through, as Mann (1986: 217) notes, 'contracts, government records, army drill manuals, coffeehouse business discussions, academies of notable officials'. A literary tradition in 'national' languages in the European states soon eroded cultural particularism, and a system of national military conscription, replacing the local recruitment of ancient military units, also helped to overcome 'peripheral' or local identities.

Modern states are also distinctive in that they are 'built' or 'made' purposefully and operate with reference to some idea of an end to which they are instrumental. This is a particular connotation of post-revolutionary regimes. Political leaderships involved in revolutions must be regarded as actors struggling to assert and make good their claims to state sovereignty, not simply as representatives of socioeconomic interests but as claimants for state power (Skocpol, 1979: 164). The social and occupational backgrounds of such leaders is conducive to a view of them as 'state-builders' rather than as representatives of classes, for they tend to come from the ranks of the relatively highly educated groups orientated to state activities or employment and somewhat marginal to the dominant classes and government elites under the old regimes.

The French Revolution, for example, resulted in a professional-bureaucratic state rather than a 'bourgeois' or 'capitalist' state. While the simplification of property rights and the reduction of trade barriers certainly facilitated capitalism, the most marked developments were in state organization, which became more centralized and which introduced nationwide systems of law, customs and taxation. State finances under Napoleon, for example, became more a form of public administration than private capitalism, with the growth of a Treasury and full annual accounts of the nation's finances.

The government took control, too, of education, making it more selective, centralized and elitist, and it provided a reservoir of talent from which state administrators and experts could be recruited. They were needed, too, as the number of bureaucrats multiplied during the Revolution (from 50,000 to 250,000) with the emergence of a stronger and more autonomous state. Bureaucratization and 'democratization' were exemplified in the professionalization of the officer corps and the emergence of a national army.

The nineteenth-century French state indicates one particular form that the emerging western nation state took as it centralized and legitimated its powers. It differs from a more liberal, parliamentary outcome, as found in Britain, which arguably may have been more suitable for the furtherance of capitalist industrialization. Abstractly, however, the French state was not untypical, for the state generally became structured as a formal complex organization, with offices hierarchically arranged and with an organic division of administrative tasks guided by general laws that 'depersonalized' decision-making.

A feature of the more marked liberal design which steadily emerged in the nineteenth century was the process through which some matters came to be accepted as public and others as private. Commercial interests were especially concerned to limit the powers of state activity and wished the state to establish parameters within which business activity could be left relatively untrammelled.

Moreover, the new bourgeois classes in Britain were quick to turn to parliament to reform and unify the existing and localized forms of social control that did not fit well with the needs of an expanding industrial economy. Before the 1830s the largest towns, such as Birmingham and Manchester, had no police because these towns had no political representation in general, while the police system, under the aristocratic and

---

Box 2.7 Corporations

Originally a mercantilist notion, a 'corporation' referred initially to an exclusive grant (generally a monopoly) by the state to a private company for the purpose of providing something that was in the interest of the whole society. Clearly it was a means of restraining trade in which corporations received rights to develop essential parts of the economy on behalf of the state. Railroads, for example, were incorporated because of their 'public' character. (This model of business development has been known as the 'state concessions' model, in which companies were regulated by the state in return for market opportunities in key areas of life, and which has in a modern sense returned as a paradigm for the public regulation of the privatized industries.)

Corporate charters in this old sense were very difficult to obtain, inevitably, and in England it required a private Act of Parliament. However, the rising industrial capitalists gradually succeeded in having it accepted that 'corporations' were private and unexceptional, rather than public and special. It came to refer to any group of people who obtained limited liability from the state in pursuit of their private advantage. This greatly facilitated the growth of the joint-stock companies and the development of business regulation through company law – which was based on the autonomy of the company and its owners – rather than more directly by state intervention. Yet the important point is to recognize that it was political action that brought about the change. To place limitations on state prerogatives required state interventionism. The liberal state was not a completely *laissez-faire* state, but one in which government intervention may be required to create or maintain the conditions for economic accumulation.

amateurish control of the Lord Lieutenants, concentrated its strength in the rural parish, rather than in the new industrial towns where it was needed. Not only were the bourgeoisie increasingly successful in ensuring that the magistrates for the industrial towns were chosen from themselves and not the gentry, but the strengthening of the metropolitan police and the reforming and centralizing of the administrative structure of the English prison system helped meet industrialists' demands for increased efficiency, competency and professionalism in the operation of state functions. The establishment of elected local authorities in Britain in the nineteenth century also helped to involve businesspeople and middle-class professionals more directly in government in pursuit of their interests, and to reduce the predominance of landowners and gentry, as well as their practices of patronage and corruption. Moreover, despite a growth in the public regulation of business and professional occupations in response to the social and other conditions of nineteenth-century industrialization, informal self-regulation by state-backed associations ('clubs') and gentlemanly ideals were generally regarded as the prime instruments for ensuring appropriate economic and social standards (Moran, 2003).

Inefficiencies in political administration had been most marked at national level during the eighteenth century in what became known as the civil (that is, non-military) service. Offices were often sinecures, and could be bought and sold, or passed around the scions of leading families. It was the need to regularize the state's finances for war, and to ensure the efficient extraction and administration of taxes, that led to reform and to a more meritocratic and standardized approach to crown employment. This is best captured in Britain in the Northcote–Trevelyan Report of 1854, which called for a more unified service based on open and competitive entry and promotion, and which confirmed the 'intellectual' and policy-making role of 'top' civil servants in serving government ministers. The aim was to produce an organization with features of the legal–rational bureaucracies that were to be outlined by Weber (1968) as a superior form of efficiency.

This feature of the liberal state indicates its 'two faces' of freedom and regulation. As we shall see, although the design of the liberal constitutional state provided enhanced individual autonomy, particularly in the economic sphere, it also allowed for state regulation in the interest of new 'corporate, joint-stock' actors, as well as devising instruments of surveillance, socialization, and pacification for growing populations that were subject to the inequalities and misery of industrial capitalism. Labour discipline or career aspiration could not depend on the free play of the market alone, but depended in considerable part on traditional attitudes, mainly religious, backed up by state controls utilizing the increasingly available techniques for the measurement and management of popular behaviour.

Liberalism and representation

In considering the second major feature of the nineteenth-century liberal constitutional state – the 'representative' nature of its claims to legitimacy – there is recognition that the claim to supreme authority, or sovereignty, is no longer based upon the hereditary rank of a monarchical lineage but lies in the nature of the relationship between the rulers and the ruled. That is, sovereignty is based on the people. More particularly, it comes to be seen as founded on consent, which raised the question of how extensive and on what basis should be this consent. It is helpful at this stage to distinguish between economic and political liberalism. Economic liberalism was prompted by the apparent separation of the state from society, especially from the economy, and is often associated with the economic individualism of Adam Smith (1776) and David Ricardo (1817) and a British school of political economy. It focused on the concept of free trade and the related doctrine of *laissez-faire*, and opposed the tendency of governments to regulate economic life through interventionism and protectionism. Individuals with property, in this view, had the right to engage in commerce and industry without excessive state restraint. The main purpose of state behaviour is to meet and conform to the economic and social needs of individuals.

The state, in this conception, is vital for economic growth but is also the source of economic decline. It should demonstrate a level of institutional autonomy sufficient to ensure a minimalist *laissez-faire* stance. As such, the state should be confined to a specific role, that of enforcing the general rules that govern civil society. This involves the creation and maintenance of private property rights, a system of law, including company law, and military and police forces to guarantee order and security. Any wider state interventionism (including widespread taxation) is economically deleterious because it distorts prices and hinders the price mechanism in optimally allocating resources, thereby debilitating the prospects for national economic development. This by no means implies a weak state, for the state may require considerable powers to enforce such rules. But it does imply a 'restrained' role that precludes detailed interference in civil society. Moreover, as well as seeking to dismantle barriers to trade internally, such as forms of collectivist organization like the guilds and increasingly the new trade unions, economic liberalism sought to eliminate or reduce the hindrances to trade between nations, perhaps reflecting the growing strength and prosperity that flowed from both imperial expansion and Britain's maritime supremacy.

Internationally, economic liberalism holds that free trade is conducive to peace and stability between nations who, rather than being prone to jealousy, will seek to advance their interests through cooperative trading agreements. Interventionist (authoritarian) states, however, have a tendency to economic nationalism and tariff protectionism that undermines commercial interdependence, heightens conflict and leads to wars. In turn wars further hampered economic development because they then require heavier taxation and debt to pay for basically unproductive expenditure. None the less, for much of the nineteenth century Britain remained largely protectionist, and even after the adoption of more explicitly free trade policies, protectionist sentiments were not always far removed from the surface (as witnessed, for example, by calls for imperial or empire tariff preferences by Joseph Chamberlain and others at the turn into the twentieth century and beyond).

Political liberalism refers much more explicitly to the relationship of the individual to the state, and particularly to the issue of government by consent. Perhaps espoused most fully in the American Revolution, it stresses the rule of law, individual liberty, constitutional procedures, religious toleration and the universal rights of man (*sic*). It opposes the inbuilt prerogatives, where they survived, of kings, nobles and bishops. The possession of individual property was seen, too, as laying the foundations of civic responsibility and stability. Consequently, while happy to reduce the powers of absolutism, adherents of political liberalism were not inclined to radical forms of egalitarianism or extensive democracy.

The legitimacy or authority of state power that derives from political liberalism finds initial expression in the early 'social contract' theorists and their speculations on the limits of state power. It was founded in opposition to the dogmas of religion and on the principle that knowledge should be tested in reasoned discussion by individual subjects who act rationally. For Hobbes (1651) the limitations of the state were more implied than explicit: individuals had a moral obligation to obey the state's commands and laws as long as the state preserved their security. For later theorists, such as Locke (1689) and Montesquieu (1746), these limits were more pronounced, for they regarded the state as only one of the associations of individuals, and one without any extensive claim over them. Constitutions, it was argued, should seek to prevent accumulations of power preferably through institutional checks and balances, or by a confederation of states.

These essentially negative concepts of government complemented the view that civil society was the sphere of individual liberties and that governments should limit themselves to promoting the conditions of, particularly, economic liberty. As a result, liberals took to democratic ideas rather grudgingly, as a possible means for protecting individuals from an ever-powerful state. Democracy was less important morally than instrumentally, as a device for subjecting state actions to rational discussion, usually through parliamentary assemblies. It at least enabled the unwashed majority to learn something about the benefits of liberty and the rule of law, and indeed to participate sufficiently to be able to defend them vigorously, and before political demagogues and others stirred them to class frenzy and other disagreeable mass passions. Even so, liberals such as Mill and de Tocqueville wanted constitutional safeguards in democracies for the rights of minorities, and were concerned that democracy would also lead to standardization, the decline of local community, and a general 'dumbing down' (although, of course, they did not use such a term). In the nineteenth and early twentieth centuries, imperial and capitalist expansion and the tremendous increase in trade and productive output, seemed to liberals to be sound evidence that liberalism worked and that the whole population would benefit from liberalism's general raising of living standards. In Chapter 8 we return to the philosophies of liberalism, including its modern variants, and discuss them in greater detail.

The state as a moral community

In contrast to Anglo-American liberalism, a continental European tradition, associated with Hegel (1821) and Rousseau (1762), has regarded the state less negatively and as a higher moral community, an end in itself, which should actively seek to counter the harmful effects of civil and market society. They, particularly Hegel, have seen the state as a rational agent for progress in ways beyond the capacities of individuals operating in markets. Markets provided only a limited form of reason, that which was configured by self-interest and the alienation of commodity forms. Modern states were purposeful instruments that enabled people to shape their world in an ethical manner. Arbitrary power, as with the liberals, was distrusted, and parliamentary states, with highly educated and professional bureaucrats, were likely to prove the most effective internally but also victorious in inter-state wars. They have the best prospects of ruling justly in the interests of all subjects.

Dyson (1980) has noted that the idea or concept of the state lacks precision and significance in American and British experience in comparison with that of continental Europe. The view of the pluralistic character of public authority, found in the 'stateless' English-speaking societies, contrasts strongly with that of the integrated 'public power' of continental Europe, where it is often defended in highly abstract and impersonal terms.

However, liberalism is not the same everywhere. English liberalism, for example, differs from American liberalism in its peculiarly feudal connotations that preserved the notion of the traditional accumulation of specific rights or 'immunities', rather than couching them in terms of universal rational or legal principles. In England these rights were established as unwritten constitutional conventions so that the legal privileges of the landed nobility, if not the king, would not be jeopardized.

Once the notion of rights is formulated in universalistic terms, it becomes logically difficult to impose limits on political participation, especially as the legitimacy of the state is apparently founded on the voluntary consent of all citizens and its purpose is to safeguard their natural rights (Gamble, 1981). Consequently, in the nineteenth century, liberal constitutionalism was broadened to include a notion of representation that was more compatible with that of democracy. However, as we have seen, in its commitment to the efficacy of rationalism and science, liberalism inevitably recoiled from the idea that the simple majority principles of democracy provided 'sound' decisions or ones that were well-informed technically. The principles of liberty and rationalism proved more important to most liberals than the idealization of democracy, and this was a position that socialism sought to exploit. The increasing juxtaposition of legal equality, and increasing social and economic inequalities in industrial capitalism, generated discussion as to which inequalities were the most intolerable, or at least were priorities for remedial action. It was gradually established that equality was not provided sufficiently by freedom of contract alone, but requires social and political rights as well. These ideas were expressed particularly through notions of citizenship which were developed in the twentieth century, and which we look at later.

Cartels and monopolies

By the turn of the twentieth century the emergence of large firms in a number of advanced economies cast doubt on the competitive aspects of market relations as outlined in liberalism. Relations between such companies, and their control over markets, seemed to become increasingly power-based and characterized by cartelization and monopolization, in which one or a few firms dominated. Moreover, the emergence of employers' associations as well as trade unions added dimensions of collective negotiation and bargaining into the essentially individual market relations held to exist between capital and labour. For some, such as Schumpeter (1942) and Galbraith (1953) in the US, this was not an undesirable state of affairs. Only monopolies and large corporations were likely to possess the research and development and other resources to maintain innovation, value, and concern for employees, especially as technology became increasingly important.

For liberals, however, the decline of market competition was likely to stultify trade, induce complacency, and lead to national protectionism and possibly economic or military wars. During the Roosevelt 'New Deal' years before the Second World War, and after the economic crises and scandals of the 1920s and its Great Depression, liberals and more modern parts of business in the US turned to the idea of independent regulatory authorities for economic sectors as a means by which the state could (neutrally) help sustain the conditions of economic competitiveness and efficiency, but without resorting to socialist-like interventions, such as the public ownership of key parts of the economy. Poggi (1978: 124) points out that the impact of these collectivist developments on the state-society line in Europe can be seen in that the rules on such matters as collective bargaining and much welfare legislation came to form a body of law (for example, labour law) that straddled the divide between private and public law. Moreover, the increasing involvement of these new economic organizations in a developing arena of 'pressure group' politics, often to be found 'behind the back' of parliament and operating within government bureaucracies, turned apparently private interests into quasi-governmental agencies. At the same time, the growth of state operations produced new sets of bureaucratic interests that competed for a share of the social product with the private sector. We will look at some of these issues more closely in Chapter 5. But to complete our story we need to give consideration to countries outside west Europe.

The state outside west Europe

The development of the modern state outside west Europe had a number of particular characteristics. For example, in the case of China and Russia, revolutions generated party-led state formation and, in the former, involved mass mobilization. Also distinctively, following the Second World War, we see in eastern Asia – in countries such as South Korea, Japan, Malaysia and Singapore – a form of 'directed capitalism from the state' (Weiss, 1998), a kind of half-way house between outright state control (as in early Germany and Russia) and western, relatively state-free capitalist development, with a key purpose being the stimulation of manufacture. It will be useful to look at some of these cases in more detail, partly because they indicate how their state development and structures differed from those in the West, and partly because in virtually every case they indicate the increased interplay of international forces, models, and rivalries in state construction throughout the nineteenth century, an interplay which accelerated throughout the twentieth.

China

We noted earlier, in discussing the fifteenth-century development of the modern western state, that China at that time was a rich civilization with a sophisticated state bureaucracy and possessed many of the conditions that could have led to capitalist and state development along western European lines. Imperial China established some elements of a modern state structure ahead of those in the West (albeit within an empire), including functionally defined and highly specialized civil and military bureaucracies, and with state monopolies over the production and distribution of key commodities, such as salt, water, and bronze (Miller, 2000). By the turn of the nineteenth century China had a state system that had existed for over 600 years, and which reached its heights during the Qing dynasty, which was established by the foreign invasion of a collection of tribes from the north-east region of Manchuria (the Manchus) in 1644.

Traditional China reached its highpoint in the eighteenth century, by which time it was one of the strongest and best-endowed countries in the world. Its rule by a scholarly official class of Confucian-trained gentry administrators seemed to admiring westerners to epitomize the rational ideas of the Enlightenment (Hunter and Sexton, 1999: 7; Moise, 1994; Fairbank, 1992; Spence, 1991). Yet Confucianism, at least as interpreted by the imperial state, lacked the challenge and 'fizz' of western rationalism. The emphasis was rather on order, hierarchy, obedience and correct behaviour, both in family and social life and in the relationship between the ruler and the ruled. Perhaps even more relevantly, there was no notion of individual or social rights governing political relationships, although this seems not to have deterred fairly regular peasant revolts (Randall, 2000: 209). (See also Chapter 8 for a discussion on whether Confucianism is consistent or not with western ideas.)

Running its wide internal imperial system, not least with persistent centrifugal tendencies making it difficult to rule over a large and dispersed area, served as an important break on any outward or market-expansionary ambitions that the dynasty may have had. Despite its highly advanced form of administration, the late imperial state had a poor capacity for extracting resources and revenue from the populace, which meant that it lacked the means to redistribute resources to needy sectors or to invest in strategic priority projects (Shambaugh, 2000: 5). Consequently China never industrialized when the West did. While science was highly developed, there were few incentives to create the investment to give it commercial application, and merchants remained rooted at the bottom of the stratification system.

Over those years of relative peace and prosperity, China's economy was agrarian and characterized by rice-producing peasants oriented to local markets and towns. The state system was a centralized administrative structure, under the rule of an absolute and legally unlimited emperor, and was generally staffed by the scions of wealthy families who had passed through a rigorous, Confucian-based examination system, which held together an essentially localized society. Moreover, imperial China saw its rule in ways unlike that of the clearly territorially defined and sovereign states of Europe. China felt itself to be the centre of the civilized world – the 'middle kingdom' – with a theoretically all-powerful, if geographically constrained, emperor directly descended from heaven, who felt no need to treat with other states on an equal basis.

The imperial state went to considerable lengths to ensure that officials operated in areas other than from where they originated; in order to avoid cliques or the build-up of local as opposed to system-wide interests, officials were moved around on a regular basis. While the top literati staffed the imperial administration, which never reached down as far as the village or market town, other officials, such as the county magistrate, functioned locally and often formed effective alliances with landowners and others in the raising of taxes.

During the nineteenth century, however, this relatively cosy state of affairs was challenged by constant intrusions from foreigners, initially from Russia but then from the growing industrial nations of the West. Led by Britain, western nations fretted at restrictions on trade in China and successfully agitated for their control of parts of Chinese territory (such as Hong Kong), for jurisdiction in a growing number of treaty ports, for the right to station troops in China, and for exemption from Chinese laws. This fuelled a hurried colonial race for trade and influence in China, involving the British, French, Russians, Germans, and the Japanese, which a declining imperial regime was unable to confront successfully.

The decline of the imperial state system and an inability to repel foreign raiders followed the humiliating conclusions to the Opium Wars of 1839–42 and 1856–60. The peasant revolt that comprised the Taiping Rebellion of 1850–64 had led to bloody civil war and famine and almost engulfed the regime. To survive it was forced to accept foreign military aid. Population growth ran up against the declining availability of new lands and the limits of a traditional economy, while imperial fiscal and tax policies became debilitated by increasingly independent provincial rulers keeping revenues for local use. The national civil administration progressively lost its grip on the country.

The weakness of state capacity was highlighted by the failed reforms of 1898, which followed defeat in war by a fast-modernizing Japan in 1895.

These attempts at change in China were influenced by the Japanese Meiji reforms, European industrial and military strategies, and American science and education. These provided the link to the modernizing and nation state-building actions of subsequent regimes, particularly Mao's in the 1950s and 1960s. The immediate outcome was regular, often peasant-based rebellions, and an increasing reliance on local gentry and officials for the maintenance of order, until the collapse of the regime in 1911. However, although the various forces that coalesced to defeat the aristocratic Manchus could agree on the need for a replenished national unity, the mix of gentry, military officers, local officials and others could not agree on the type of constitution to reflect this. The result was thirty years of 'warlordism' by local chiefs, characterized by intermittent and destructive wars and national disintegration, exacerbated by repeated foreign incursions, particularly by the Japanese during the Second World War, before the peasant-backed Communist Revolution of 1949.

As in the French and Russian Revolutions, the Chinese Revolution instigated the building of a much larger state administration, more powerful and bureaucratic than before, under the control of a political party that relied upon the mobilization of the masses, especially the peasants. While it is possible to find other examples of revolutionary parties that purport to rule on behalf of a particular class (as in the case of the Soviet Union and its 'proletarian state'), in China we witness the attempt to involve the revolutionary class – the peasantry – through widespread mobilization. The regime rested on the distinction between government, responsible for administrative functions, and party, which had the 'higher' revolutionary tasks of policy-making, coordination and supervision. It was an apparatus that functioned hierarchically at all the levels, from the national right down to the village. At the same time the state extended its reach into new areas of activity, such as economic production, education, and the social services. And in comparison with the earlier scholarly, exam-based bureaucracy, selection for office depended more on political and class criteria than qualifications. Offices at all levels were incorporated within an overall organizational control, with positions made distinctive from personal or private interests and assets, unlike the earlier systems of rule. A consequence was the general elimination of local powers and provincial oppositions, and a national unification under a party-state committed to industrialization and modernization under its controlling hand.

Russia

In the sense of 'world time', it would have been difficult for the 1949 Chinese Revolution not to have been profoundly influenced by the earlier Russian Revolution of 1917, despite the more agrarian class structure of the Chinese example. Both, after all, shared a commitment to socialist transformation under a party-state committed to state-controlled industrial development. And, in the early years of the new regime in China, the Soviet Union supplied considerable guidance and assistance – too much eventually for Mao and his colleagues, who became concerned to develop a pathway better suited to the particular needs of China (avoiding especially over-reliance on rapid urbanization and heavy manufacturing), and who became suspicious of the shared nuclear interests of the Soviet Union and the United States.

The Russian imperial state in the nineteenth century had introduced significant modernization and reforms, as well as protecting itself from the predatory incursions of faster-developing nations. It had become more militarized, industrialized and bureaucratized than imperial China, utilizing a range of western innovations and techniques. However, defeat in the Crimean War both prevented access to a sea base for the navy and revealed weaknesses in an imperial regime dependent on a traditional serf-based economy. Russia's landed aristocrats, following the mandatory requirements of Peter the Great that they undertake lifelong military or state-administrative careers, had become state dependent but economically weak. Defeat highlighted, too, the significant industrial and military advances of competitor nations, as later did humiliating defeat by an Asian power – Japan – at sea in 1904–5.

Consequently, the imperial regime found itself unable to reform landed structures or, despite considerable state-induced industrialization, to conduce a productivity spurt that would enable it to catch up with the West. The defeats and strains of the First World War compounded the shackles of a backward agrarian economy and paved the way for the Bolshevik uprising. What followed, particularly under Stalin, was a collectivization of agriculture as a means of feeding the towns and cities and also supporting the state drive for heavy industrial development. A key aim was to provide military protection against marauding capitalist societies, particularly as found in the encircling European system of states. However, while the party took the commanding role, as it did later in China, the rapidly expanding and bureaucratized state system never sought mass participation or perpetual struggle along Maoist lines as a means of revolutionary purification. Rather, a new class of professional experts and party elites generated a form of stratification, with access to privileges and rewards, not unlike the patterns to be found in the capitalist West. Control and repression, and the abolition of civil society associations, became ruling techniques in support of the party-state (Skocpol, 1979; Moore, 1967).

Japan

We have noted that a faster-modernizing Japan in the late nineteenth century was able to inflict military defeat on both Russia and a more backward China and that the latter contributed to the Chinese Revolution. The origins for this disparity between the countries can be traced in part to the Tokugawa regime in Japan that ran from around 1600 until the middle of the nineteenth century, and which unified Japan. It did so by mitigating if not entirely overcoming a system of warring barons and, through its bureaucratic and centralizing reforms, ensured a level of internal peace and outward protection from foreign invasion (McCargo, 2000; Pyle, 1996; Allinson, 1997). During the two centuries when Japan was relatively isolated from the world, the Edo 'shogun' – a local and hereditary commander-in-chief – effectively ruled, despite formal subordination to the emperor, and successfully under-mined the landed aristocrats by rearranging the latter's domains and forcing them to divide their time between Edo and home ('alternate res-idence'), an extravagance that contributed to their indebtedness. McCargo (2000: 15) describes the system as a 'feudal-central hybrid', with a firm regime and a control of the aristocracy that allowed space for the rise of a merchant commercial class, particularly in cities such as Osaka. This dispensation was imposed on a cultural form of feudalism that, unlike that in the West, laid less emphasis on reciprocal rights and obligations and more on loyalty and duty to superiors.

External incursions and the rise of commerce undermined these arrangements. In opening up Japan to foreign trade, not least under the promptings of the Americans, the regime considered that this would create a strong Japan, capable of matching western economic and military power, as well as its science and technology. It led, however, to the 'restoration' of the Emperor Meiji, and it was the Meiji government (1868–1912) that followed which effectively led the way for 'moderniza-tion from above' (Moore, 1967). This involved a form of centralizing and enlarging state with which to propel industrialization in order to meet both the military and economic challenges of other, faster-industrializing nations. Japan sought to learn from the western imperial powers and adopted a range of different institutional models from a variety of coun-tries. A Japanese 'Enlightenment', based on a belief in progress by emu-lating western examples and rationality, also helped to create Japan as the first non-western industrial nation. Although the Meiji rulers gave prior-ity to a state-led process of industrial development, it would be wrong to ignore the role of a growing class of commercial entrepreneurs. The state facilitated as much as it directed or controlled.

It was a regime in which a strong state was backed by increasing measures to create a powerful sense of national identity, through policies such as conscription for all men over twenty, new national holidays associated with imperial dates, 'morally' controlling new schools curricula and emphasizing loyalty to the emperor and family, incorporating traditional localities into a national administrative structure, and opening up the bureaucracy and making it more meritocratic. The promulgation of the 1889 Constitution symbolized the establishment of the first modern nation state in Asia (McCargo, 2000: 20; Gluck, 1985: 42–72). It borrowed from German legal and political ideas, and established a bicameral legislature, albeit with limited suffrage. None the less, as a Constitution imposed from above rather than as a consequence of major domestic pressure, it seems doubtful that the new representative institutions changed much, and they may be regarded as mainly emblematic. Rule continued to be exercised by a small elite. Business remained largely dependent on the state and deferential to governmental and feudal statuses and culture, at least until the more rapid period of industrialisation in the inter-war years of the twentieth century. Yet even these limited political reforms met resistance and were not maintained, and democracy faltered and eventually ran into the barrier of the great worldwide economic depression of the 1930s.

The Meiji and subsequent regimes saw the build-up of military strength as a major source of both industrial development and national identity-building, and also as a means of 'imperial catch-up'. The defeat of the Russian navy in the Russo-Japanese War of 1904–5 reinforced imperial ambitions and militarism, not least because the defeat had been inflicted on an important western power. Yet the victory was not without its costs, and subsequent Japanese feelings of vulnerability helped reinforce military and imperial ambitions. The result was a totalitarian war regime and economy that led to eventual defeat in the Second World War and the post-1945 adoption, under the aegis of the United States, of a more liberal democratic constitution.

The United States

The United States, of course, by 1945 had become a well-established liberal state. Mann notes that civil and political rights had been promulgated early although the notion of social citizenship was much less regarded than it became in Europe. The state was not interventionist:

> Interest group conflict was predominantly left to the economic and political market places, its limits defined by law. However, collectivities could legitimately exploit their market powers, and operated

under rules [in which] ... individuals and interest groups, but not classes, could be accommodated within the regime. (Mann, 1996: 129)

Although it took until the 1960s for blacks to obtain the full benefits of civil and political citizenship, by the 1840s all white, adult males had achieved the vote, a good half-century before anywhere else. One outcome was that labour was absorbed early into the liberal arrangement; trade unions became accepted, provided it was clear that they were operating in the interests or on the instructions of their individual members (after a ballot, for example). Trade unions were simply another interest group, although it did mean that they could still be disruptive if they chose to exercise their market power irrespective of a wider public interest. However, although the United States witnessed violent attacks by some employers on strikers and others in the earlier decades of the twentieth century, class struggle and socialism has never featured, and the minimal welfare state is seen as a safety net to catch the really desperately unfortunate, and particularly what has become known as the emerging 'underclass'. Britain, however, adopted what might be described as a mix of the liberal and the welfare state 'reformist' approaches, particularly in the aftermath of the two world wars.

Conclusion

In this chapter we have described the development of the modern state, and we have focused particularly on the emergence of the liberal or western model. The liberal state is characterized by an apparently sharp differentiation between the realms of state and society, with the former characterized by binding commands and the rights and duties of civil and political citizenship, and the latter as a voluntary realm of affinities, interests and ideas. Public action on economic matters consists largely of the construction and management of legal, fiscal, monetary and financial frameworks for the land, labour and capital markets.

Although the liberal state is supportive of capital, the extension of the state's activity in the nineteenth century, not least in response to demands from the growing business classes for security, services and protection, also contained attendant potential dangers for capital. Notions of equality and civic rights, despite the individualistic twist given them by liberalism, paved the way for increased demands by the disadvantaged and disenfranchised. A developing capitalism implied a growing working class and new, more intensive forms of social fissure. Social and political demands from an increasingly large group of the population inevitably confronted business with a potential threat in a political system where government power was gained by voting (that is, by numerical) strength.

The development of the modern, increasingly powerful state during the latter part of the nineteenth century induced conflicting responses from businesspeople over the extent to which the state should actively secure the basis of successful capital accumulation through increased economic interventionism in the market. Alongside was the question of attitude to be adopted towards the working class – should it be recognized and incorporated, or should the class basis of politics be resisted, as it was in the United States? These questions surfaced early and more insistently in Britain where the working class so quickly became a majority. No class of peasants, no smallholders or other potential 'tools of reaction' could be drawn upon, as they could in most of continental Europe, to provide the social basis for a democratic organization against the interests of the working class.

The dilemma in Britain was whether to aim for a thoroughgoing market society, based upon individual desire to accumulate, as in the US, with its denial of special class interests, or to seek the gradual incorporation of the working class as a privileged interest into the corporate body as a means of securing social stability and a 'moderate' labour movement. The result was an erratic, and some would argue basically inefficient, path that oscillated between liberalism and collectivism.

However, we have also considered, admittedly briefly, forms of state- and nation-building that have not followed the liberal model. In Japan, Germany and the Soviet Union, for example, a strong state was a primary driver for industrial take-off, and this turning away from liberalism had major consequences for the type of centralizing and dictatorial political regimes that ensued. In China, party elites were relatively successful in mobilizing the masses, especially the peasants if not the working class, to smash existing state and elite structures, and in creating a one-party socialist regime, at least for around 30 years.

Yet one overwhelming impression still remains. Whatever the historical and political differences underlying variations in both state-society relationships and nation state formation, state apparatuses can look remarkably similar. They are hierarchical institutions, bureaucratically organized, formally 'disinterested' but prone to the maintenance of privilege for their occupants and their families (through education and other 'cultural capital' devices), and to occasional corruption. Above all, states stimulate passionate debates as to their general worth for economic and other development, particularly in matters of taxation, public spending, and regulation, veering between claims of 'parasitism' to moral worthiness and economic effectiveness.

At the back of these similarities is the inter-state system that has been, and continues to be, significant in explaining nation state formations. From military warfare to economic competitiveness we see the clash of nations shaping state institutions, their purposes and funding, and the nature of social change, from the relatively peaceful and prosperous, to the radical and revolutionary. But ideas, too, play their part. Modes of statehood become either accepted wisdom, or prudently accepted exemplars, that help the nature if not the wealth of nation states to converge. And, of course, with economic globalization and the rise of supranationality at the regional level, such as found with the European Union (EU), we see worldwide forces that appear to make the 'outside' of the state more potent and significant than its 'inside'.

But, before considering those processes in more detail, we must examine some other key parts of the 'state story', particularly as these concern the democratic nature of a state's political arrangements, and, before that, how the modern state has been interpreted in some of the important theories on the subject.

Chapter 3

Classical Theories of the State

Marxism
Elite theory
Weber
Theories of the state as a beneficial social instrument
Conclusion: classical state theories reviewed

The nature of state power and its relationships to society was a central theme in nineteenth- and twentieth-century classical sociology. In particular the impersonal and public character of legally regulated governmental authority, apparently quite distinct from the self-interested or communal forms of action in civil society, generated controversy as to its neutrality or partiality for different social interests. A related issue was whether the modern state was judged to be beneficial for society or rather a parasitic, alienating and ultimately dislocating force.

In considering nineteenth-century interpretations of the liberal democratic state, we find critics of capitalist democracy from within liberalism itself. John Stuart Mill, for example, although no advocate of social and political equality, regarded the potential for participatory representative democracy as likely to remain largely unfulfilled unless the extensive social and economic inequalities of capitalism were mitigated substantially. However, advocates such as Mill of constitutional liberal democracy and the extension of citizenship rights took the individual and his (less often her) interests as the touchstone for democracy. 'The people' were a collection of unique individuals who required the means to pursue free choices with as little interference from the state as was compatible with a well-ordered, property-owning national community.

As we shall see in more detail in Chapter 8, theories of the state had developed in the West in the two centuries or more prior to Mill that were distinctly less individualistic in their conceptions of 'the people'. Increasingly we find the concept of 'the population' emerging as an appropriate object of rule. It was a category that initially was interpreted in territorial terms and as appropriate for developing 'nation states', but which increasingly came to be seen in a more social way. That is, 'the population' came to be seen as consisting of a number of social categories – the poor, the old, and so on – which required the state to be more discerning in its policies and treatments. With the increased availability of investigatory techniques and empirical data to rulers, the state became more knowledgeable and, in contrast to Mill, 'societies' were regarded as more than simply a collection of equally regarded individuals.

Emerging social science accounts of the modern state, however, were also less inclined to accept the notion that one starts from an analysis of the individual. This was most clearly articulated in the writings of Marx and Engels. As Held (1983: 25) observes of their position:

> It is not the single isolated individual who is active in historical and political processes, but rather human beings who live in definite relations with others and whose nature is defined through these relations.

Marxism

At around the mid-point of the twentieth century about a third of the world's population lived under Marxist regimes, while many other countries, especially in the developing world, were sympathetic to such governments. By 1990, however, Marxism appeared to be an exhausted ideology as many nations, in eastern Europe particularly, turned more towards liberal democratic forms. What was Marxism's view of the modern world, and particularly the state, that proved to be so influential, if not especially durable?

For Marx a crucial methodological starting point is the distinction between 'appearance' and 'reality', between what lies on the surface and an often hidden or deeper essence that explains the surface phenomenon. Scientific method lay in recognizing that life is not quite as it appears – it can be distorted by self-serving or ideological accounts, for example – and the task of the scientist is to get behind these smoke-screens and to uncover the real story (the essence) and to provide a scientific explanation. The method for uncovering the causal source of social phenomena is based on class analysis. In contrast to liberalism the focus is not on the individual but on the social nature of people's activities, or more specifically on differences between social classes.

In capitalism, this refers to the postulated exploitative and systemically conflicting relationship between the private owners and controllers of production, on the one hand, and wage-labourers (the 'proletariat'), on the other. The proletariat – unlike pre-capitalist craft-workers or skilled artisans – no longer owns the tools and other means of production in order to engage in economically rewarded activity. These have become owned or controlled by others who seek to organize work more economically and with more imposed and supervised discipline within factories and other sites of productive property. In order to live the proletariat is forced to sell its only remaining 'commodity', its labour power, to these owners. For doing so, it is compensated in the form of wages, although their value, in the Marxist view, falls far below the actual productive value of the labour expended. The difference in the cost (to the owner) of labour, and the price that the owner is able to obtain for its product in the market, is the surplus or profit that is appropriated by the capitalist.

Although it could be argued that this profit is a reward for the entrepreneurial risk taken by owners, and also for their discharge of management functions, and is also necessary to ensure continued investment in the production process, and therefore the maintenance of jobs and the means to life for workers, the picture painted by Marx is rather different. It is one of structural or 'objective' (that is, endemic) class conflict arising from the needs of owners in competitive markets constantly to accumulate capital, to maintain and improve profitability, and to keep costs (particularly wages) as low as possible, in order to stay in business.

To reprise, Marx offers a method that distinguishes between 'superstructure' (appearance or surface visibility) and 'base' (reality or the essence) in that the former is explained ('reduced') by the latter. And the essential base and cause is the class struggle within the dominant mode of production. While it may appear that workers, for example, individually and voluntarily enter personal contracts with the owners of capital in order to obtain employment, and that such arrangements are therefore reasonable and just, the hidden reality is that they are compelled by the nature of class relations to undertake positions in circumstances where a fair return for the value that they create is denied. Rather, the capitalist owner creams off as much as possible in the form of profit. And whatever the charitable or generous individual disposition of the owner may be, the cut-throat and highly competitive nature of capitalist activity leaves the owner no option but to increase profits and lower costs in order to survive and to prosper.

Marx extends this analysis to a consideration of the role of the state in class-based societies, and particularly in capitalism. As all phenomena are determined by class relations, it follows that the state cannot have an independence of these either. State administrators' claims to being objectively neutral for all social groups, in Marx's view, are examples of ideological distortion. Class interests provide the 'realm of necessity' to which the state must conform. That is, the nation state has a class purpose.

Marx basically offers a view of economic activity in which profit availability is fixed and one person's profit is at the expense of someone else's. The notion of expanding profitability through investment, thus allowing higher returns to labour as well as to capital, is regarded as impossible as owners are forced continually to reduce the costs of production, particularly labour, which over time is exacerbated as capitalism exhausts opportunities for profits. Consequently, in this view, economic or class dominance requires political dominance, as class tensions domestically and the requirement for new and profitable markets internationally, are likely to generate on a regular basis the need for an exercise of state force. The state, in its defence of private property in capitalism, becomes inextricably fixed to particular economic interests, although it takes on an autonomous and neutral appearance, acting apparently on behalf of the general public.

Marx's critique of the individualism of liberalism and liberal democracy is aimed at the view of the state as a neutral or even moral defender of a public interest, and which is contrasted with the self-interest of private behaviour. This is another example of appearances not being matched by reality. Not only is the state's claim to impartiality argued to be incorrect, for it serves the interests of capital, but Marx also asserts that the liberal and continental interpretations of the state as a distinct and autonomous public realm, separate from society, has the ideological effect of defining class power as an individual matter in the realm of the economy. That is, socio-economic relations are perceived as a myriad of private arrangements, and as not matters for politics or the state that lie 'above' such concerns. Thus, economic inequalities in the liberal perspective are regarded as the natural or spontaneous consequence of the markets for capital and labour, governed by the impersonal laws of supply and demand and encapsulated in individual agreements or contracts freely concluded, and not, as Marx countered, as the result of class rule by the state.

In the Marxist tradition, justice, which is seen in liberalism as taking a prime position, is regarded as an unnecessary notion in post-capitalist communist societies. It is only needed in social systems where there are flaws to correct. All talk of rights within liberalism and capitalism, and of the notions of justice and equality that guaranteed rights, was anathema to Marx, for this reason: rights are merely the right to be unequal (Kymlicka, 1990: 162), and thus will not be necessary in a state where capitalism has given way to communist equality. Marxism rejects liberal notions of justice, such as the position advocated by Rawls (1972), that justice requires an equality of resources, that is, an equality of private property. Instead Marxism sees the *elimination* of private property – not its *equalization* – as the only path to 'justice'. This position on justice enables Marx to develop a rationale for the contention that the history of all societies prior to communism is a history of class struggle.

As Kymlicka (1990) argues, this means that theories of wage labour (inevitably exploited or alienated) become the fundamental justification for communism.

Capitalism for Marx was doomed to destruction, since the owners of the means of production were in the minority (a minority destined to shrink in size), and eventually the proletariat (growing in numbers) would seize control of the means of production, which would become common property. The socialist phase would eventually give way to a communist phase in which private property would be eliminated. Consequently, with the abolition of private property and class relations, the state would 'wither away' as it no longer had a class exploitative role to fulfil. Or would it?

Different state models in Marxism

It is now commonplace to recognize that the accounts of the state in capitalist society advanced by Marx and Engels were incomplete and not especially consistent. In some works, such as *The German Ideology* (1846) and *The Communist Manifesto* (1848), the emphasis appears on the state as a simple, non-autonomous agent of the dominant capitalist class (its 'executive committee'). In their more empirical studies, however, such as *The Eighteenth Brumaire of Louis Bonaparte* (1852), the state appears to have a measure of independent power. The very size and scope of bureaucratic institutions are seen as giving the state the power not only to steer social arrangements but also to constrain the bourgeoisie. Capitalists only rarely rule directly. The political governance of the landed aristocracy on behalf of the bourgeoisie in Britain in the nineteenth century is a case where rule is exercised on behalf of an economically ascendant class, which at least leaves some 'wriggle room' for disagreements between state rulers and capitalists.

A more important issue in the later work of Marx and Engels is to account for the reasons why state bureaucracies function on behalf of the bourgeoisie in capitalist society. It cannot be as a result of a common or shared social background because, as Marx himself noted, there are instances where this is clearly not so. In any case, such 'individualistic' explanations do not get to the heart of the structural compulsion of class dynamics. The answer rests largely on the dependency of the state on capitalism to provide the means of material existence and, therefore, social order. Although the level of autonomy enjoyed by state executives varies according to such factors as location within the world economy and military rivalries, as well as class forces and relationships, state bureaucrats generally a have distinctive interest in preserving the status quo and the dominant mode of production.

The analysis of the Paris Commune and its operations (1870–1) offered by Marx in *The Civil War in France* (1871) is interesting in providing one of the few accounts of how public affairs could be administered under socialism, and also in its influence on Lenin and others in the aftermath of the Russian Revolution of 1917. Harding (1984) suggests that it offers one of two contrary models of the state in socialism. One is where the state machinery is regarded as a source of alienation and needing to be 'smashed' in favour of self-governing people's communes (such as in Paris following the uprisings in 1870). The other is where the state is regarded as a necessary instrument in the dictatorship of the proletariat and for the construction and defence of socialism, not least in the context of a hostile, predominantly capitalist world (as found in the Soviet Union under Stalinism).

Understandably perhaps, Lenin, in *The State and Revolution* (1917), was initially attracted by the first model, in which the state is regarded as not capable of being reformed. The Commune model became the practical programme of the Russian Bolsheviks in their first years in power, during which factory councils and soviets (communes) provided a form of popular self-administration, and which aimed at effectively dismantling the state. Yet it was a model that was unable to withstand or manage the repeated economic and administrative crises that beset the Soviet Union following the ending of the First World War. Lack of food turned the peasants back to growing for themselves, thus starving the towns and industrial workforce, while the extensive seizure of property and factories by local committees added to managerial dislocation.

The result was the increased attraction of the second Marxist model of a strong state dedicated to the 'dictatorship of the proletariat' through a party-led bureaucracy, and meeting the requirements for powerful central instruments of planning. The primary purpose, as prosecuted in ruthless fashion by Stalin, was to secure the means of material existence for the people as a whole, not to give them direct participation in decision-making. Socialism was thus defined as state ownership of production in the name of the working class – if not directly by it – and legitimated as the form of administration that was best able to achieve technical efficiency and economic growth.

Soviet Marxism

Marx's theories were designed with western nation states in mind. In line with a fairly strict evolutionary theory, he believed that the replacement of capitalism by socialism/communism was a prognosis for the West; Russia and China barely concerned him, as he thought that such traditional 'backward' societies were not ready for the evolution to communism (for Marx, history in Asia had 'gone to sleep'). There was not, therefore, within the body of Marx's work, any obvious blueprints for socialism outside of developed capitalist systems and in countries such as Russia, a gap that was to be filled by Lenin.

Lenin's major contributions to the development of the Soviet version of Marxism lay in his definitions of party and state. The party was conceived of as a centralized body, with representatives (cells) in every important institution, whose job was to act as a relay between the authoritative centre and the periphery. Lenin's theory of the party has sometimes been described as *vanguardism*: the party is not broad-based in social composition, and certainly not full of labourers, but is made up of professional, intellectual revolutionaries who can dictate the direction of the socialist revolution. The party were the representatives of the masses, and could see what needed to be done better than they themselves, could; thus the masses owed them their support (Lenin, 1902, 1904/1967a,b).

The party uses the state to further the revolutionary cause. Lenin's famous notion of the 'dictatorship of the proletariat' (Lenin, 1905/1967c) essentially gives the party *carte blanche* to use all the powers of the state to further the revolution: in the transitional stage of socialism immediately after the 1917 Russian Revolution, Lenin clearly thought that the end justified the means.

Trotsky (1970) also dealt with the issue of how Russia could 'fast-track' the revolution. In Marx's theories, it is clear that communism follows capitalism, yet Russia was still a feudal state, with barely any developed capitalist modes of production. Trotsky thought that the revolution in Russia could succeed, but it required an international effort such that Russia could encourage and draw from successful proletarian revolutions in west Europe. If Russia remained alone, she would be destroyed by international capitalism, and international socialism was the key to success. In this policy he fell out with Stalin, who thought it better to concentrate on building socialism in one country. Stalin, as we know, proved victorious, and after Trotsky's exile, Russia became increasingly isolationist.

Stalin made his own contributions to Soviet Marxism, especially through the so-called 'second revolution' of 1928. This plan focused on boosting the Soviet economy through industrialization, but the goal was mainly to be achieved by enforcing the collective ownership of farms, and breaking down any notions of private property among the peasantry. Stalin explicitly moved from such Marxian notions as the 'withering away of the state' as he sought to justify the expanding size of the Soviet governing bureaucracy, and the increasing use of police to ensure a kind of ideological homogeneity in the Soviet Union.

Despite these contributions from Trotsky and Stalin to Marxism, they have proved less significant than Lenin in analysing a major feature of the modern world – the development of colonialism and imperialism, and the operation of capital on a global stage. In *Imperialism, the Highest Stage of Capitalism* (1916), Lenin argued that imperialism was the consequence of an ineluctable process of capitalist development. For Lenin, at the end of the nineteenth century, capitalism passed into a new stage, in which industrial and financial capital had fused. There now existed financiers and bankers who lived off the income derived from the profit on the shares that they owned in industrial companies, and who exercised dominance through the new joint-stock companies with which they came to control industry. Lenin argued that these financiers exported their capital in order to get the best rate of profit, as backward countries had little capital and profit rates there were consequently higher. Colonies were the monopoly outlets for the export of capital. At the same time the growth of 'monopoly capital' – merged and large companies dominating their sectors – created the urge for them to dominate foreign markets, too, especially through directly investing capital abroad. Aided by governments, these increasingly large corporations helped to divide up the world politically and economically. British companies could monopolize British colonies, French companies the French colonies, and so on.

Thus, for Lenin, capital dominates the state to such an extent that the state will do what is necessary to maximize the profits to be made from investments. The monopolies in a country look to the state to protect their markets from acquisition by competitors; that is, from other national monopolies. They need to ensure that normal business conditions are maintained in the areas where they are operating, that law and order is operating, that contracts can be made and enforced, and that there is a communications infrastructure. For these reasons a colonial state is needed to guarantee the conditions necessary for overseas capitalist development. However, for Lenin, this was a 'last gasp' strategy for an overripe capitalism that was fast running out of investment opportunities. It heralded the final stage in the capitalist mode of production prior to the socialist revolution. The state, in this view, was not sufficiently powerful or autonomous to reform capitalism in a social democratic fashion, as social democratic writers such as Hobson (and later Keynes) believed.

Chinese Marxism

In China, there was a political shift from a form of feudalism to a Chinese or homegrown version of Marxism (Dreyer, 1993). In the early feudal period, we see many techniques for social ordering, classification and government derived from the ethos of Confucianism, especially played out in family-based collective organizations or groups that revolved around social status and self-mastery (Dutton, 1992: 350). In the Chinese Marxism model there was a conscious reactivation and renewal of the values of collective life.

While there are many similarities in the systems of feudalism and of Marxism in China, the differences are none the less striking. While the classical feudal period stressed the family, the Marxist regime stressed the labouring population. This latter emphasis in turn gave rise to more systematic attempts by it to govern the economy. While some of these shifts look temptingly like those we have seen in the West, we need to tread carefully here.

First, liberalism has never had much appeal in China: both the feudal and the Marxist systems did not conceptualize the individual in anything like the way it was understood in the West. Confucianism, which influences both models, was not about universalism in individuality (something which was a premise of western liberalism), but about stressing differences and particularities in status and in family position which added up to a community (feudal) or collective (Marxist) order (Mauss, 1985). Marxism allowed China an alternative to the exhausted patriarchalism of its earlier feudal dynasties:

> while dynastic patriarchalist forms of government were bankrupt, the western-influenced advocates of liberalism were always foreign aberrations. Marxism offered an alternative to both, and, in the process, transformed the subject of 'feudalism' – which was the family – into a subject central to all conceptions of Marxism: the collective labouring class. (Dutton, 1992: 13)

So while it seems likely that the current integration of China into the liberal world marketplace will continue apace, especially now that China has joined the World Trade Organization, it is unclear to what extent China will become 'liberalized'. Eastern Europe, as we have seen, presents a different case, in that the forms of individualization which liberalism presents as an alternative to communism are recognizable to the inhabitants of those territories. Soviet communism stressed the collective just as much, if not more, than Chinese communism (and in fact Chinese Marxist collectivism owes much to the Soviet example), but the continuing legacy of Confucianism in China militates against the forms of self that are consonant with liberalism ever being realizable.

Box 3.1 Non-western theories

As well as in Chinese and particularly Confucian ideas of power and the state, we can find radically different perceptions to those found in the West in Islam. The notion of nation state, although borrowed from western beliefs and practices, is not the most important way in which the Islamic world conceptualizes the division of power blocks. Islam is understood as a civilization, a reasonably coherent entity, although divisions within it are divisions of orthodoxy, rather than national boundaries. There are also zones outside of civilization, divided into those areas with which Islam has friendly relations, and the 'infidels' with whom they are at war (Ali, 2002). The point is that the state has nothing of its western power in the Islamic nations.

The western state developed its power as an 'atheistic' autonomous entity, with its own non-divine, thoroughly rational rule system. The governmental rationality of the Islamic world is one that has never embraced the western separation of the state from its divine origins. A small piece of evidence for this is the neo-Arabic word *dustur*, translated as 'constitution'. To a westerner this might appear evidence for a western-style understanding of political life, but in fact it is a word that refers back to the Qur'an as a 'holy constitution' (Kurdi, 1984). Tibi (1998: 119) argues that in fundamentalist politicizations of Islam, not only is the state rejected, but so too is the free individual, since the human being is a creature of God.

Islamic politics, then, presents an entirely different rationality of the state. Tibi (1998: 69) argues that attempts to emulate the West have typically been military. This has come down to Islam attempting to understand the technology of the West, rather than adopting its political philosophy (see also Goçek, 1987; Lewis, 1982; Ralston, 1990). As Tibi points out, when the Islamic world has had experience of the western state model, the experience has been far from happy, whether we consider 'failed development policies (Algeria and Iran) ... the effects of war and dictatorship (Iraq and Syria) ... local ethnic strife (Sudan) or the repercussions of foreign occupation (Afghanistan and the Occupied Palestinian Territories)' (1998: 119).

In the case of both China and the Islamic world, then, it seems unlikely that the western liberal state model will prevail. No doubt increasing economic trade with both these civilizations will produce further degrees of westernization, but the western ethos of individuality and free will, what Habermas (1987a) terms the 'principle of subjectivity' and which he regards as underpinning the philosophical discourse of modernity, is not a form of personhood that makes any sense. To this extent, then, we might summarize by saying that liberalism appears to have won the battle of ideologies in the West, but it has reached the limit of its powers within the territories where individualistic forms of self are dominant, but not elsewhere.

Marxist revisionism

To a certain extent, western Left intellectuals looked to the Soviet Union (more so than China) for inspiration as they tried to develop critiques of liberal democracy, and it is fair to say that many of them overlooked for far too long, in the face of increasingly damning evidence, the horrors of Stalinism. The Soviet Union was just too different in the end for its fortunes to impact on the governmental possibilities of the West, and when the Soviet Union fell in 1991, it was easy (perhaps too easy) to conclude that western liberalism had seen off its major alternative (Fukuyama, 1989, 1992). Indeed, many of the interesting developments in theoretical Marxism in the West were increasingly unconnected with what was going on in the Soviet Union, in China, in Cuba, or in any other state where Marxism was being tried out.

Consequently, in recent decades, Marxist views of the state have undergone a range of sophisticated, if not always astoundingly transparent, revisions. A primary aim in these accounts is to modify Marxism to offer a less reductionist theory of the state, by drawing on the notion of 'relative autonomy'. Thus state actions are not always a direct correspondence of the dominant class but may vary, for example in times of exceptional societal tension. Yet, even here – 'in the long run' – the state eventually and always functions to support the dominant class. That, after all, is the core of Marx's theory of the state. The notion of 'relative autonomy' in Marxist revisionism may be regarded as thus seeking to preserve the fundamentals of Marxism in the face of historical and empirical complexity.

Partly these revisions were influenced by Gramsci (1971, 1978), writing in the 1920s and 1930s, but significantly influential in western Marxism thirty to forty years later, not least in the development of eurocommunism. Gramsci advances the concept of 'cultural hegemony' to make sense of the apparent enthusiasm of the working class and others in the West to keep supporting the bourgeoisie and other so-called forces of reaction, including the state, when such support was against their 'objective' interests. Cultural hegemony is the means by which a dominant class's worldview could become widely accepted.

Hegemony is constructed initially through the concessions of the 'relatively autonomous' state to the subordinate classes, such as in welfare reforms, which help to disguise capitalism's class exploitation. But it is then continued normatively. This involves the organization of popular culture and its direction and appropriation for class goals (such as with 'nationalism'), and which, according to Gramsci, operates primarily through the ideological practices of institutions and groups in civil society, such as the schools, media, the churches, or political parties.

Social practices come to represent and to reconstruct capitalist class goals as perfectly sensible, 'common intelligence', 'taken-for-granted', everyday ideas. These socialize and integrate subordinate classes into accepting the capitalist state. Such processes are preferred by dominant interests to the exercise of force that happens in more precarious times. Gramsci, in such an analysis, tends to blur the distinction between the state and civil society (by assuming that the state includes all agencies involved in hegemonic mediation), and the notions of 'false consciousness' and 'objective interests' are also highly problematic and potentially unverifiable. But he importantly helped move Marxism away from regarding state institutions as always directly reflecting (in a 'one-to-one correspondence') simple class interests.

For Gramscian euro-communists the task was to use techniques of mass communication to allow Marxist ideas to become ideologically dominant for the proletariat. This is a world away from Bolshevik revolution. Not unlike Gramsci, the Parisian Marxist Louis Althusser, in the 1960s, was especially interested in the concept of ideology and helped contribute to quite a resurgence of Marxist theorizing of the modern state. Althusser developed a theory of state apparatuses of two kinds: those that are repressive, such as the army, the police, and so on (and which correspond to state apparatuses in classical Marxist models), and those that are ideological, such as politics, religion, the education system, the media, and so on. For Althusser (1969, 1970) the educational system is the most important of the ideological state apparatuses, since it is through education that capitalism and its values are reproduced.

Both Gramsci and Althusser focus on the role of knowledge in the maintenance of existing social relations, and to this extent they borrow quite heavily from a liberal framework. The fundamental techniques by which liberalism seeks to govern are by equipping citizens with the ability to self-govern. Gramsci and Althusser recognized this and, in developing a critique of liberal capitalist states, attempted to consider how it might be possible to equip citizens to think in other ways. While this critical endeavour is still alive, and to a certain extent is continued in what is sometimes called 'post-Marxism', it resembles liberalism in its commitment to individual self-realization.

Althusser (1969) also engaged in seeking to overcome 'base-structure' reductionism in Marxism by arguing that the mode of production comprised three levels or regions – the economic, the political and the ideological – in which, in any mode of production, the economic assigns particular functions and powers to the other levels. Thus the state can, in some circumstances, possess a level of autonomy from economic classes (as in feudalism, for example, where the economic assigns dominance to the political level). Yet the problem remained: the dominance of the economic 'in the last instance' is always going to rule out effective state institutional autonomy.

A further influential figure was Nicos Poulantzas (1973), who built upon Gramsci's accounts of state power in explaining the cohesive functions of the state in capitalist societies and who, in an important debate with the British theorist Ralph Miliband, also helped to extend and renew theoretical work on the state in Britain. Miliband (1969) argued that, despite the formal independence of the state and it being comprised of a number of different and relatively autonomous institutions, and although governments are elected democratically, the state none the less pursues capitalist interests. It does so because its key positions are staffed by those drawn from the capitalist class or by those whose disposition is supportive of capitalism because of their socialization (in the family or from their education, for example). The respective personnel of the state and capitalist organizations have the same social and educational backgrounds – effectively they are two elites that form one caste – and their similar values, reinforced by the constraint that the wellbeing of society depends on a healthy private sector, propel the state to be helpful and non-threatening to capitalism.

Poulantzas, however, offers a more structural account of state power than Miliband, in which individuals are less significant than the overall structural logic of the system. Whatever their personal beliefs, individual state officials, for Poulantzas, have no alternative but to act on behalf of capitalist interests, even if they enjoy, in circumstances of class balance, an element of relative autonomy. As simply 'carriers' of structures, both capitalists and state bureaucrats are required to follow the logic of the system and seek to maximize profits. The competitive character of capitalism, however, can mean that capitalists often lack the unity to identify and promote their own best interests. 'Fractions' of the capitalist class can act as 'mavericks' or selfishly pursue narrow sector interests, which may be prejudicial to the capitalist class overall (by aggressively provoking working-class unity and hostility to state and capitalist institutions generally, for example). This is where the state comes in. It acts as an 'ideal collective capitalist', by insisting on reforms or concessions to labour to help preserve the long-term continuation of capitalist power.

However, as with Althusser, the concept of the state's 'relative autonomy' in Poulantzas is ambiguous and potentially circular, in that the state both can advance labour interests because it is autonomous, and yet promote capitalist interests because this autonomy is limited (Cawson and Saunders, 1983). Moreover, the explanatory burden falls entirely on outcomes for inferring the influence of classes; if policies become reformist then, by definition, it follows that the working class has exerted power, when, alternatively, it could follow the election of a labour-friendly government. It becomes difficult to empirically test for the separate causal variables in such a schema.

In the more crisis-driven, oil-price inflationary world of the 1970s and 1980s, Marxist accounts emphasized less the stabilizing and cohesive role of the state in capitalist society. In these interpretations, Offe and Habermas, among others, argued that the continued failure of state strategies eroded popular acceptance or the legitimacy of capitalist societies, leading to regular 'crises'. For Habermas (1976) this stemmed from the necessity for the capitalist state to meet what are often opposing or conflicting goals: the support for capitalist accumulation, which could mean seeking to keep wages and social expenditure as low as possible; and eliciting popular support for a neutral, welfare-supporting, democratic state, which could mean higher public expenditure and taxes. In the view of Habermas the costs of seeking popular support at times of recurring economic crises generally prove to be too expensive, and this is exacerbated with popular demands for the state to accept ever greater responsibility for correcting market and social failures. The result is state 'overload'. Offe (1984), too, sees the state as having to face in two contradictory ways, trying to support capitalist development by not intervening too much to regulate, tax or even 'socialize' the means of production, and yet having to meet the costs of rising popular expectations and demands on the state. This required the increased growth of taxation and state revenues generated from capitalist development. Yet such policies were likely to hamper capitalist investment, thus gradually reducing the capability to furnish the funds required by the state to meet increasing social expectations in the population. It was potentially a vicious cycle.

These views recognize that the state is excluded from direct control over the means of production (which are privately held) and that its own survival and funding depend on a globally competitive and well-functioning (national) private sector. Consequently the state has little option but to ensure capitalist profitability and to keep concessions to the subordinate classes – which, tactically, have to be made from time to time – within the limits of the 'logic of capitalism'. On the other hand, unlike pre-capitalist forms of state, the economically dominant class does not directly control the levers of political power and has to recognize that the state has to maintain its own legitimacy through welfare expenditure and other concessions.

Both Offe and Habermas display more concern than Poulantzas with the specific institutions of the modern state and their failures and struggles to be functionally effective. In managing the contradictory pressures on them, states are forced to become 'structurally selective' in favouring those groups, such as organized labour and large business, whose support is regarded as crucial for the maintenance of the existing order. This leads to more secretive, corporatist forms of decision-making, away from parliamentary and public scrutiny.

The recent experiences of the state in Britain and elsewhere suggest that Offe and Habermas underestimated the capacity of politicians and state administrators to overcome apparently structural deficiencies. For example, the 'privatization' and 'New Right' policies of Conservative administrations in the 1980s were not prevented by the power of organized labour or a tide of rising social expectations of the welfare state that prevented reform. However, Offe and Habermas are recognized as making important contributions to Marxist theories of the state, particularly in moving them away from rather sterile accounts of the state as inevitably, generally unproblematically, and successfully pursuing the interests of the economically dominant class directly and at every turn. More recent accounts within this tradition take this perspective forward, arguing that the national state, rather than 'withering away' has a key part in organizing the global economy, polity and civil society, and that 'it is being reimagined, redesigned and reoriented in response to these challenges rather than withering away' (Jessop, 2002: 9).

Elite theory

While liberal democratic and Marxist accounts agreed in offering an essentially confident and Enlightenment view of the future as it was glimpsed in advancing industrial societies, even if they differed over the benefits of the prevailing political arrangements, there were some who were decidedly more pessimistic about what lay in store for society. Among these were the so-called 'classical elite theorists' who doubted that good intentions and fine words would change much. Elitism is best understood as both a retort to Marxism and its claims for a future elite-free socialist society, and to theories of pluralism that formed a particular variant of liberal democratic approaches.

Pluralists have generally taken the increasing complexity of the division of labour in society, and a connected plurality of ideas and identities in the modern world, as the basis for the claim that political power should be distributed to take account of these functional differentiations. Work, social, and other voluntary groups are regarded as the elements for what could be an essentially harmonious, reciprocal and self-regulating society and polity. Multiple identities, crosscutting group memberships and diverse sources and centres of power characterize modern societies, which rules out notions of a dominant and unified ruling class, and a 'general' or 'national will', and overcomes liberal concerns about the so-called 'tyranny of the majority'. These modern multiplicities allow individuals and groups to mobilize to defend or advance their interests in ways compatible with the democratic temper. Pluralists see 'countervailing power' as a critical democratic resource for preventing despotism.

Elite theory, in contrast to pluralism, suggests that not minorities, but a minority – a ruling elite – governs in virtually all societies, and not least modern ones. And, in opposition to Marxism (or at least to its 'commune', non-state model), elites could never wither away and were not simply economically based.

Classical elite theorists

The notion of 'elite' was used initially and prominently in the works of two Italian theorists, Mosca (1939) and Pareto (1935), who focused on personality types and on the alleged psychological needs among populations for elite rule and mass compliance. It is important that we see these propositions as comprising a parsimonious or deliberately simplified view of political rule. The purpose is to avoid complexity so that the essential or bigger issues and processes can be analysed. In these theories it was asserted that some people want to govern and had the attributes to do so, while most others were quite happy to be subordinate. Consequently Mosca claimed that in all societies can be found two classes – those that rule and those who are ruled. Similarly, Pareto referred explicitly to a 'governing elite', comprised of all leaders involved in ruling a society, and a 'non-governing elite', who make up the remainder of the elites, but who are less politically active. Despite the sense of the term 'elite' as implying 'the best', neither Mosca nor Pareto assumed that governing elites, who are usually differentiated into the military, the religious, the political, the commercial and so on, were composed of the most able. While the social base of a governing elite can be open or closed, it is always at risk to being overthrown by a counter-elite, who may have superior talents or be better organized. Indeed, history can be characterized as a virtual revolutionary cycle of elites.

The claims of the 'classical elitists' – that elitism is inevitable – may be regarded as a critique of liberal notions of democracy and its assertions for political equality and representative government, and also of the Marxist belief in the prospect of a classless, non-stratified socialist society. Instead of focusing solely on economic processes, as the Marxists were inclined to do, the elitists suggested that organizational dynamics and the psychology of the masses, particularly in large-scale urban and industrial societies, made ruling elites an inescapable part of the landscape. Any other claim was a 'myth' to propagate the leadership claims of a rising counter-elite. Yet the claims of Mosca and Pareto are very broad and sweeping and as such difficult to rebut. In their alleged universality, however, they are bound to ignore historical examples where, for example, the masses become organized and control the elite.

A more powerful rejoinder to Marxism from within classical elite theory came from Michels, who developed what he termed the 'iron law of oligarchy' in his book *Political Parties*, published in 1911. Michels had serious reservations about the possibilities and desirability of classical participatory democracy in increasingly complex and bureaucratized societies and argued that the very structure of an organized society gives rise inevitably to an elite. Even in organizations dedicated to preserving internal democracy, such as social democratic political parties, the necessity for technical expertise and efficiency in modern environments eventually leads to greater leadership power and restrictions on membership participation in key policy-making.

Weber

Michels was strongly influenced by the work of Max Weber who, if not directly part of the classical elitist school, certainly offered the major response within classical sociology to Marxism's claims that state institutions were derived directly from class relations. Weber argued that classes formed only one dimension of the distribution and competition for power and leadership in societies. Status groups, often characterized by a particular form of lifestyle, and political parties, competing to take over governments, were just as important in modern systems of stratification.

It was inescapable to Weber that a key feature of the power of the modern nation state was the ability to generate strong feelings of national identity that could be mobilized in times of war and external competition. But this could not be construed as simply the consequence of capitalist imperialism, for Weber recognized that the nation state had its origins in the pre-capitalist, medieval conflicts between absolutist rulers in northern Europe. Moreover, the growth of bureaucratic administration and the development of central state institutions laying claim to the monopoly of legitimate violence within a defined territory, Weber's definition of the modern state, he regarded as subsequently evolving with capitalism in a mutually supportive way in the core western European societies. The modern state did not simply reflect the evolution of capitalism, nor did it simply reflect the interests of the capitalist class. It generated it own interests. However, capitalism did significantly boost the process of rational and bureaucratic administration in both the private and public spheres. Companies and government departments alike were operating similar rule-following and office-oriented ways. Nor was all national rivalry to be reduced to the play of economic forces. The competition and conflicts between states could be a vibrant characteristic of the modern order, often supplying politicians with the popular support and leverage required to keep the deadening grip of bureaucratization and officials at bay (Gerth and Mills, 1958).

Weber was extremely critical of the view that state systems could be cast aside with the end of capitalism and the growth of socialism. He regarded modern state institutions as essential for ordering complex societies whatever their political colouring. The introduction of a socialist society, despite the aims of its progenitors, would not overcome the need for a state to order an increasingly differentiated society, but would rather simply extend the process of bureaucratization. Weber regarded socialism as likely to prove even more tyrannical than capitalism. Rather than socialism being able to overcome the state, its commitment to equality was much more likely to result in the extension of the universalistic, rational-legal criteria associated with state growth and bureaucratization. The dictatorship of capital would simply be exchanged for the dictatorship of the state bureaucracy. Nationalization and state ownership of production was likely to result only in a more officious, rule-bound and ineffectual senior management.

As Held (1983: 35) indicates, Weber believed Lenin to have confused and conflated two separate issues on the state: its class nature, and its 'technical' role in securing social order and the administration of public life in complex modern societies. Moreover, as we have noted, bureaucratic organization with its advance in administrative efficiency ensured that that it was not only the state that was increasingly characterized by bureaucratic organization, but also companies and associations in the private sphere. Weber thus anticipated a steady convergence in rule by officialdom in modern industrial societies, not only between capitalist and socialist forms of governance, but also between public and private organizations (Gerth and Mills, 1958).

Weber may be described as a pessimistic liberal who felt that individualism, freedom of choice and social differences were being eroded by large-scale social forces, particularly by the rise of big organizations, in virtually every sphere of life. The growth of office hierarchy and pyramidal authority, the spread of impersonal written rules, the decline of both arbitrariness and discretion by officials, the growth of qualifications for employment and a decline in patronage, the public rather than private ownership of the means of administration, the extension of technical specialization and calculated, science-based efficiency, were regarded as aspects of the development of rationalization to be found in all the major institutions of western capitalist society. Rationalization was corrosive of traditional values and belief systems, such as religion, but this was a mixed blessing. It was good that metaphysical illusions and their restrictions on human potentiality had been stripped away; but po-faced intellectualism hardly provided existentialist support for individuals as a replacement.

The result of these developments was a form of moral relativism, with all values objectively valid, which meant that liberalism and democracy could only be defended on methodological grounds – procedurally – rather than as essentially superior in the realm of values. None the less, democracy, albeit defined in a fairly limited fashion by Weber as a regular competitive arrangement for ensuring that the best leaders are chosen, was still the preferred regime – not least because it produced politicians with the skills, charisma and oratory to keep bureaucrats and similar unaccountable functionaries in their rightful place. The crucial choice for Weber was 'between bureaucracy and dilettantism' in the field of administration; bureaucracy might have its pathologies, but its alternative was likely to produce amateurish inefficiency. As the technical superiority of bureaucratic organization ensures its continued growth in increasingly complex, differentiated societies, it provides officials with the potential for wielding enormous influence through their control of information and knowledge. How was this influence to be constrained?

In Weber's view it was crucial that effective leadership in modern nation states continued to be discharged by politicians, who were sensitive to social and moral values, and not by soulless officials governed by dispassionate technical criteria. A strong parliamentary democracy was vital in enabling potential political leaders to become steeled and tested in public debate and communication, and to be in a position to control officials. Weber believed that politicians should always guard against national goals becoming usurped by private and bureaucratic interests. However, in common with the proponents of liberalism, Weber also recognized the desirability of a strong private sector both as a counterweight to possible state authoritarianism and as a vital source of change and new ideas.

Nor was direct democracy any longer feasible for the management of large modern societies. It was administratively inefficient, unstable, unlikely to facilitate compromise, and was subject to capture by unrepresentative minorities. Representative, parliamentary government and a competitive party system were still likely to be best in securing the openness, contestability, leadership training, and negotiation essential for liberalism, although Weber felt that the extension of the franchise was leading to the decline of parliament and the rise of the mass party and the career politician. Moreover, electorates exhibit little capacity for wider democratic participation, nor did Weber feel that they would be developed by the experience. Leadership choice was quite enough of a role for most people.

Despite the importance of Weber's analysis of the state for contemporary analyses, it invites some criticisms. For example, Weber tends to overlook the problematic nature of bureaucratic control in modern organizations, especially the ability of subordinates or clients to use their 'everyday knowledge' of on-the-ground operations and practices to circumvent central direction and hinder the implementation of decisions. As we have seen in more recent times, 'command and control' can often be ineffective and need to be replaced by more delegated or local team- and initiative-based organizational processes. It is not clear, either, why the electorate should be confined to a minimal political role and seen to be capable of distinguishing between potential leaders, yet not capable, apparently, of a more substantial political involvement generally or of thinking through important political issues. There is a case for suggesting that wider forms of political participation may be systemically efficacious and individually developmental. Nor does Weber examine more empirically and historically the varieties of representative democratic systems to be found in the world and that could have implications for his universalistic – that is, unvarying – views on both organization and democracy (Held, 1996: 175). However, Weber provides significant insights into the development of democracy and the state, particularly the likely direction of socialist regimes.

Theories of the state as a beneficial social instrument

A major challenge to the optimistic individualism of classical liberalism throughout the twentieth century from within the social sciences was a more fatalistic view about the inevitable growth of organization and the state. This can be found particularly within the school of thought associated with Weber. Here, as we have seen, the extension of bureaucracy and the managerial and hierarchical arrangements typified in the modern state were located in the dominance of the principle of rationality to be found increasingly in virtually all walks of life.

However, it would be wrong to classify all challenges to liberalism and its view of the state in this pessimistic manner. More optimistic perspectives of the beneficiary potential of the modern state can also be found, and they underlie the emerging theories of a more caring and welfare state at the turn into the twentieth century. Here the state could correct the perversions of liberal market society and respond to the demands of both capitalism and mass democracy for increased rights and social protection for the mass of the population. In turn, popular mobilization for war efforts in countries gave impetus to the idea that the state 'owed' its peoples more than before.

An initial concern, however, lay in understanding how social order itself could be maintained in societies that were rapidly industrializing and becoming more populated in large urban centres. For the French sociologist Emile Durkheim, the more specialized, complex and advanced a society, the greater the extension of the state as it undertakes more tasks and subjects their fulfilment to centralized and homogenized coordination. In contrast with pre-industrial societies, where social control and stability are established culturally and 'mechanically' through external moral constraints, in industrial society the functional deployment of tasks through the division of labour provides an 'organic solidarity' as a result of social interdependency. Moreover, as traditional, collective, and rather repressive cultural values lose their hold, the state is enabled to develop as a separate and identifiable structure and become the brain or guiding intelligence for society (Durkheim, 1933).

As befits a functionalist theorist, with the view that all social phenomena have socially useful consequences, intended or not, and living in France, a country with a strong state tradition ever since Napolean and the French Revolution, Durkheim is disposed to a favourable view of the state's secular and 'scientific' development. He places great store in the emancipatory functions of the state for individuals, who are enabled to become free of the bright glare of traditional and – to Durkheim, oppressive – social customs and groups. In his view state officials assume responsibility for rationally advancing the 'universal interest' with an impersonality that distinguishes their behaviour from the rest of society. However, Durkheim was aware also, like Weber, of the potential dangers to individual liberty from too powerful a state. 'Pathological' state forms could develop particularly where societies lack intermediary groups or associations that are able to place a constraint on arbitrary state power.

Social democratic theories

Even more activist perspectives on the modern state and its ability to promote economic and social good than found in the work of Durkheim is located in social democratic theories and their efforts to reinterpret classical economic and political liberalism, not least in the context of the growth in international trade and national rivalry. This is epitomized in the work of the British analyst Hobson (1902, 1915, 1920) writing, not insignificantly, from within the dominant world empire of the time.

Anticipating the later theories of Keynes in the UK, Hobson recognized the necessity for a more interventionist state in domestic affairs – not least in managing the economy – and he also articulated the notion of what came to be termed 'liberal internationalism' in which states are able to cooperate in pursuit of world government and global peace.

Hobson's position rested on a rejection that capitalism was automatically 'self-regulating' (as posited by Adam Smith and David Ricardo). He argued instead that it required political intervention nationally and internationally to be stable and effective. The domestic capitalist market, in Hobson's view, has the tendency to produce a skewing or maldistribution of income that leads to general and severe underconsumption of goods and services, as the wealthy have too much money, a large proportion of which they inevitably save, while the rest have too little, and cannot afford to purchase that which is produced and which they also need. This insipid domestic market sparks the imperialist search for new and more profitable markets overseas, which leads to economic and then military conflict between the colonial powers.

Classical liberalism, in this view, neglects the role of accumulating, unearned and surplus income by domestic capitalists (often in sectors where entrepreneurs enjoyed some form of legal or natural monopoly), which they save rather than reinvest. The consumer power of the working classes is thereby severely constrained, preventing them purchasing the goods and services necessary to sustain demand and profitability in the economy. Consequently capitalists look abroad for better markets and profit opportunities. Capitalists in other national economies do the same; the result is increasing conflict and eventually war as political elites are enlisted to defend new monopoly interests abroad. Moreover, imperialism actually makes the situation worse. Success overseas leads to further underconsumption at home, the diversion of public expenditure into military procurement, and the subsequent crowding out of welfare spending.

The solution for Hobson was to forget about *laissez-faire* and to think about the need for social-democratic state intervention, initially to tax unearned surplus income, and then to distribute it more widely through progressive taxation and welfare expenditure. This would stimulate overall demand. Thus capitalism and class conflict, unlike the view found in Marxism, was open to reform by an enlightened state. In turn, the state would be free to control capitalist interests domestically, promote international free trade, and secure worldwide peace.

Keynesian theory

The post-Second World War period saw a shift in the style of western governments, whether they were from the Left or the Right of the political spectrum. State involvement in production and industry increased dramatically, and in Britain and elsewhere, the extraordinary conditions of the war economy were built upon as (especially, but not exclusively) heavy industry was taken into public ownership. The lessons of the war economy and of the inter-war Great Depression were that it might be possible and desirable to plan and manage economic demand to a much greater extent than was typically understood under classical liberal systems.

Allied to this planned economy were a number of social intervention-ist measures, including the provision of public housing, public health and welfare services, social security, and public education schemes. Governmental intervention in the wider economy, however, was limited to modifying market or exchange mechanisms, and private capital was still the driving force behind production. All of this came together in what is sometimes called the 'mixed economy', in which an attempt was made to reach a consensus between capital and organized labour, around the goals of full employment (or at least low unemployment), low inflation, steady economic growth and a trade surplus. Keynesianism was an attempt to use the state through fiscal and mone-tary instruments to help establish a mutually supportive relationship between economy and society.

John Maynard Keynes developed his macroeconomic theories in the 1920s and 1930s – a crucial indicator of his developing work is *The End of Laissez-Faire* (1926) – in the context of liberal failure: the economi-cally depressed western economies at that time. The argument that state economic management could and should be used to promote the well-being of the social was one that was eventually taken up enthusiasti-cally, and, of course, periodically revived (for example, by Mauroy's French socialist government of 1981–4). As a macroeconomic theory, Keynesianism did not especially concern itself with the supply side of the economy, but with the 'social end' of economic strategy, seeking to manage demand through fiscal and monetary policy. The Beveridge Report (1942) generated a way of dovetailing macroeconomics with policies of social insurance (out of this report came governmental pro-vision of health services, housing, accident insurance, workers' com-pensation, education, and so forth), and was taken up in the post-war welfare state in Britain. Similar models were constructed elsewhere in Europe, especially in France.

Citizenship

One argument for the success of liberal democracy throughout the twentieth century is that it came to recognize the important ability of the state to offset the divisive consequences of the class inequalities of capitalism through the national integration of all classes by the extension of a range of civil, political and social rights. That is, the growth of citizenship may be regarded as part of the democratic rise of the welfare state and as a key means of avoiding radical or revolutionary changes. The classic work in this vein is Marshall's *Citizenship and Social Class* (1950), whose analysis of the progressive development of citizenship can be regarded as a theory of democratic evolution (Giddens, 1994), the realization of a programme of social democratic reform, and a rebuttal of Marxist claims about the inevitability of class-based revolution in maturing capitalism. His analysis of the rights and obligations of individuals in democracies, and their rightful expectations that the state uphold these, also help to furnish reasons, other than those that we have looked at so far, why the state continued to enlarge during the post-1945 decades that marked the height of the welfare state.

Marshall defines three types of rights that correspond to three stages in the fight for citizenship: civil, political, and social. Civil rights, he argues, emerged in the eighteenth century (at least in Britain) and were constituted by the rights necessary for individual freedom – freedom of speech, thought and faith, the liberty of the person, the right to own property and to conclude valid contracts, and the right to justice. Political citizenship, however, developed in the nineteenth century and included the right to participate in the exercise of political power, as a member of a body invested with political authority, or as an elector of the members of such a body. Social rights emerged in the twentieth century with the acceptance that the full benefits of democracy could only be enjoyed when individuals had a reasonable level of economic resource and were protected from the worst ravages and inequalities of capitalism. These rights may be regarded as a 'thank you' to the weaker classes for being prepared to fight wars on the national behalf. Thus they were entitled to at least a modicum of economic welfare and security, and to live the life of a civilized being accorded to the standards prevailing in the society.

There are a number of difficulties with Marshall's account, most of them understandable given the time when it was written, immediately after the Second World War. One is that there is no reference to gender and to the lateness and often incompleteness of women's democratization. Another criticism is that Marshall's analysis is confined to Britain and it is not clear that it can be generalized to other countries. Mann (1996) suggests that the British citizenship pathway is only one among five taken by advanced industrial countries, these being the liberal, reformist, authoritarian monarchist, fascist, and authoritarian socialist. All five demonstrated the capability of elites to handle class conflicts and to direct them into less radical and more institutionalized movements.

Social rights and a welfare state were much less developed in the US than in Continental Europe, for example. Individual not class rights and a weak central state were preferred.

Conclusion: classical state theories reviewed

In this chapter we have considered a number of the 'classical' theories of the state, particularly those found in Marxism, elite theory, Weber's works, and in social democratic analyses up until around the middle of the twentieth century. All of these may be considered as helping to constitute a more sociological critique of liberal democracy, not only for its methodological individualism, but also for its undeveloped sense of the state and of its benefits. We have yet to consider some important accounts of the state that lean back towards liberalism in seeking to minimize its role, and also interpretations that examine national governmental policies as a means for understanding the state. Both approaches have been particularly influential in the US and, to a lesser extent, the UK. They rest upon a greater utilization of rational individual and behaviourist models, and we examine these in Chapters 4 and 5.

Market and individual theories in the last thirty years or so have contributed to a 'New Right ' onslaught on social democracy in some countries – not everywhere – that viewed an expanding welfare state as inefficient, unsustainable, and morally objectionable. In turn, New Right theories influenced social democracy itself and its traditional view of the state as an instrument for the pursuit of macroeconomic stability and social redistribution. 'Third Way' interpretations, as found in the programmes of the Blair and Clinton administrations in the UK and the US respectively, are perhaps the prime example of social democracy's revised approach to the role of the market in national policy-making.

Before we examine New Right and Third Way social democratic programmes, however, it is necessary to pay closer attention to democracy. We have described above how Marshall's notion of citizenship is contained within a model of democratic evolution and the extension of rights – civil, political, and social – but that the balance between these, and the historical pathways taken, vary between countries. It is appropriate at this point, therefore, to consider what lies behind this variation and whether there is a systematic pattern to it. Moreover, we need to examine whether, with the ending of east European communism, the liberal democratic model has vanquished all the other pretenders. We do this in the next chapter.

Chapter 4

Democracy and the State

The first long wave of democracy
The social origins of democracy
Class and ideology
The requisites for democracy
Second and third waves
Post-communism
Conclusion

In previous chapters we discussed some of the early origins of liberal democracy as found particularly in Britain and the US in the eighteenth and nineteenth centuries. We referred to at least an elemental affinity between individualistic notions of electoral democracy and popular sovereignty, and the rise of capitalism. During the twentieth century liberal forms of democracy spread throughout the world – not evenly or in a straightforward linear manner, but in 'waves' (Huntingdon, 1991; 1996). It has been estimated that in 1996, 117 or 61 per cent of the world's 191 countries (at that time) were formally democratic, which compares to only 41 per cent ten years previously. Since 1974–5 and the demise of authoritarian regimes in Spain, Portugal and Greece, over 30 countries have made the transition to democracy, including a number following the collapse of the Soviet Union and the fall of communism in eastern Europe between 1989 and 1991. The main exceptions to these trends are the Muslim and Arab states of the Middle East and those found in sub-Saharan Africa. And, of course, the country with the largest population in the world – China – is not a liberal democracy.

An interesting question is whether this increasing worldwide adoption of western-style democratic arrangements reflects the extension of capitalism into global forms or whether other factors may lie behind it. That is, does capitalism tend to generate democracy? In China, despite the increasing marketization of its economy, and its entry into the World Trade Organization, there appear to be few signs of change to its closed system of party-led socialist rule. But elsewhere, liberal-democratic regimes seem to have become more prevalent, in part encouraged by conditions attached to loans and other forms of financial assistance to countries from international bodies such as the International Monetary Fund, the World Bank, and the European Union. The constitutional rule of law, the protection of individual liberties, and the use of free and fair elections to choose and change governments seems to have become very much the norm by the turn into the twenty-first century.

As a consequence, some have felt able to pronounce 'the end of history' and the final victory of capitalist and liberal democratic ideologies in the world in its struggles with socialism, fascism and other forms of authoritarianism (Fukuyama, 1989/1992). By this is meant an ideological convergence or consensus has emerged on the best means to run advanced modern economies, a model comprised of a mixture of a market-based economy and law-bound constitutional government and representative institutions. While in this view wars and conflicts in the international system would continue, they would lack ideological significance, all the big issues in history having been resolved.

Leaving aside some of the problems found within many contemporary liberal democracies – falling participation in political parties and at elections, the blanketing use of 'spin' and other media and marketing techniques to sell almost identically 'packaged' parties and policies, persisting revelations of both corporate and political corruption, and the rise of various social movements often well outside the national and other parameters of conventional politics – the Fukuyama thesis appears remarkably premature and optimistic. For some, indeed, a rising China and an increasingly radical Islam are seen as examples of something much more apocalyptic and as setting the scene for a 'clash of civilizations' based on cultural conflicts. Set-piece, full-scale battles over values and ideologies are forecast to become the order of the day in this perspective (Huntingdon, 1993). Yet, while this view offers a useful corrective to Fukuyama, many of the major conflicts in the world since the fall of the Soviet Union have not been full-scale clashes of ideology as such. They have involved territorial and nationalistic claims, rather than 'ideas', where boundaries are not clear-cut but permeable and fuzzy, such as in the former Yugoslavian Federation.

Rather than the 'end of history' and a 'clash of civilizations', it may be best to examine recent political system changes more routinely. There is little doubt that arrangements other than liberal democracy have rather disgraced themselves in recent years. State socialism, at least in east Europe, has appeared unable to compete with the economic productivity, and the ability to create and meet consumer demands, of the West. Fascism and its Nazi authoritarian variant were unable to avoid defeat in war, while military and other dictatorships have not been up to the task of running increasingly complex and querulous societies. On the other hand, liberal democracies have sustained their legitimacy in the context of advancing capitalism and, in some key instances, in the face of challenges from increased migration and multiculturalism. Their emphasis on individualism and formal equality matches both the temper of capitalism, and that of 'anti-authoritarian' postmodernism in thought and culture. In turn, the increasing practice by international institutions to withhold full legitimacy and recognition (and aid) from states unless they demonstrate commitment to democratic norms and procedures has also assisted the transposition of such practices on a worldwide basis (Beetham, 2001).

The issue may be less the numerical quantity of liberal democratic regimes than understanding quite what contemporarily the description means. Undoubtedly, some political administrations might be classified on minimalist grounds as a liberal democracy (as holding open and regular competitive party elections on a basis close to a universal franchise), but may be lacking a wider practice of respect for basic rights. Worryingly, since the early 1990s, a declining proportion (from 85 per cent in 1991 to 65 per cent in 1996) of formal democracies in their actual behaviour are rated as 'free' (Diamond and Plattner, 1995). Often it would appear that while a system may have the state dimensions of liberal democracy it may lack its civil society characteristics as expressed in economic and political rights, and in a range of voluntary associations. It may also lack a free and uncorrupted media and other forms of institutional accountability (Potter, 2000:5). For both full and partial liberal democracies, an overriding challenge is posed by the power of transnational corporations and supranational entities, and the 'anti' movements they help to generate, and it may be that formal variations between political regimes may become less salient than their respective abilities to meet successfully or otherwise wider global forces.

Yet, for our purposes, it is still instructive to look at the development of democracy and its various forms and interpretations, and not least the economic and other conditions that historically lie behind these processes.

The first long wave of democracy

As we saw in Chapter 2 it was in Europe and the US that the early notions of representative, parliamentary and liberal democracy were formulated; indeed, their institutional forms began to develop in the English civil conflicts of the seventeenth century and the French and American Revolutions of the eighteenth (Goldblatt, 2000a). We noted the spread of literacy and education as part of the process of nation-building in the eighteenth and nineteenth centuries, and the increasing fiscal imposition by states on their populations as a consequence of the need for higher taxation to fund military projects. At the same time the growth of capitalist industrial society, first and furthest in Britain, was the basis for new social classes, who were well placed to organize (especially in the urbanizing centres) and who were increasingly likely to demand greater political rights.

Although early theorists, such as Rousseau in France, emphasized the necessity of equality and direct political participation for the democratic development of the individual and the health of the community, these ideas were seen as not confronting the challenges of fast-growing and rapidly populating nation states, whose very size appeared to rule out intimate forms of political engagement. Consequently it was in the liberal tradition that the notion of representative democracy was formulated to handle the relationship between the impersonal, public nature of the territorially defined state, and the individuals – the 'people', the 'citizens' – emerging from the more particularistic, traditional, local, religious, unreflective loyalties and commitments of an earlier age. A private sphere of family and business interests was appearing that seemed characterized more by reason, choice and civility than previously, and which was felt to need protection from the arbitrary and despotic claims of Church and monarch. And increasingly this protection seemed best afforded through constitutional and legal arrangements that would both limit state interference in the daily lives of individuals (especially male property owners) and allow the beneficent influences of competitive market economies to be maximized. What were the protections – the provision and maintenance of natural and inalienable rights for the individuals that comprised the people – that would need to be matched by corresponding duties and obligations?

For Hobbes (1642, 1651), caught up in the passions and struggles of the mid-seventeenth century English Civil War, the primary requirement for the state was to ensure security in the face of the essential warlike and self-interested 'state of nature', which was the 'normal' condition. It was in the long-term interests of the people to agree to place their

---

Box 4.1 Huntingdon's waves of democratization

First, long wave 1828–1926. Examples: USA, Britain, France, Italy, Argentina, the overseas British dominions

Second, short wave 1943–62. Examples: West Germany, Italy, Japan, India, Israel.

Third wave 1974–. Examples: Portugal, Spain, Latin America, Asia, Africa, East Europe

See Huntingdon (1991) for a full account of these 'waves'.

rights (natural and pre-existing to forms of rule as such) in a single, powerful 'authority' as this would be the only way to guarantee peace. Although Hobbes regarded the office of the sovereign as needing to be absolute, undivided, and self-perpetuating, it is important to recall that the state's right of command and the subject's duty of obedience depended on a 'contract' based on consent that could be withdrawn if the ruler was not delivering the goods (Held, 1996: 77).

Locke, however, went much further. Unlike Hobbes, Locke (1689) was less interested in the security of a powerful ruler than in ensuring that the state only interfered where it had to (in preserving 'life, liberty, and estate'). This entailed more constraints on the scope of rule, and the proviso of the granting of only conditional assent by the people, who would keep regimes under regular scrutiny to make sure that they kept to their defined roles and promises. Locke increasingly felt that a separation of powers (a 'mix') would be good practice in helping the discursive rationality of parliamentary monarchy, with the main estates of the realm – king, Lords, and Commons – sharing the exercise of power. However, it was Montesquieu (1764) who was to formulate this idea in the institutional ways – the threefold distinctive powers and interdependency of executive, legislature and judiciary – that were to have such a profound influence on those who were to write the principles of the American Constitution in the third quarter of the eighteenth century.

It is not hard to imagine why a preoccupation with confining the involvement of the state to a relatively minor role might come to appear inadequate in the face of a rapidly developing capitalist industrial society. Before long the social problems associated with poverty and urbanization would lead to demands for greater state intervention by the entrepreneurial classes on behalf of their workers and others. Added to the pursuit of overseas commercial opportunities and continued geopolitical warfare needs, the middle classes were bound to have to construct a finely judged balance between the pros and cons of state activism and state abstention.

This balance can be found in the works of Bentham, Mill and the Utilitarians:

> Tied to the advocacy of a 'minimal state', whose scope and power were to be strictly limited, there was a strong commitment in fact to certain types of state intervention, for instance the curtailment of the behaviour of the disobedient. (Held, 1996: 96)

Thus the provision of security, through the extension of prisons and administrative discipline, for example, was regarded as especially vital in advancing the happiness of the greatest number and, when such policies were proving successful, the citizen should support the state.

Initially, in Britain, it was the new merchant and commercial classes that made the running in seeking both extensions to the franchise and reform of elections and representation. They were preoccupied mainly with redressing the overwhelming influence of the landed aristocracy by having property qualifications for the vote widened and the House of Commons strengthened by a less patronage-based arrangement for constituency elections. Predominantly, however, they looked for a dispensation that would defend individual natural rights and commercial opportunity through minimal state intervention.

With the growth of the working class, the middle classes in manufacturing and the professions also had a class balance to strike. Disenchanted with the power and corruption of the landed classes, they were also fearful of the financial and other consequences, such as the threat to individual natural rights, of extending the vote to the proletariat. The aim, shared with the equally apprehensive landed classes, who, in any case, had become fairly well embourgeoisified themselves, was to manage the process through gradual reform and incorporation, not least through recruitment to the established Liberal and Conservative parties, and to avoid revolutionary socialism. Consequently, in the first Reform Acts of the nineteenth century, property qualifications were used to limit the franchise on the grounds that property owners had a clear stake in the system and that this also inclined them to act 'responsibly'. At the same time the landed aristocrats calculated that conceding on middle-class interests would help preserve the broad essentials of existing arrangements and help ward off stronger democratic claims for the extension of the franchise. The Great Reform Acts of 1832, 1867 and 1884 saw the extension of the vote to around 40 per cent of the male population, based increasingly on notions of individual rights, rather than property qualifications, although it was not until 1919 that close to universal adult suffrage was achieved, while women had to wait until 1928 for electoral equality.

The process involved an increasing struggle by the working class and their supporters to dispense with property qualifications in favour of 'one person (initially one man), one vote'. Liberal democracy came to be characterized by the proposition that all individuals were free to elect their own representatives, a direct link between state and society that was seen to ensure government by consent. And while the middle and landed classes worried about possible assaults on liberty and property, and the demise of the liberal state and the competitive market society with the extension of democracy, they eventually came to see democracy as invaluable.

The liberal idea of constitutional checks and balances – not only a separation of powers but a compulsion for them to be dependent on each – was most formally institutionalized in the US:

> The constitution of 1787 established a popularly elected federal (national) legislature and executive, alongside a powerful and independent judiciary, and entrenched a series of universal civil and political rights into the American polity. (Goldblatt, 2000a: 48)

Although the US extended the individual franchise furthest and fastest in comparison with elsewhere, property qualifications continued to exist, although they were progressively removed, while women, native Indians and blacks continued to remain on the electoral outside. Women were to achieve the vote after the end of the First World War but effective black political rights were not secured until after the Civil Rights demonstrations of the 1960s. Although the Civil War (1861–5) destroyed the national political ambitions of the non-democratic, plantation elites of the South, federalized and decentralized constitutional arrangements in the US – which had been purposefully designed to build-in protections for individual rights against popular democratic demagoguery – allowed 'space' for the long-term persistence of anti-black practices and denial of democratic rights at local state level. Congress was repeatedly stymied by senators from the eleven Confederate states blocking moves to give practical effect to nineteenth-century federal legislation proclaiming universal voting rights.

In France, democracy was less linear in its progress, and the country veered between republican democracies and authoritarian monarchies. Although there was a period during the French Revolution of 1789 when a radical programme of republican universal suffrage looked likely, reaction, defeat in war (by Britain), and 'strong-man' Bonarpartism helped reinstate an authoritarian constitutional monarchy. Repeated uprisings ensured that a democratic constitution and universal male suffrage were not implemented until 1875, following the collapse of the old regime after defeat in the Franco-Prussian War of 1870–1. However, full universal suffrage in France was delayed for a further seventy years.

German democracy is less easy to account for, not least because Germany as a united nation state was not created until 1870, under the leadership of Prussia. However, universal male suffrage came early – in 1871, when it was wider than in Britain or the US at that time – yet German political institutions were only partially democratic. Power was highly centralized and secretive, with extensive monarchical powers, which meant that the executive and the chancellor were appointed by the king and not by the elected Reichstag. Prussian influence continued to dominate, especially at local level, and in the military. Property qualifications for elections remained formidable hurdles, and some groups, such as the Socialists and Catholics, were repressed. It was not until defeat in the First World War that a democratic constitution was finally formed, although its existence continued to be precarious and subject to authoritarian interruption, until it finally succumbed to the Nazis in 1933.

By 1926 a number of countries had become democracies in Huntingdon's so-called 'first wave', including the US, Britain, France, Italy, Argentina, and British dominions abroad, such as Australia and New Zealand. A real dilemma for most became whether the most effective approach was to incorporate labour and its allies as virtually an equal partner in state management – as a class or estate – as tended to happen in continental Europe, or whether their involvement was to be liberalized – for their members to be treated as individuals like others, as citizens and voters, the situation that occurred in the US. The notion of the 'rule of law' became critical in maintaining liberal constitutional concern that individuals needed protection from arbitrary state officialdom and that all citizens were equal in political and legal terms. The 'rule of law' also was regarded as helping to preserve liberal rights from democratic processes – from the possible tyranny of the majority. Liberal representative democracy consequently became more limited in its scope than espoused by advocates of more direct and participatory democracy, and also in the clear restrictions that it placed on the legitimate range of state involvement.

The social origins of democracy

Although classical theories are important in helping to understand the relationship of the state to wider social forces in emerging democratic societies, and in formulating key concepts and analyses, it is clear too that the route to the democratic world was not singular but comprised of a number of pathways. An important approach that seeks structural and general theories about the political development of different societies over different historical periods, but based on secondary analyses of key historical work, and on the broad political consequences of varieties of socio-economic constellations, is found in Barrington Moore's classic account of the *Social Origins of Dictatorship and Democracy: Lord and Peasant in the Making of the Modern World*, which was originally published in 1966.

Moore seeks to explain why the processes of industrialization in England culminated in the establishment of a relatively free society in which the toleration showed by the landowning classes is a significant element. Crucially, and ironically, it derived from the 'legalized violence' of the enclosing landlord, which finally destroyed the whole structure of English peasant society embodied in the traditional village, and eliminated the peasantry as a factor from English political life. It thus removed a huge reservoir of conservative and reactionary forces of the kind that continued to exist in Prussia and France, where the landed classes, such as the Prussian Junkers, relied on repressive political action to sustain a declining and outmoded agricultural economy. In England, by contrast, the elimination of the peasants provided the basis for a successful agrarian capitalism.

Moore's approach to the whole issue of the rise of dictatorship and democracy in the modern world rests on three key axioms. First, that it is possible to take a comparative and generalizing methodology (of the kind usually to be found in the social sciences) to historical development and to come up with suggestive accounts and explanations. They may lack the detailed introspection of more discrete historical enquiry, although making as much use of such studies as possible, but they may in their sweep generate more complete accounts of epochal change. Second, Moore seeks to show the importance of economic factors, particularly the interplay between key socio-economic classes, in explaining political and related phenomena, such as the emergence of democracy, and of authoritarian, fascist and communist regimes. Third, in contrast to classical Marxism, although accepting its emphasis on the socioeconomic, Moore aims to show that the linear, one-outcome, and historical revolutionary claims for 'maturing capitalisms' made by the Marxists are untenable. Rather, capitalist development is seen to be directly associated with maturing and strengthening democracy (not with socialism), and the routes to the modern world are diverse and not pre-ordained. Moreover, in the emergence of western parliamentary versions of democracy, and in the dictatorships of the Right and Left (fascism and communism), the key classes are the landed upper classes, the peasantry, the state and the bourgeoisie, rather than the working class.

The democratic-capitalist route is seen to occur when there exists a relative equilibrium between the state (the monarch in its earliest forms) and the landed upper classes and when a strong and independent urban bourgeoisie is thus able to strongly influence national policy, either by successfully enlisting the landed elite to its positions, or by effectively eliminating them. In England, the commercialization of agriculture was the outcome of an alliance of the urban merchants with the landed classes. It involved the enclosures movement (effectively the 'privatization' of common land) and the transformation of the peasantry, partly into an urban proletariat and partly into a stratum of independent farmers. The democratic-capitalist outcome flowed from a marketization that started under the influence of an increasingly commercially-minded landed class which, instead of fighting the growth of the bourgeoisie, allied with its emerging elements, not least in restraining and influencing the power of the monarch/state. The key factor was a broad balance of power between the state and social forces.

In France, however, where a further variant of parliamentary democracy eventually developed, although following a process of revolutionary upheaval, a key variable was the destruction of the economic power of the landed classes. Here, unlike in England, these classes did not seek to encourage the commercialization of agriculture but rather aimed to intensify traditionally repressive methods of extracting the surplus from the peasants. The result was not only an overall addition to the tensions underpinning the French Revolution of 1789, but also a rising cry from the peasantry to be allowed to possess their own property. This latest demand added to the list of revolutionary grievances and fanned the Revolution's fires. Although the peasantry eventually recoiled from the excesses of the Revolution, and indeed contributed in the later stages to the reaction to it, this was not before the power of the landed upper classes had been destroyed and the peasants had been turned into farmers.

In America, which Moore regards as a third variant of capitalist democracy, the peasantry did not exist, although there was a conservative landed upper class in the south utilizing labour-repressive plantation agriculture. However, the power of this group was eventually eliminated by a coalition of northern industrial bourgeoisie and western independent farmers. As Gill (2000:99) observes:

> the crucial point about these three patterns of reaction to agricultural commercialization is the destruction of the conservative power blocs based in the countryside ... the key to the non-democratic paths is the failure to destroy such power blocs.

We are here mainly concerned with this first route to liberal democracy. Box 4.2, however, indicates the different class relations and state forms found in the other two main pathways, fascism and communism. Again patterns of domination in the countryside are a key variable.

Skocpol: states and social revolution

It is arguable that the emphasis placed by Moore on economic factors in explaining developments in political structures may underestimate the independent effects of changes in state organization as an important determinant in political change. In comparison to Moore (but also to

---

Box 4.2 Barrington Moore's three paths to modernity

1 The democratic-capitalist route: occurs when there is a rough balance between the state and the landed upper classes and when a strong and independent urban bourgeoisie is thereby able to establish its control over national policy, either by winning over the landed elite or by destroying its position. The commercialization of agriculture is sponsored by the bourgeoisie, either in alliance with the landed upper classes, as in England, or by destroying the economic power of the latter, as in France.

2 The fascist route: comes about when the landed upper classes sponsor agricultural commercialization through a tightening of controls over the peasantry exercised in part through the repressive apparatus of the state. The urban bourgeoisie is politically and economically weak, relies on this conservative alliance between the landed upper classes and the state, and fails to exercise any significant influence on national life.

3 The communist route: the likely outcome where the urban bourgeoisie is weak, the landed upper classes do not promote agricultural commercialization, but market relations intrude into the countryside. If the peasantry is cohesive, the connection with the landlord is weak (as in the case of absentee landlords) and the peasants can find allies with the organizational skills, peasant revolution is likely to lead to a communist outcome.

See Gill (2000: 97–8) for a concise account of these routes.

---

liberalism and Marxism), Skocpol (1979) asserts that social change (analysed by studying social revolution) cannot be explained by a focus on national economic forces or class struggles alone. Rather, state autonomy and the military requirements of the international system of states play larger roles. State institutions have interests at variance from dominant economic interests (not least in imposing the taxation needed to engage in warfare) and can introduce reforms to strengthen state power that may be objected to by the economically ascendant. Moreover, state rulers can fight wars, lose, and be deposed, thus preventing them protecting the economically dominant or their mode of production – even in the 'long run', as Marxists claim. Such factors as state administrative efficiency, political capacities for mass mobilization, and international geographic position may be as relevant as the conditions of domestic economies or international economic positions in accounting for the comparative strengths and weaknesses of nations.

Modern social revolutions provide particularly good examples of this, for defeats in war, threats of invasion, and struggles over colonial controls have directly contributed to revolutions by undermining existing state authority, thus providing opportunities for successful revolts 'from below'. More generally, as we have noted, state organizations, rather than merely reflecting dominant economic interests, may run counter to them. They may consume more resources, perhaps in military adventures, than dominant economic interests may feel is compatible with the need for economic reinvestment. Revolutionary crises tend to happen when old-regime states fail to meet the economic and/or military challenges of more developed states, and lack the capacity to carry through political reform in the face of entrenched landed interests more concerned with preventing increased taxation or in using possession of state offices to procure revenue in a manner that maintained the domestic status quo.

The differential spread of military capacity among states and the basic military challenge of the stronger states led to war and revolution. A backward France confronted a more advanced Britain; China faced the might of the western nations; and an under-resourced Russian state failed to match the advances of a unified Germany after 1870. The dilemmas for rulers faced with intensifying military competition from nation states that had greater power based on capitalist breakthrough were huge and required the rapid marshalling of immense social resources to carry out major reforms. Consequently states needed quite high levels of domestic institutional autonomy to push through economic and fiscal changes against resistance so as to enhance their military power base. If they failed to overcome these domestic constraints, the result was likely to be war or revolution, as occurred in Russia and China. In these inadequately centralized states, tax collection could not be extracted directly and rulers relied for its collection on local and provincial classes, who failed to pass on most of the tax take but rather used it to improve their own power rather than that of the central authority. The result was further fiscal debilitation centrally and the added inability for the regime to compete internationally. In Russia, however, the problem was less an issue of entrenched dominant classes than the inability of the state to modernize agriculture and produce a more buoyant tax base.

'Revolutions from above' in Prussia and Japan showed that these modernization and fiscal tasks were not impossible, although it still needed authoritarian political rule to extract more from a declining economic base to compete in the inter-state system. At a later stage in such 'revolutions', and with the support of a weak commercial bourgeoisie allied with the landed upper classes, the state directly supports capitalist development in several important ways, not least as an engine of accumulation through the introduction of armaments and heavy industrial needs. The political result is a regime with an authoritarian military ethic unfavourable to democracy.

In France, however, the old regime was unable to overcome this dilemma, and it succumbed to the opposition of politically powerful landed upper classes, which resisted the King's efforts at reform. As we noted in the second chapter, France remained predominantly an agricultural society in the seventeenth and eighteenth centuries, with a torpid economy featuring a complicated mix of property interests that ruled out any rapid change to capitalist agriculture or industrialism. A large peasant sector stayed in place from which was drawn a surplus through a mosaic of rents and dues, enforced in part by legal institutions heavily influenced by the dominant classes and backed up by the monarchy, neither of which had any interest in reform. The eventual breakdown of this economic system and the inability and unwillingness to reform it were key factors in the demise of the royal household and the subsequent social revolution (Skocpol, 1979: 64). Yet, in the aftermath of social revolutions, such as the French, it was the political elites rather than the unwitting revolutionary classes that emerged to build up and direct the state, and to implement the economic and administrative reforms against weakened social groups that would make the state more competitive internationally.

In returning to Moore, we conclude by noting that in his outline of the different historical pathways to democracy – and to dictatorship – Moore helps the move way from 'straight line' explanations of the rise of the liberal-democratic state. Emphasis is laid instead on the variability in patterns of modernity. For later authors also the compelling and competitive nature of the inter-state system – although less economically constituted – remains a key causal factor (Skocpol, 1979; Gilpin, 1981; Tilly, 1975). In one important account, however, it was the internal mix and balance of state/military coercion and capitalist development (neither just one or the other) that was viewed as especially promising for liberal-democratic development (Tilly, 1990).

Class and ideology

Barrington Moore's analysis has been subject to considerable debate and some criticism. A recent compelling review, plus several theoretical propositions of his own, has been provided by Gill (2000). He points out that although a powerful independent bourgeoisie is essential for the democratic path, Moore provides no clear method for establishing the political and economic strength of this particular class. The danger is that the dominance of the bourgeoisie – or indeed any class – may be inferred from the primacy of a particular set of ideas that are then assumed to 'belong' to a particular class. Thus, when liberal ideas are influential, this is regarded as a sign that the bourgeoisie are in the ascendancy. The problem, however, is that classes can espouse different ideas and political programmes depending on the range of alliances available to them and the relative strength of other classes. Thus, while in England, America and France, where industrialization proceeded initially on the basis of small and medium-sized entrepreneurs acting largely free of the state, their interests were defined in principles largely consistent with democracy. These included individual freedom, a limited state, and so on. However, in other countries, the bourgeoisie may not have espoused such views and may have allied with more conservative or reactionary forces, such as landowners or the state, and adopted their conservative and nationalist philosophies, because of their own weakness, not least in the face of a growing urban and working class. In Germany, for example, which started the process of capitalist industrialization late, and in the context of stiff colonial competition from England, France and then, later, the US, the role of the state in driving this process was crucial. As a consequence the bourgeoisie's interests were best advanced in Germany by supporting the state, and its conservative supporters and their illiberal ideology, rather than opposing it on the grounds of the need for market freedoms. Indeed, Moore's own case studies, of Japan, Russia and China, as well as of Germany, suggest that the bourgeoisie are just as tempted to join conservative and reactionary coalitions as liberal ones.

Others have also criticized Moore for underestimating the role of the working class in the path to democracy (Therborn, 1977). Generally it has been resourced and organized better than the peasants and spatially it can be found – at work or at home – as being less close to conservative ideologies than those groups to be found in the countryside. However, according to Rueschemeyer *et al.* (1992), the working class has normally needed partners in other classes to promote democratization, which often has meant a tempering of aims so as not to frighten particularly the middle class. A further point is that Moore's analysis stops some way short in historic terms of the stages where democratic or other outcomes are actually being achieved. Both Germany and Japan, for instance, today would be classified as democratic, while communism has since fallen in Russia. Rather than fascism or communism being final end states, they have proved to be transitional.

A further key factor in explaining how the broad historical and socioeconomic forces outlined by Moore actually operate on political development – the triggering processes and political actions that are largely ignored by Moore – is the strength of civil society. Gill (2000: 109) suggests that the capacity of organized forces from within civil society is important, not least because this is often the location of the development of working-class organizational resources and a source of political power. Urban-based, manufacturing development tends to magnify the influence of bourgeois and working-class forces, as it increases organizational capability and instruments of disruption (such as within the extended division of labour). Conditions of industrial concentration, levels of communication, and urban-based organization for the working class are also likely to influence its sense of itself as a class with common class interests and consciousness.

It is this realm of civil society that is important, not least when it is recognized that most authoritarian regimes have sought to constrain civil society by imposing restraints or prohibitions on autonomous organizations. Thus, in the transition to democracy, a critical factor is whether civil society has been allowed to develop and has created the fertile soil for independent political organization. In turn this generates a public sphere within which political issues are discussed and interests pressed, activities that, crucially, are recognized as legitimate by existing regimes. For Gill, it is not enough, therefore, in studying the movement to democracy or dictatorship to look at the interplay of elite groups; it is essential to examine the conditions of civil society forces, too.

The requisites for democracy

Alongside accounts of the origins of democracy, as exemplified in Moore's classic work, the post-war period after 1945 in political sociology saw also a search for the social, economic, political, and cultural 'prerequisites' of liberal democracy – those factors that particularly *maintained* democracy. In the 1950s and 1960s, political sociology in both the American and the European traditions became marked by an academic orthodoxy that was characterized by two main assumptions, and which reflected a convergence of classical European 'grand theory' with the more micro, empirically detailed concerns of the Americans with the psychology and otherwise of the 'ordinary citizen', not least at elections. The first assumption was that the liberal regimes in most of the western industrial nations were as democratic as one could reasonably expect. The key issue was to identify how such regimes could be stabilized and their examples furthered elsewhere. Second, it was assumed that social processes largely determine political arrangements and that the answer to the issue of stabilizing liberal democracy lay in establishing the social causes or requisites of democracy.

An early critical influence on these ideas, not least, as a European migrant to the US, because of his interpretation of Weberian state sociology within the US context, was Schumpeter. His *Capitalism, Socialism, and Democracy*, published in 1942, is notable for his minimalist view of democracy, shared with Weber, that it was a procedural arrangement, namely competitive party struggles for the people's vote, which was none the less welcome because it allowed people some influence over political decisions. It was a prosaic, unsentimental view of democracy as a political market place, based on selling and buying at periodic elections, except that in comparison with the economic market, the buyers were irregular and rather passive consumers. Most people did not want more participation than this, being far more preoccupied with family and leisure pursuits, which was just as well as they were predominantly fairly ignorant of what constituted wise decision-making, and could easily be roused by demagogues. Romantic classical ideas of fully participatory democracy, drawn from Antiquity, were no longer feasible or desirable.

Although Schumpeter's pared-down portrayal of democracy has been criticized for over-simplicity and ignoring the democratic educative gains from wider forms of political participation (Pateman, 1970), and for wrongly deriving the 'ought' (normative) from the 'is' (empirical) – see Duncan and Lukes, 1963 – he claimed that there was sufficient evidence to show that people are easily led and manipulated by non-rational forces (not least through the expanding use of advertising), that they are broadly uninterested in politics, and that often unaccountable 'experts' can make better decisions, and have them readily accepted by the people, than those taken by democratically elected politicians. Electoral democracy and the operation of competing political parties he regarded as probably the best means for ensuring that the wide span of individual interests is broadly converged programmatically and acted upon by those best positioned to do so.

The behaviourist tradition in American political sociology, which was primarily an orientation to collect and evaluate data according to the methods of research generally found within the natural sciences, including the use of surveys and statistical analyses to focus on observable behaviour, provided a number of studies to test Schumpeter's propositions after the Second World War. They looked at electoral behaviour as an important empirical referent for democratic theorizing, and studies by Lazarsfeld *et al.* (1948) and Berelson (1954), among others, challenged many traditional assumptions about the discerning, rational voter found in conventional democratic theory (although not in Schumpeter's work). Most voters had preformed ideas and choices that were largely unaffected by party campaigns, and their views were often contradictory. Consequently, like Schumpeter, behaviourists argued that classical participatory notions of democracy as a means for arriving at good, consensual-based decisions, and for promoting a sense of tolerance, citizenship, and personal efficacy, needed revising along more realistic and elitist lines.

The implications of electoral studies for democratic theory were explored by Robert Dahl in his classic work, *A Preface to Democratic Theory* (1956), in which he advanced a modified pluralist concept of democracy as polyarchy, or the rule of multiple minorities. In an interesting addition to Schumpeter, Dahl argued that elites competed in the public policy process and not just in elections, a conclusion he found supported in his study of urban politics in New Haven (*Who Governs?* 1961). Dahl found support for the pluralist view that the city's political system revealed multiple coalitions trying to influence public policy. Control over decisions by different sector interests, when analysed, indicated a process of interest bargaining and resolution through government offices. The result was a 'competitive equilibrium', with policy outcomes that were generally beneficial for the people. Political power was found not to be equally distributed as in formal 'classical democracy', nor cumulatively structured in a few hands, as with an oligarchy or an elite. Groups could be freely formed and used to mobilize interests.

Dahl, in further revising both classical and also simple 'realist' electoral models, was more concerned that polyarchy might lead to gridlock, the cancelling out by various 'veto groups' failing to compromise and agree, and floating free of their member's interests and becoming too powerful, than being bothered by the old liberal bugbear of a tyrannical majority trampling over individual liberties. The prerequisites for an effective polyarchy included a broad consensus or agreement on values – including the rules of procedure and on the parameters of policy options and their scope. The more of these, the better established was a democracy.

Dahl's work was subjected to various criticisms, not least by elite theorists. Radical elite theorists, such as Burnham (1941) and C. Wright Mills (1956), argued that power in the US was passing into the hands of unaccountable, silent and impersonal elites, predominantly composed of military, corporate and political cliques, with similar backgrounds and values – a 'power elite'. Empirically, urban analysts writing from within the elitist paradigm, and using rather different methodologies (based on 'reputations' for having power, rather than analyses of actual decision-making, as employed by Dahl), claimed to discover, not open, multiple and competing groups, but small groups of cohesive, think-alike individuals running things political and economic (Floyd Hunter, 1953). Some argued, too, that there were groups so weak that they could not get their points of view to be taken seriously, and that political leaders are adept at mobilizing bias – in the media and in policy procedures – to 'screen out' a consideration of radical or potentially upsetting matters. Studying 'non-decisions' may be as important as studying decisions in seeking the location and exercise of power (Bachrach and Baratz, 1962; Lukes, 1974). More recently, however, Dahl (1985) has recognized that social inequalities can be so great that they threaten the political equality of the democratic process.

Dahl's pluralist theory has been influential in highlighting the role of groups in explaining policy processes as well as their importance for democracy, and has helped to modify the individualism of classic liberalism by regarding groups as more effective and able to represent individuals. But his proposition on the necessity for democratic values and economic development for the maintenance of democratic political systems also exemplifies a key strand in the American sociology of democracy. Two works are of crucial influence in this tradition. Almond and Verba's *The Civic Culture* (1963) sought to demonstrate through cross-national surveys that democratic regimes were sustained by a 'civic culture', operationalized as a mix of participative and deferential attitudes in its citizens, that allowed citizens to trust their government, but also to feel competent enough to challenge it where necessary. However, whether culture of this sort precedes democratic structure, or whether the former flows from the latter, is highly uncertain in their analysis.

A rather different approach to establishing the social bases of democracy was advanced by Lipset, who sought to provide an alternative socioeconomic explanation to that of Marxism for both the origins and the maintenance of liberal democracy. In *Political Man* (1960), Lipset argues, having distinguished between stable and unstable democracies and dictatorships in terms of periodic changes of government, and taking wealth, industrialization, education, and urbanization as indices of economic development, that in every case the average level of economic development is higher in the more democratic countries. The theoretical interpretation of these correlations is that increased income and better education lead to a less radical and evolutionary perspective among the lower classes, creates a middle class that acts as a buffer between the lower and upper classes, thus reducing class conflict, and generates a range of intermediary associations between government and elite. Moreover, democracy also leads to greater wealth and prosperity, which in turn reinforces belief in democracy, thus adding to its legitimacy.

In a subsequent work with Rokkan, Lipset extended his analysis to take more account of the role of political variables in influencing system outcomes (a criticism of his earlier work), by accounting for variations in European party and political systems by referring them back to the historical conflicts and cleavages faced by all advanced European societies; that is, subject versus dominant cultures, churches versus secular governments, rural versus urban, and workers versus employers (Lipset and Rokkan, 1967). Responses to these dilemmas help explain how viable and democratic political systems are forged in the face of the fissures and divisions of interest produced by industrialization. A crucial factor identified was the 'non-cumulation' and resolution of essentially non-bargainable cleavages – those centred on religion, language and culture – before these have the opportunity to overlay the essentially secular and bargainable cleavages over economic matters between employers and workers in advanced capitalism.

Underlying the sociology of democracy at this time was a further set of assumptions that seem to confirm the important role of groups and established elites in protecting democracy. This was a fear of the rise of what was described as 'mass society' (Kornhauser, 1960). The increasing 'privatization' and 'individuation' of increasingly non-active, mass media-influenced populations was regarded as making them ripe for mobilization by non-democratic and totalitarian leaders who had mastered the techniques of modern communications. Protection by more civilized and established elites, along with ensuring that civil society maintained high levels of social interaction and participation in community and interest groups, were the most potent antidotes.

We shall see that these medicines have not been in ready supply in recent years. Although totalitarian 'coups' may no longer be high on liberal democracy's 'worry agenda' there is continued concern at the increasingly powerful role of the mass media and the apparently accompanying decline in community activities. However, before considering these matters, we need to conclude with an outline of the second and third 'waves' of democracy, to bring the picture up to date.

Second and third waves

The nineteenth- and twentieth-century processes of democratization (the 'first wave') generated counter-cyclical periods of crisis and decline (Huntingdon, 1991). After an initial period of extending franchises and the introduction of more democratic political institutions following the First World War, there was a marked reaction in the inter-war period. Italy, Germany, and Argentina were among the countries that reverted to authoritarianism in the period leading up to the outbreak of the Second World War in 1939. By then Britain, Switzerland, the Benelux countries, and Scandinavia retained the only functioning democracies in Europe. Four main factors have been identified as being particularly important in explaining this turn of affairs (Bessel, 2000).

The first can be traced to the consequences of the First World War. Its social, economic and political dislocations debilitated the legitimacy and effectiveness of European democratic regimes, not least their apparent helplessness in reintegrating large numbers of demilitarized soldiers back into productive civilian life, and in coping with the pension and other requirements of the dependents of the many who perished. Second, economic recession, unemployment and, at times, periods of both severe deflation and inflation made the task of ruling democratic regimes much more difficult, and the problem of attaining consent for tough decisions on expenditure priorities that much harder. Third, the rise of labour, not least as a consequence of increased democratization, posed major challenges to democratic regimes and generated 'Rightist' reactions that led to the development of fascism and the Nazis. Moreover, the domination of the German Nazi regime during the Second World War years helped extinguish a number of the European democracies. Finally, a contributory factor if not vital on its own account, was the increase in national and nationalist tensions that added to the overall stresses that democratic governments were under. In contrast, where democracy survived – in the US and Britain and, to some extent, in France – it benefited from being associated with victory in the First World War and from the 'dug-in' nature of existing democratic political institutions and culture. Political parties, especially of the Right, such as the British Conservative Party, were able to incorporate and control groups that gravitated to the authoritarian and extremist right in other countries.

It took the impact of the Second World War, and not least the impact of emerging American hegemony, which favoured democratic constitutions – a feeling reinforced by the growing anti-communism of its foreign policy as the Cold War intensified – to kick-start the process of the second wave of democratization in Europe, including in Germany, Italy and Austria. In those countries the experience of fascism and its subsequent defeat in the Second World War had significantly reduced the attractions of authoritarian regimes. However, in Portugal, Spain and (later) Greece, authoritarian regimes were found until well into the 1970s. It took capitalist development, the attractions and increasing influence of the democracy-encouraging European Community, and, in the case of Portugal, military crisis in its colonies, to undermine authoritarianism. The ability to compromise in negotiations by the democratic opposition and to secure alliances also facilitated the path to democratic transition in these countries. In a number of ex-colonies, especially those of Britain and France in Africa, one-Party and other forms of non-democracy were also conspicuous. Elsewhere, the success of the USSR in the Second World War and the Cold War stand-off with the West helped to ensure that eastern Europe experienced state-led socialist regimes until 1989, and in a number of them democratic oppositional movements were suppressed over that period (Goldblatt, 2000b). Yet it was the economic and military success of the West, which eventually the Soviets could not match, perhaps as much as ideological conviction, which clinched the democratic route to the modern world in the post-1945 years. It was responsiveness to that success which reinforced the third wave with the post-communist democratization of the last decade of the twentieth century.

The third wave

In recent years the relationship between economic development and democracy has been regarded as looser than that originally outlined by Lipset. Indeed Lipset has come to regard the relationship as highly prob-abilistic and largely suggestive rather than particularly causal (Lipset, 1993). Huntingdon might also be classed as a 'modernization' theorist, as behind the notion of democratic waves is a view that they are largely propelled by increased global economic prosperity. For example, one factor behind the second wave of democracy in the 1960s was unprecedented global economic growth, which raised living standards, increased education (and a culture of political toleration), and greatly expanded the urban middle class in many countries.

However, Huntingdon is careful to recognize that it requires political leadership for favourable conditions to become realized in new democratic arrangements. Moreover, the relationship between modernization and democratization was perhaps strongest during the first and second waves but is likely to have become attenuated subsequently as a range of other factors have gained salience, not least the notion of global emulation – the search by states for respectability and international funds, for example – which Huntingdon describes as 'snowballing' (Huntingon, 1996). We have seen too, from our analysis of wider comparative and historical studies, such as those of Moore, Skocpol and Mann, that certain historical periods appear more conducive than others in facilitating democracy, not least when it involves the impact of war. A regular feature of accounts of democratization tends to point out that one of the most advanced economically of countries – Germany – took a considerable time to achieve democratic institutions, while one of the world's poorest – India – democratized relatively early, in part because of its colonial heritage (Randall, 2000).

A further counterpoint to modernization accounts of democratization is found in those works which look more closely at the factors involved in the transition and consolidation of democracy. Rather than background or structural explanations these tend to look more directly at agency – the actions of elites and opponents – and at more explicitly political processes. Influential here has been the work of Rustow (1970), and also the analyses of authors adopting much of his approach, such as O'Donnell *et al.* (1986), Mainwaring (1992) and Linz and Stepan (1996). For Rustow the 'routes' and stages to democracy emphasize the need for national unity, a failed or non-resolved first political struggle, a decision phase, often involving compromise, and a concluding routinization stage when the practices, ideology and institutions of democracy are firmly established. For the later theorists, too, whether this process occurs, however, generally depends on the strategies and actions of political elites; some behaviours are conducive to democratization, such as the easing of repression and the introduction of political liberalization (as occurred in the final years of east European communism), while others are not (such as the presence of 'hardliners' in the elite and 'radicals' in the opposition, which tends to result in crackdown or violent change). In a comparative study of transitions in Latin America and southern Europe, O'Donnell and Schmitter (1986) indicate that the typical beginning of the transition to democracy is a period of liberalization. This tends to involve the authoritarian rulers extending a level of civil and political rights to individuals and groups. This creates the space for further oppositional political activity and at least nascent political competitiveness. However, if attempts at pluralism remain controlled within a single dominant party, rather than multiparty arrangements, the process is unlikely to provide much of a breathing space or legitimacy for the incumbent regime (Sorensen, 1998).

The 'transition' or political elites approach has been regarded as particularly appropriate for the analysis of democratization in Latin America. O'Donnell (1996), for example, suggests that many of the new democracies in Latin America (and elsewhere) face special problems that are generated by their 'delegative' character, in which presidents often operate with few 'horizontal' constraints, but personalistically and paternalistically. That is, formal political institutions are weak (especially legislators and courts) and possess little consensual commitment. The result is that it becomes harder for public policy to be forged effectively within extensive state dialogues and bargaining, and in ways that overcome protracted economic and social problems. There is therefore a propensity to rule by surprise and decree, which reduces stability and democratic institutions, even if it may occasionally produce moments of decisiveness. Compared to parliamentary forms, because of their directly elected character, presidential regimes can assume plebiscitarian and undemocratic characteristics (Linz, 1990).

In many ways the haphazard and cyclical development of democratization in Latin American countries may be regarded as a disappointment.

Geographically situated close to the US, the region seemed to offer encouraging signs of democracy in the nineteenth and early twentieth centuries, not least with the introduction of constitutional civilian rule. But economic depression after the First World War and the 1929 Wall Street crash made this increasingly unstable. In subsequent decades, especially after the Cuban socialist revolution in the late 1950s heightened regional insecurity, military intervention and state-led development and authoritarian populism – involving state-controlled associations and unions, and hostile to political competition – were more the order of the day. Landed elites remained powerful and the peasantry and growing working class stayed largely outside the state system. However, from around 1980 Latin America became part of the third wave of democratization as a consequence of mainly elite-controlled forms of liberalization and compromise, and successful economic performance. However, its consolidation appears less entrenched as a result of the factors examined above, and the persistence of corruption, clientelism and widening social inequalities (Cammack, 2000; Little, 2000).

Liberal democracy has also struggled to take root in Asia. India and Japan provide the earliest examples of such regimes, although a number of Asian countries have moved towards democratic or partially democratic regimes as part of the second and third waves of world democratization. In some cases external influences and the impact of war provide the explanation. In Japan, the American Occupation, which commenced after victory in the Pacific in 1945 and which continued until 1952, imposed a western-style democratic constitution, which stripped the emperor of all powers and located sovereignty in the Japanese people, who elected a parliament (Diet) to which the cabinet was accountable. The Americans extended the franchise, re-established the rights to form parties and other groupings, and reformed land ownership and education, among other changes. Yet the emerging Cold War, and the need by the US to secure Japan as a major counterweight to communism in the Pacific area, led to a downgrading of democratization goals and the build-up of Japan's economy and self-sufficiency. The result today is a slightly uneasy combination of a democratic constitution, one-party rule, and decisions often emerging as a consequence of rather secretive elite bargaining and patronage (McCargo, 2000).

Elsewhere in Asia, democracy has often appeared late. In South Korea and Taiwan, for example, the legacies of Japanese colonial domination produced a lengthy period of authoritarian rule (from 1945 to the early 1980s) before rapid capitalist development, a decline in the power of the military as a consequence of the easing of Cold War regional tensions, and the development of democracy as part of the global third wave, helped create more propitious conditions for democracy, although not before quite sharp clashes between protestors and the authorities. The rapid and successful state-directed industrialization of east Asian societies such as Japan, South Korea and Taiwan, but also elsewhere, such as Singapore and Malaysia, has led to the view that the state bureaucracies in those countries possessed high levels of autonomy. They are 'catalytic states' – not simply passive in the face of economic globalization, but able to act as catalysts for the internationalization strategies of corporate actors (Weiss, 1998).

Such states offer a range of incentives to finance overseas investment, to advance technological alliances between national and foreign firms, and to promote the regional relocation of production networks. They have been able to impose performance targets on business, been prepared to withdraw support from ailing companies, backed strategic winners by diverting resources from consumption to production, and operated efficient public corporations (Amsden, 1989; Wade, 1990). Others, however, have questioned the above proposition by pointing to the influence of non-state actors in some instances, such as the role of the *chaebol* or big conglomerates in resisting efforts by the Korean government to rationalize the car industry. They suggest that the state was only able to exercise the leverage that it did because it was 'connected' to key social groups and was able to enlist their support for national objectives rather than it being 'autonomous' (Evans, 1995; Hobson and Weiss, 1995).

In India it would appear that a combination of internal and external influences helped produce a democratic outcome. India's political culture, as formed by social diversity, an element of social pluralism, and the lack of a centralized hierarchy in Hinduism, proved receptive during the long period of British colonialism to liberal democratic values and institutions, and was sustained by the emergence of a dense and autonomous civil society and the rise of a democratically-inclusive and dominant Congress Party (Randall, 2000).

In recent times, following the attacks on the US in September 2001, the role of Islam in the apparent lack of democratic impulses in Middle East countries has received more attention. The depiction of women as inferior to men and the consequent denial of democratic rights were highlighted particularly under the Taleban regime in Afghanistan. Moreover, the perspective of most Islamic movements has been largely undemocratic. Yet in many instances Islamic movements find themselves in opposition to well-entrenched reactionary regimes and they have often been subject to coercive repression, while in some partial democracies such as Malaysia there has been a level of Islamic incorporation within democratic arrangements. None the less, a history of longstanding conflict between Islam and the West has not made Islamic movements naturally incline towards western forms of political rule, and this is reinforced by the continued virulence in the relations between Israel and some Muslim and Arab states.

Post-communism

The fall of communism in the Soviet Union and other parts of east Europe has been a major boost to the recent third wave of democratization, and has been a significant world event. The result of the downfall of these authoritarian regimes has been the introduction of either liberal democracy or partial democracy, apart from the continuation of authoritarian regimes in a number of states to the south of Russia and bordering Afghanistan (such as Kazakhstan). The primary reasons for these transitions were the inability of the Soviet Union to compete economically or militarily with the United States and, reinforced by the Soviet defeat in seeking to subjugate Afghanistan, a change in its policy towards the maintenance of the regional communist bloc so that controls on its satellite countries were much reduced. At the same time a number of the east European countries faced similar internal problems associated with poor economic performance, but also increased demands for civil and political rights for individuals and parties (and, in the case of Solidarity and Poland, independent trade unions). Prior to this, over a number of years, the Soviet Union had been forced to intervene military to put down revolts in Czechoslovakia and Hungary, and to threaten to do so in Poland.

A quickening process of political liberalization in the Soviet Union and elsewhere proved impossible to contain within the dominance of the ruling communist parties, both within the main countries and as a model for elsewhere in the region. None the less, the pattern of democratic development has varied, with the more socially and economically advanced countries – the Czech Republic, Hungary and Poland – among the earliest and deepest with their reforms. Explanations for these differences appear to rest upon a number of factors and interpretations, which mix modernization and transition approaches with the specific historical and other patterns to be found within each of the countries (Lewis, 2000). In this context the notion of 'civil society' has been used to give some theoretical coherence to these explanations and to provide a connecting point between structural conditions and political actions leading to changes in regime (Gill, 2000). This may be particularly appropriate as the concept of 'civil society' received greater attention following the emergence of Solidarity in Poland in the early 1970s when its intellectual founders applied the term to their efforts to organize people independently of the totalitarian state.

Essentially, civil society refers to the associational space that lies outside the state and in the voluntary sphere of society and to its sentiments based on interests, affinities and ideas. A strong and vibrant civil society is seen as providing that balance in the relationship between the state and society that many theorists regard as particularly facilitative of democratization, as well as providing the channels for articulation, legitimation and resolution that are seen to be characteristic of both successful social and political change and also the operation of stable democracies. The vibrancy of personal engagement is the key, and some have argued that the decline in trust in US democracy in recent years is as a consequence of the growth of single-issue national organizations, and the substantial drop in participation in voluntary associations (Putnam, 2000).

These views are associated with the view that democracies require, not only high levels of economic and intellectual property, but *social capital* too. Social capital is a stock of resources, like other capital, which has been built up over many years and which can be used to generate 'returns', such as competent democratic performance (Bagnasco, 2001). A democracy is better secured in this view by being embedded in a dense network of civil and voluntary associations that generate social capital and close links between civic life and state institutions (Ray, 2001).

Particularly influential has been the work of Robert Putnam (1993) on the comparative institutional performance of regional government in Italy in implementing political choices. Despite a common institutional structure, Italian regions differ in their political culture. Those with a civic tradition of mutual trust, tolerance and solidarity (within which private interests are mediated) have a higher social capital and consequent political performance than other regions. Values, norms, and networks, which comprise social capital, have the causal primacy, not the institutional structures or the presence of democratic arrangements themselves.

Putnam's thesis has been taken up more generally as displaying a compelling link between associational activity and social trust on the one hand, and democratic development on the other. It lies remarkably in line with earlier US political sociology, including the work of Almond and Verba (1963) on 'civic culture', and that by Lipset (1960) and others, who argue that regime legitimacy and effectiveness go 'hand-in-hand' (a phrase that hints at the difficulties none the less in isolating the independent from the dependent variables). As with earlier 'mass society' theorists, such as Kornhauser, Putnam, in a later work on the US (Putnam, 2000), worries about the increasingly private and individuated leisure activities of ordinary citizens (for example, 'bowling alone'), in an age of mass media and consumerism. These provide opportunities for governments and others to bypass democratic, communitarian processes for more authoritarian ones. The aim must be to see how civil society, and community activity and association, may be reinvigorated in pursuit of healthier, more participative democracies.

Although Putnam's approach has been criticized as ignoring such other factors as 'institutional design' (Lowndes and Wilson, 2001), for neglecting the relative role of employment, education, family, and friends (Newton, 1999), and for its society and non-state centredness (Levi, 1996), it remains an influential part of an increasing literature connecting democracy with the vitality of civil society.

One of the most obvious features of the post-communist European transitions was that they all occurred at around the same time (between 1989 and 1991). As Gill notes, this indicates a common external opportunity presented by the collapse of the Soviet Union, but the different pattern of outcomes suggests that internal factors were also at work. This difference stemmed from the historic conditions in the different societies, especially levels of social capital – the extent or otherwise of central control and the corresponding development of civil society forces and political organization.

More specifically, Gill (2000: 216) suggests that the former communist countries can be divided into two categories: those, such as Hungary, Poland, Czechoslovakia, East Germany and Yugoslavia, which possessed autonomous organizations pressing political demands; and those, such as Romania, Albania, Bulgaria, and the Soviet Union, where such activity was very limited or negligible. In part, these differences reflect pre-communist legacies, but largely they reflect the development or otherwise of

> a bourgeois middle class with the resources, commonality of interests, and opportunities to unite in defence of those interests. The bourgeois middle class has been crucial because it has been this group which has sought to pursue its economic interests by carving out a space autonomous from state control, and thereby creating a shell within which autonomous social organization could blossom. (Gill, 2000: 217)

Moreover, when such a class is based in a few large cities, communication is easier because of the concentration of people and the more developed technical infrastructure, thus facilitating civil society organization. In this third wave example of democratization it would appear that conditions were supportive for the middle classes to be the pivotal agents of democratic change and proponents of liberalism, although in Poland the skilled working class was instrumental in starting the process of democratic change through the creation of Solidarity and the call for independent trade unions.

Conclusion

In this chapter we have looked at the development of liberal democracy throughout the nineteenth and twentieth centuries. We have used Huntingdon's notion of 'waves' to indicate that the process of democratization can fall back as well as advance. However, we have identified three such waves, culminating in that associated particularly with the decline of east European communist regimes. Additionally we have looked at classical sociological interpretations of liberal democracy, their interpretations of the claims that it makes, and their theorizing of it. We noted the importance of considering more general theories within the context of historical analysis and how this not only points to critical differences in the routes taken by countries to the modern world, but also indicates the multicausal nature of that change, including socioeconomic and military developments, within an increasingly inter-state system. The convergence of European and American political sociology in a 'sociology of democracy' orthodoxy post-1945 was identified as significant for marrying micro, empirical processes with grander theory, and for seeking to validate more minimalist models of democracy. It helped to evaluate the impact of civic culture and socioeconomic development for democracy, and to confront liberal democratic individualism with more group-based and policy-making approaches. Finally, we introduced notions of 'civil society' and social capital as playing a part in recent democratization, although we drew upon examples from around the world, including Asia and South America, to highlight also the importance of wider regional and colonial factors, in both impeding and facilitating the introduction and maintenance of liberal-democratic regimes.

In the next chapter, some of these themes will be picked up again, notably the significance of an extending state apparatus for democratic and economic wellbeing.

Chapter 5

The Interventionist State and its Critics

The Keynesian welfare state
The Cold War convergence thesis of East and West
The post-1945 state in the West
New Right
Social democracy and the Third Way
Networks and governance
The regulatory state

By the 1970s a strongly interventionist or welfare state model seemed to predominate in many developed liberal democratic countries, with the US apparently the significant exception. For the most part this took the form of considerable state-provided social services, such as health, education and unemployment benefits, extensive state involvement in the economy through public ownership of key services, such as the water and energy industries, and through the wide use of fiscal (tax) policies for both the pursuit of macroeconomic stability and wealth redistribution, and, finally, at the political level, through the incorporation into the state system of interest groups considered important to the maintenance of political order and authority. Even in the US, without a tradition of public ownership of vital economic sectors, the development of state-backed independent regulatory agencies to overcome market perversity and to implement social rights objectives, such as for health and safety, indicated a more activist state than hitherto.

We should note that that the 'Keynesian welfare state' (Jessop, 2002) did not arrive in the 1970s unexpectedly or as the result of some form of 'big bang'. It had built up over the years. In the first industrial nation – the UK – we can see throughout the nineteenth century increasing attempts by governments to regulate a variety of social conditions: at work, through controlling the length of the working day and bearing down on the abuse of child labour, particularly in the factories; in health, through, for example, compulsory vaccination to halt infectious disease and supervised by local boards; in housing, by allowing local government the powers to buy dwellings (often to tear them down to clear slums in the growing urban areas) and to provide council

111

accommodation to tenants for rental; and through the provision of several pieces of education legislation aimed to ensure compulsory but free basic schooling. In the period before the First World War, further social reforms were enacted, including on old age pensions, and sickness and unemployment insurance, while, following the experience of mass unemployment in the inter-war years and the horrors of the Second World War, from 1945 further social measures were enacted. National insurance was unified and extended to provide income protection in the event of job loss, illness, or old age, a national state owned and delivered health service that was essentially 'free to all' was introduced, and educational reforms aimed at enhancing working and other lower-class achievements were implemented. Moreover, levels of taxation were raised considerably to finance these changes, while at the same time securing a redistribution of income and wealth on more egalitarian grounds. Between 1910 and 1975 the amount of public expenditure growth on social services as a percentage of gross national product in the UK rose from 4.2 to 28.0 (Ling, 1998: 75).

Yet critics argued that high levels of direct taxation (on salaries and wages) were a disincentive to hard work and ambition, thus curtailing the individual enterprise and corporate profits needed by the economy in an increasingly competitive world, and that an overblown state hampered the efficient allocation of resources and rewards that a healthy private business sector required. Too much bureaucracy and 'red tape', it was alleged, would stifle economic development and actually reduce the funding available for social expenditure. These were claims picked up in the 1970s by a variety of 'New Right' critics of the Keynesian welfare state, and which we discuss later in the chapter. There were many critics on the Left, too, who increasingly felt by the 1970s that the welfare state was not delivering on its promises, with poverty only marginally moderated – at best – and with the middle rather than the working classes taking advantage of higher benefits and increased educational opportunities. But why, if this was the case, did the welfare state grow to such an extent and over quite a lengthy period, and in many countries other than the UK?

In part, particularly in the earlier stages, it followed the efforts of the traditional governing elites – aware of the growing numerical size of the labouring classes in an age when individual votes were beginning to matter politically more than ever – to buy off the working class and avoid socialist take-overs. In this sense it was anticipatory and concessional. Subsequently, as social democratic and labour parties representing the working classes and the trade unions obtained political power, their programmes of reform became a primary factor. However, by the 1970s, a form of consensus appeared to operate, in which parties of both the Left and the Right agreed that the key policies and entitlements of the welfare state should not be challenged. Both accepted the necessity for 'Keynesian' economic policies that required an interventionist and activist state to manage the economic cycle through demand and fiscal instruments, and to maintain full employment. The idea that the 'supply' side – the workings of the labour markets, the practices of trade unions, and provision for education and training – should be reformed, did not constitute part of the prevailing governing orthodoxy.

The Keynesian welfare state

The Keynesian welfare state may be considered at three levels: the economic, the social, and the political. A brief examination of each level enables us to build a more comprehensive account of its development.

Economic

At the beginning of the twentieth century, even in Britain, where strong advocacy of free trade was to be found, the economy was looking less and less like the liberal model. Large companies were increasingly dominating their sector, including as monopolies, and the quickening of international trade only seemed to reinforce these tendencies. The First World War also offered a model of capitalism that differed considerably from the liberal design, for by 1918 the state in Britain had succeeded in coordinating for the first time the most important sectors of the economy in order to maximize war production, and had become the largest employer. It had experienced in war the requirements of 'creating' public opinion and the need for an increasingly formal network of information gathering (Middlemas, 1979: 20). The War also created the need for new organizations for the representation of industrial interests, as the state had relied heavily on the cooperation of business. By the 1930s labour had also developed organizationally to match employers' associations.

The Second World War intensified these developments. Increasingly the governing approach was to 'manage the economy' rather than leaving it to the market. The experiences of the inter-war worldwide economic Great Depression and the recognition that national governments could use fiscal and monetary instruments much more aggressively to manage consumer demand (Keynesian strategies), allied to the experience of wartime planning and controls and the recognition that mass war mobilization required more state focus on the rights and welfare of the population, led to the rise of state and corporate planning.

We noted above how social legislation was increased in the decades before the 1970s, including in areas such as employment, health, education, housing and pensions. Inevitably this also impacted on the economy, through increasing levels of taxation, particularly on businesses, by encouraging employer–trade union negotiation in the workplace, by increasing costs and bureaucratic book-keeping, and through the tightening of labour markets with full employment policies that helped to raise wage rates and trade union power and reputation. Additionally, utility charges from the state-run monopolies for the private sector could be high, particularly as their main purpose in the setting and administration of price levels appeared to be raising a return for the Treasury. Nationalization of the means of production was a significant characteristic in Britain and other capitalist economies where major sections of industry were taken into public ownership, especially heavy manufacture, energy and communications. Moreover, long-term corporate planning could be disrupted severely by the 'stop–go' switches of government macroeconomic policy between growth and recession.

Yet we should be careful against assuming that the economies of all countries with developing welfare states operated according to the same model. We have noted above, for example, how the US differed from the UK and the rest of Europe in disavowing the public ownership of key industrial sectors and opted instead for regulatory intervention through independent agencies backed by law for the implementation of governmental economic and social policies. And both the US and the UK possessed economic institutions that, in turn, differed from those found in continental Europe, particularly in the extent to which 'non-market' or social considerations entered corporate decision-making (De Jong, 1996).

The 'Anglo-Saxon' type of free market capitalism is one in which the company is organized by its owners on a public basis, through stock exchanges, which supply capital on a risk basis for a return, a system which ensures that management is a distinct function to that of ownership. Owners (shareholders) can sell the company to others if they are dissatisfied with their returns, or if they are disenchanted with the management, or simply on an investment opportunity cost calculation. Typically, neither suppliers of loan finance (banks), or employees, who are regarded as simply a hired production factor (a cost), are represented on the board of directors or have a say in management. Regulation occurs through company law which stresses the autonomy and self-responsibility of shareholders.

In the continental model, employees are not simply a production cost but are seen to share social and corporate responsibilities. Moreover, as public capital is often less important than family or corporate ownership, take-overs are therefore more contested, and the state is seen to have legitimate rights to intervene where social factors demand that it does. Regulatory state intervention is regarded as necessary for overcoming the social and economic distortions of the marketplace, which are not viewed as playing out to the maximum benefit of all, as the Smith–Ricardo propositions would have it. Essentially, the state is seen as bringing wider, non-market values to bear, which are not generated by capitalism alone and which lie outside company law.

In Anglo-Saxon models, by contrast, the market is the source of economic values while the state is a potential distorter of the market mechanism and a hindrance to the benefits that flow from its unimpeded operation. However, the 'privatization' of key parts of the economy under Conservative administrations in the 1980s and 1990s in the UK, led to recognition that company law and existing forms of self-regulation of the business sector were insufficient for the protection of employees and consumers in the circumstances where public monopolies became private sector ones, and where they also tended to cover some of life's essential services, such as water and electricity. The result was steadily more hierarchical and codified forms of state intervention (Moran, 2003). Moreover, a range of social directives from the EU in recent years, aimed at increasing social protection for employees, have also served to weaken purer forms of the Anglo-Saxon model in the UK.

Social

We have described above the social legislation, and some of the reasons for it, as it helped comprise the development of the welfare state in the UK. However, as with the economy, we need to recognize that the social dimension of welfare state models also varied between countries. In the Scandinavian parts of north Europe, for example, the welfare state system emerged as a means of making welfare provision universal and 'de-commodified' – that is, free and enjoyed as inalienable social rights. It also extended further to the middle classes, rather than seeking to target (and to contain) welfare benefits according to an individual's 'means'. De-commodification refers to the process where a service is provided as an entitlement or as a right, and as a means for escaping market dependency, and is not moderated by the ability to pay (Esping-Andersen, 1990). In liberal welfare regimes, however, as generally found in the UK and the US, there is much more limited provision of universal or free services on social rights grounds, and a greater use of the market for rationing claims for welfare payments and thus for reducing or constraining costs.

Yet we have to be careful not to overstretch national comparisons. Even in the UK, the National Health Service (NHS) that was introduced in 1948 was closer to the Scandinavian model than to the Anglo-Saxon. The NHS provided free health care to those in need with resources guaranteed by the state from general taxation. And rather than the price mechanism allocating resources, these were planned and administered by state officials, while medical buildings, such as hospitals, were owned by the state, which also provided the major source of income for medical practitioners. As Moran (1999: 27) notes, the command and control model of the NHS is rather a 'policy surprise' in the liberal welfare UK context, for it 'marginalised private provision and established common access as an implied principle of citizenship'.

Contemporary debates in the UK focus on the extent to which the NHS should be more 'marketized', including providing patients with the ability to choose between providers on a more competitive basis, along the lines found in some other countries. These include discussions on funding and whether US and continental approaches should be adopted, being seen by some as offering greater diversity, efficiency and individual choice through the use of occupational and other private insurance schemes.

Two points are worth taking from this discussion. First, that the welfare model varies between countries, and, second, that within such structures, governments have the ability to introduce exceptional models (such as the UK's NHS) for particular sectors, albeit in difficult times, such as following war. Moreover, even in the most liberal of welfare regimes, as found in the US, there has been in recent years an increase in state intervention to control the funding and other autonomies of medical professionals, albeit through the use of private third-party procurers and managed healthcare schemes (Moran, 1999: 120).

Political

Although the powers of the state expanded greatly in the inter-war years, it was less the growth of an all-powerful central authority than the development of shared powers between the public and private sectors. The welfare state was also a 'franchise state' (Wolfe, 1977), parcelling out state power and responsibilities to semi-governmental private agencies. The result was a state-backed system of self-regulating business and professional associations, operating an informal and 'club-like' control over their affairs, including restrictions on competition, that helped protect oligarchy from both democratic mass politics and the challenges of the economic market (Moran, 1991, 2003). This applied to a range of economic and professional sectors, such as financial services, the universities, and medical associations. In time these arrangements came to be severely challenged by the growth of a regulatory state in the latter years of the twentieth century, and which we outline towards the end of this chapter.

At the national level the welfare state was characterized by a formal 'tripartism' between capital, labour, and the state. It was a part of a 'deep strategy of crisis avoidance' (Middlemas, 1979: 8), and involved a triangular cooperation at the industrial level, as the trade unions and employers' associations gradually became 'governing institutions' in alliance with the government, rather than operating as just interest groups. They came to display some of the characteristics of the state, which, for its part, welcomed moves that helped it avoid and control a myriad of individual labour demands. This emergence of 'corporate bias' in British politics reflected a distinct concern for the maintenance of social order, in an increasingly conflictful and less deferential age, by public administrators who increasingly valued the arts of good public management, 'not by invoking authority ... but by the alternate gratification and cancelling out of the desires of large, well-organized, collective groups' (Middlemas, 1979: 18).

However, the 'corporatist bias' in Britain in the 1930s, referred to by Middlemas, should not be confused with the corporate state found in German Nazism or Italian fascism. Whereas the UK accepted the international economic order, the necessity of trying to maintain a liberal polity and capitalism, and operated more by 'light touch' statutory back-up for self-regulating 'private government', the German and Italian systems were much more 'statist' in their subordination of the economy to government. Fascism sought to concentrate power in the state, crushing groups such as trade unions, political parties and the churches. Its doctrine of national self-sufficiency, or autarchy, was part of the attempt to insulate the nation from the depressions and slumps that characterized the world economy in the inter-war years.

The Cold War convergence thesis of East and West

In the post-1945 years, as the Soviet Union emerged as a major advanced industrial society, various writers, some influenced by both Weber and elite theorists, suggested that its political and economic processes were little different to those found in western welfare state societies, despite Soviet claims to be pursuing much more egalitarian socialist policies. It rested on the view that the welfare state in the West was moderating the worst features of capitalist economies – owners, but particularly professional and well-educated managers, were now fairer and less rapacious – while the economic system in the Soviet Union was being forced to acknowledge market forces and economic and other inequalities as essential for the provision of incentives and the attainment of the economic performance and consumer affluence of countries in the West. Less charitably perhaps, some on the Left in the West, particularly associated with Trotsky's advocacy of international socialist revolution, rather than Stalin's 'socialism in one country' approach, regarded this convergence as a consequence of the Soviet Union having perverted the aims of the Russian Revolution of 1917. It had become simply a form of 'state capitalism' like many other capitalist societies, with the difference only that in Russia a state bureaucratic class, rather than private owners, owned and controlled the means of production.

A number of non-Marxist convergence theorists, however, influenced particularly by Weber, suggested that there was an evolutionary tendency for all industrial societies to converge into a single type (Parsons, 1966; Galbraith, 1967; Clark, Kerr *et al.*, 1973). As western societies were becoming more planned and managed by bureaucratic elites, so the Soviet Union, with the rise of technology, the growth of bureaucracy, and the ideology of technical rationality, was becoming like the West. For functionalists, this process of industrialization in both the East and the West reflected a high level of structural differentiation and 'adaptive capacity' within all advanced societies (Parsons, 1966). In this view, modern technology and science imprints common social patterns onto the division of labour and relationships between groups in all advanced societies.

Cold War convergence theories were convenient to both the Left and the Right in western countries and were adapted for domestic analyses of contemporary capitalism and how western relations with the Soviet Union should be conducted. For the moderate Right convergence justified claims that modern capitalism was no longer controlled by uncaring, greedy entrepreneurs but was managed in a benign and class-neutral way by expert managers and socially responsible shareholders, who were found particularly in the leading positions of the larger corporations and the increasingly powerful pension funds. For the social democratic Left, convergence theory sustained a belief that peaceful coexistence with the communist empire was possible, although this involved turning a blind eye to Soviet trampling of individual and national sovereignty rights.

A major difficulty with a convergence interpretation based on the view that modernization, and its twin pillars of industrial development and bureaucratization, would lead to moderate and technically efficient societies in both East and West, is that quite wide variations in systems of social stratification can exist between industrial societies, and patterns of distribution can be altered quite radically by political regimes (Parkin, 1969). None the less, patterns of occupational recruitment, educational achievement, and social mobility in the old Soviet Union did reveal the almost universal tendency for those in privileged positions to ensure at least a headstart for their children, despite the ruling ideology of socialist egalitarianism (Lane, 1985). But this was more a consequence of political class privilege and its protection than the result of industrialization. An important element, despite the positive discrimination in favour of the working class in the allocation of education places by the Soviet state, was the 'cultural' as opposed to economic capital possessed by the educated political and middle classes in the Soviet Union, which was handed down to offspring in the form of encouragement and preparation for education.

The post-1945 state in the West

A feature, therefore, of western capitalist societies in the three decades following the ending of the Second World War was the inexorable increase in state involvement in the economy. The state's share of employment increased considerably and its proportion of overall expenditure steadily expanded, partly as a consequence of the state's role in 'transfer payments', such as social insurance, where the state 'collects' resources and then re-directs (rather than 'confiscates') them. The relative individual affluence, growth in world trade, and generally favourable economic circumstances for many countries in the West in the thirty years following the War until the mid-1970s meant that this level of increased state involvement in the economy was regarded relatively benignly. A consensus operated whereby all governments adjusted levels of demand in the economy to meet the prime Keynesian objectives of economic growth and a trade surplus, as well as full employment and low inflation. However, the consequences by the 1970s were often quite different, with 'stagflation' (stagnation and high inflation), rising public deficits (leading to high public borrowing and interest rates), rising taxes, and trade-union militancy in the face of increasing difficulties by economies in maintaining full employment, not least in the face of radical hikes in oil prices from, especially, Middle East producers. Trade union power itself had been ratcheted up by full-employment policies leading to tight labour markets and rising wages and salaries.

In some views these developments reinforced 'corporatist intermediation' in the realm of interest group politics, and offered a major challenge to pluralist accounts. By the 1980s the pluralist view of the pressure group world and its benign and open influence on democratic processes had undergone serious criticism and revision (see Schmitter, 1974; Panitch, 1976). The end of rapid growth in the world economy, mounting inflation, rising welfare expectations and increasing levels of unemployment, provided conditions which led to the view that pluralism created an unstable system of representation with destabilizing effects on governance and economy. However, these views were not uniform, and continental countries, especially if they were governed by social democrats, were more inclined to accept the advantages of corporatist welfare state arrangements than the US or, later, the UK.

By the 1970s, labour groups had become more concentrated, bureaucratized and professionalized. Both unions and business were powerful interest groups confronting each other and, with the state, participating in a new form of 'tripartite' governance that required the state to become even more involved with managing the economy than hitherto. For writers such as Schmitter, influenced by the 'crises of capitalism' analyses of fellow German theorists, Habermas and Offe, new forms of interest group intermediation with the state provide a better basis than pluralism for explaining the processes of advanced monopoly forms of capitalism and the increased social and economic coordination which added to the system's regulative capacities. Corporatism, in his view, differs from pluralism in the amount of decisional authority a group acquires from the state and the role of interest groups as co-responsible 'partners' in governance and societal guidance. Thus corporatism involves not just bargaining between the state and functional groups but also the implementation of public policy through the groups themselves. Moreover, not only do such interest groups represent or advance their members' interests, but they are also prepared to enforce on their members compliance with agreements reached with the state, and perhaps other groups, in the 'national interest'.

In comparison with pluralism there is an assumption in corporatism that the state more actively forms and sustains the system of interest intermediation and is deeply interested in its outcomes. It is not the essentially passive recipient of the demands of organized interests. Inevitably corporatism raises questions of representation and accountability within groups, matters that tend not to be regarded as such significant issues in pluralism. Rather, in pluralism the existence of groups is explained by the rational calculations that a self-interested individual would make about the utility of associating with others to pursue objectives. This calculation includes the availability of 'selective incentives' to motivate membership (cheap holiday offers, for example) as well as the pursuit of collective goods, such as better environmental protection (Olson, 1965).

In corporatism, however, the leaders of organizations may have to strike a balance between membership demands and the requirements of public policy. There may be inherent organizational needs in interest associations that lead away from pluralism and towards corporatism, such as the offers of additional resources by the state on a more reliable basis. Consequently, organizations have to balance a concern with the 'logic of membership', the structure and kind of membership interests within an organization, and the 'logic of influence', which ultimately is concerned with the conditions and processes of gaining political influence with the state (Streeck, 1982).

Corporatism, however, at the national as well as at the sectoral levels, has slipped back since the 1980s, with the growth of more market-focused governments which have been concerned to 'roll back' the state and to reduce the power of trade unions and professional bodies, although this has occurred less in parts of central and northern Europe (Swank, 2002). But corporatism had already shown weaknesses as a form of state policy before the advent of such administrations. State control over both big business and organized labour had proved limited and problematic, while 'hands-off' state licensing of associational self-regulation was proving increasingly ineffectual in protecting consumers and reducing costs, not least where the welfare state rather than the individual consumer was the main purchaser. Mostly, corporatist processes were secretive and generally outside parliamentary scrutiny – indeed they were regarded as symptomatic of the decline of parliamentary democracy and sovereignty. Labour organizations often struggled to ensure agreement and compliance by members for government policies, especially those constraining incomes, in so-called 'social contract' arrangements. Even when labour leaders secured compliance from members, business came to feel the outcomes of agreements to be too costly, while citizens, consumers, and those on pensions and other fixed incomes were among those who became hostile to what was regarded as the over-privileged position of trade unions and saw in it a major cause of rising inflation from which there was little protection.

Corporatist theories of interest intermediation and national policy-making were challenged on two fronts. First, by strong advocates of the market who, while accepting much of the corporatist analysis, found this to be a source of great alarm and who, rather than favouring corporatism as a way to secure political advantages – welfare and social order particularly – felt that it needed to be confronted and dismantled in order to reverse economic decline. Second, and related to the need to regain state power in order to dismantle corporatism, by advocates of the view that the state needed to become more authoritative, although in a regulatory rather than the hitherto public ownership manner. This second position particularly characterized the Thatcher administrations in the UK from 1979 to 1990.

Moran's (1991) analyses of the financial services sector in the US, the UK, and Japan illustrates this second point – the movement from corporatism to state regulation. He utilizes the notion of 'meso-corporatism' to explain the prevailing arrangements prior to the 1980s between government, and self-governing and self-regulating associations. The term refers to the appropriation of a regulatory role by such private bodies (and its granting by governments) and their effectively becoming authoritative in the eyes of the state, and how this position helped such associations in restricting competition in the sector, including on prices and market entry. The revolution ('big bangs') in financial services saw these rather cosy arrangements break down in the wake of scandal, the resultant interest by politicians to protect the standing, standards and efficiency of markets in an increasingly globally competitive economy, and the challenge and influence of American financial institutions, not least in exporting more juridical forms of regulatory surveillance from the US. Meso-corporatism consequently became replaced in the 1980s by direct supervision and monitoring of the sector by the state and legal regulators in all three countries, which involved more bureaucratic and accountable procedures being adopted.

With the increased economic problems facing many societies from the mid-1970s onwards, capital and labour became sharply divided, and corporatist arrangements were seen to be uncertain and contributing to the state's declining authority and capability. The relative autonomies of state and market seemed endangered by the close corporatist fusion of the two. The issues became one of 'state overload' and 'state crisis', for which the 'New Right' felt that they had the answers.

New Right

It is often claimed that there is both a logical and historical connection between the development of capitalism as an economic system, and the growth of liberal constitutionalism as a political arrangement. Specifically, the democratization of liberal regimes with the extension of political and other rights, and the development of electoral politics, are clearly linked to the individualism and demands for market freedom of the bourgeoisie. Competitive capitalism, it is argued, provides a necessary if not sufficient condition for competitive politics.

So-called 'market society' or New Right theorists, such as Friedman (1962), Nozick (1974) and Hayek (1976, 1979) suggest that the freedoms to be found in both the political and economic sphere in these circumstances confer general, cross-class benefits. The separation of political and economic power allows the existence of distinct and counterbalancing spheres – that of economic interest and political authority. Economic power can be used to prevent the abuse of political power, and political power can be used to offset deficiencies in the market. Power thus becomes dispersed rather than centralized. New Right theory clearly stands in a line back to classical liberal thinking.

Consequently, it is argued that competitive capitalism works best on behalf of the general wellbeing if state interventions are limited and broadly confined to ensuring the conditions for successful and expanding capitalist enterprise. Political and economic affairs are most effective when they are matters of individual freedom and initiative. In fact, the notion of 'social class' is regarded as an invention, as the only 'real' political and social entities are individuals. While a pure *laissez-faire* economy was accepted as a chimera, state interventionism should be specific, fine-tuned, remedial and authoritative. At the very least governments should seek the maintenance of social order and should provide a minimum safeguard for the economically and socially dependent, such as the infirm or the unemployed. However, the emphasis wherever possible should be to allow the market to provide the bulk of such social provision through private insurance and other schemes. Thus, 'New Right' theory accepts that some guarantee of 'social reproduction' must be provided by the state, and that interventionism is required to maintain the conditions in which competitive capitalism can operate, such as through the provision and maintenance of an appropriate legal and monetary framework. In their concern with individual freedom, New Right liberals, however, can be distinguished from conservatives, who tend to adopt a more paternalistic moral view that the state must reinforce efforts at constraining and regulating individual desires, and that it is not sufficient to leave moral judgements to individuals provided that they do no harm to others.

In this New Right view, the modern welfare state by the 1980s had become over-mighty, threatening liberty, and needed to be cut down to size. Hayek was a highly influential advocate of this approach. In his 1944 book, *The Road to Serfdom*, Hayek had launched a critique of Nazi Germany and the Soviet Union as examples of where excessive state control can lead, although he was also critical of milder 'welfare state' approaches. In later works Hayek regards the 'market' as a spontaneous social order (Dean, 1999: 157), which is the product of 'cultural evolution', and as a consequence is not sensibly regulated by governments. Rather individuals require protection from the state through legal frameworks and laws.

Hayek has been described as calling for a return to 'legal democracy' (Held, 1996: 257), in which formal and legal rules are used to protect individuals from governmental decision-makers – who claim to regulate on behalf of the people but who cannot hope to know the myriad wants and needs of so many individuals – and from the dangers of arbitrary and oppressive majority rule. The aim must be a rule of law in which governmental interventions must be restricted to the rules which serve individuals in their pursuit of their particular ends and which guarantee 'life, liberty and estate'. The key mechanism for dynamic and responsive 'collective choice' is the free market, which may not be perfect, but is more likely to reflect individual interests than is governmental decision-making.

In the US, however, a rather different approach to the view that the state and the economy were distinctive sectors and best kept apart was adopted by the so-called 'Chicago School', associated particularly with the works of Gary C. Becker (Becker, 1964, 1976). In this view the 'market' was sufficiently strong and superior that its rationality could be extended to the public and social realms – including crime, family life, government departments, and so on. The starting point for their radical reconceptualization of the social lay in the idea that all rational behaviour is about deciding which resources are best devoted to which ends. As a result, all human behaviour (or at least rational human behaviour) could be understood as economic behaviour.

The notion of choice is pivotal for the Chicago theorists: it defines the rational human and provides the basis for overcoming notions of the 'social' found in the social sciences. Life, effectively, is an entrepreneurial economic enterprise, and the emphasis shifts from Keynesian safety-net provision to individual responsibility for one's own life projects. Along with the works of Hayek, and also Friedman (1962), these ideas had a marked influence on the Thatcher Conservative governments in the UK. They reinforced the introduction of market processes (competition, consumer choice, budgetary discipline, accounting and audit) into areas previously protected by notions of professional 'expert knowledge' and state-supported social objectives. The aim rather is to establish goals and targets to be achieved, including through the processes of accountability and delegation, rather than close or intimate confrontation between the governors and the governed. Expertise was tied to the demands of the market not to 'arcane' and self-serving professional knowledge. And lower levels of personal direct taxation increased scope for individual choice while reducing state expenditure (which 'crowded out' private and corporate investment and decision-making).

Although such notions for some had been regarded as long outdated, and out of kilter with the global, monopolistic forms of corporate capitalism that characterize the modern world, they were significantly influential in a number of governments of the 1980s and 1990s. Britain, Australia, New Zealand, and the United States led the way in seeking to strip away many of the state's functions in the economy, preferring instead to place greater trust in the market. Leaders such as Thatcher and Reagan were also sharing technical (if not political) anxieties with writers on the

Left who were concerned with the alleged 'contradictions' and 'crises of capitalism'. The Leftist writers in particular had increased doubts as to whether the state in capitalist societies could reconcile its twin aims of supporting, on the one hand, capitalist accumulation (including the need to keep labour and welfare costs reasonably low), and, on the other hand, maintaining popular support through continuous increases in social expenditure. At the same time, the failures of the socialist bureaucratic Soviet Union and its satellites reinforced the concern on the political Right that the policy problems of the state lay as much within the state itself and its overextension as with the changing nature of its external environment.

The outcome was a reorganization of the machinery of the state itself with the implementation of such policies as the sale to private purchasers of state assets, the dismantling of regulations restricting competition in markets, and the setting up of specialist regulatory agencies in areas such as banking, health and safety, and the physical environment, thus making them allegedly free from partisan political control and able to neutrally and 'technically' guide policy. In the UK, a further development was to ensure that within government strategic policy was the preserve of ministers and top civil servants whilst operational matters were hived off to operational agencies. Additionally we find income-tax cuts, public expenditure reductions, and an emphasis on monetary as opposed to fiscal instruments in fine-tuning the economy.

The aim was to reduce public expenditure, but in particular state welfare – on the grounds that it created a dependency culture, that such policies generally supported the relatively well-off middle class consumer and the public sector employee, rather than the working class, who were often in greatest need of such support, and that these beneficiaries had a vested interest in talking up 'social problems' and bloating an already 'overloaded' state. Moreover, market advocates found somewhat surprising support from many sections of the working classes who, rather than following the lead of Marxist-reading western intellectuals and supporting socialist revolution, were showing interest in supporting political moves to lower income tax. Rising incomes were taking them into areas of high marginal taxation, too. So, individual choice was to be promoted (for example, in parents choosing schools), and 'internal markets' introduced into the running of public services to make them – it was claimed – more efficient, competitive and consumer-oriented. The last two decades of the twentieth century have generally witnessed the view that the management of the public services needed to be less rigid and more entrepreneurial – rather more, it was alleged, like that found in the private or commercial sector.

The result overall has been the popularity of the view across a wide political spectrum that the state's role in the authoritative steerage of society and economy should be much more modest than hitherto. It should become more of an enabler, a partnership-former and coordinator than the all-singing and all-dancing versions of the state found in both West and East in the middle years of the century. Policy was best served by being the product of 'public/private networks', operating forms of 'soft' bureaucracy rather than command and control, and with markets having much more influence. Government decision-making was to be more inclusive of societal groups and be thus better described as 'governance'. We shall see, however, that, in effect, the state's role was reduced much more modestly than was claimed, with often the form of intervention rather than its amount changing, and, in some cases at least, involving re-regulation and heightened state intervention with the growth of new instruments and agencies.

Lightening up the state by selling public assets, or contracting the provision of public services to private companies, are policies not always taken for ideological reasons, such as to widen share ownership, encourage individual enterprise, or reduce the potential support for trade unions or Left political parties. In some cases, such as in France, for example, socialist governments have regarded such policies as tactically useful ways of raising income, or cutting public borrowing, while in the United States there has been a long historic tradition in local government of utilizing the market in the pursuit of effectiveness and efficiency. In the UK, of course, what may have been stumbled into on tactical grounds became much more ideological in its extent. Privatization policies eventually, if not initially, came to be seen as much more part of a concerted attempt to 'roll back the state' and alter the terms of class relations (Fiegenbaum *et al.*, 1998). Yet privatization policies depended on decisive state intervention, rather than being left to private sector corporate strategies.

Comparatively, however, national differences in the approach to state-economy changes are quite noticeable. While the UK has a political tradition of strong executive rule, and the availability of world-class financial and legal services in the City of London to undertake effective privatization strategies, elsewhere more consensual or continuing 'corporatist' arrangements have made such action more problematic, and led to greater reliance on alternative and more incremental approaches than privatization of state industries. The growing role of the EU also has subjected national privatization and other national competition policies to stronger external regulation and standardization, not least in the restricting the ability of governments to use 'write offs' and other forms of public subsidy.

Thus, the goal of privatization was not a weak state, but more a move in the modes of intervention from public ownership to public regulation (Prosser and Moran, 1994). For the Thatcher government, while the aim was to reduce public expenditure, and the extent and range of state interventions, it was with the purpose of strengthening the authority of the state for undertaking its proper, albeit more restricted, role. The view was that an authoritative, increasingly centralized state was necessary for effective governance, and this had been jeopardized when the state had taken on more than it should. Consequently, in many cases, de-regulation of markets through the divestiture of public enterprise assets was accompanied by an increase in state regulatory control over markets, and the creation of new institutions and rules. The act of privatization is in itself insufficient to stimulate or kick-start a functioning market economy; rules and institutions that are effective, efficient and legitimate are also needed, so that the relations between companies, their employees, customers and lenders, are clear and well-governed. In the case of the 'privatization' of the ownership of previous state assets in the UK, the state was regarded none the less as an essential regulator that was needed to help look after the consumer interest and to restrict the power of previous state monopolies.

Although it would be mistaken to underestimate the influence of ideology in New Right governments, it was also the case that a number of key changes were also taking place in the socioeconomic sphere that supported curbs on trade unions and social expenditure from the 1970s. The remorseless decline of manufacturing industries and the growth of more mobile finance and services sectors, not least within an increasingly global context, helped to reduce the attraction and effectiveness of hierarchical, scientifically controlled, 'large size fits all' approaches to capitalism ('Fordism'). More favoured were less rigid, more devolved and intelligent teamwork structures suited to fleet-of-foot multinational corporations operating within fluid global networks, and taking advantage of the revolution in electronic communications ('disorganised capitalism', according to Lasch and Urry, 1987). Trade unionism was weakened, too, with the decline in manual work, and its militancy seemed more and more confined to the public sector.

Social democracy and the Third Way

Recent years have seen reaction to New Right regimes, but also the durability of their policies, with the election of governments committed more to social democracy and the so-called Third Way, most notably the Blair-led New Labour government from 1997 in the UK, and the two-term presidency of Bill Clinton from 1992 in the US, but also including the Australian Labor governments under Hawke and Keating throughout the early 1990s. Although not easy to define ideologically because of the strong pragmatic and instrumentalist approaches adopted, social democratic/Third Way policies seek a balance between the market and the state, and between the individual and the community. Capitalism is accepted as providing the best mechanism for the creation of wealth, but the aim is to distribute its rewards more fairly through interventions informed by strong moral values rather than just through the market, particularly to benefit the poor and the needy. Third Way values are identified as equality, protection of the vulnerable, support of personal autonomy, recognition of responsibilities as well as rights, democratization of authority, pluralism, and a pragmatic cautiousness when dealing with change (Giddens, 1994: 64).

Unlike earlier 'statist' versions of social democracy in the post-1945 years, the Third Way emphasizes a middle way between capitalism and socialism based upon communitarian values rather than state ownership of the means of production. Communitarianism, associated with the work of Etzioni (1993), seeks a stronger sense of morality based on the traditional communities of family, education and voluntary associations, and stresses internalized self-discipline. When individuals fall on hard times the wider social community has a responsibility to help put them back on track – not by encouraging dependency, but by finding the means for the person to become a contributing individual again. (The same applies to failing organizations, particularly those offering public services, even if it involves initially 'naming and shaming' through the media and the increased use of so-called 'league tables' of comparative performance). Individuals, in this view, need to be weaned away from constantly seeking new rights rather than responsibilities and to be encouraged to participate more in voluntary associations.

The purpose, unlike older forms of social democracy, is to provide better and more meritocratic means of individual opportunity rather than the creation of equality. As such communitarianism has been described as a form of 'ethical socialism'. The influence of such Third Way ideas in public policy can be seen, particularly in the US and Britain, where welfare benefits are dependent on evidence that work is being sought, or that improvement is being gained through education and training. In many ways Third Way thinking could be seen, in the aftermath of the collapse of east European communism, to accept many of the tenets of the New Right, including the need to keep public expenditure under control, to avoid the need to raise income taxes (if not other taxes), to regulate business and the professions through independent statutory agencies, to reform the public services by making them more subject to market and consumer forces, and to either privatize state functions or to lever private finance into development projects through private–public partnerships. Yet social democratic and Third Way leaders remain under constant pressure from their supporters to increase public expenditure and, if necessary, raise taxes, and this can lead to 'stealthy' ways of doing both.

Inevitably, perhaps, social democratic governments are always in danger of being accused of 'betrayal', of utilizing the idea or threat of globalization and 'there-is-no-alternative-to-capitalism' arguments as a cover for implementing market-enhancing policies (Kreiger, 1999; Hay and Watson, 1999). Certainly a number of theorists have demonstrated that social democratic policies can still be viable in the global age – indeed, when this involves expenditure especially on education and training, it can be welcomed by the big corporate players as an aid to higher-value production and national competitiveness in increasingly knowledge-based economies (Garrett, 1998; Swank, 2002). Yet, even in such circumstances, social democratic governments cannot any longer simply pursue the old political nostrums – such as commitments to public ownership and the nationalization of the 'commanding heights of the economy' – but need to explore alternative instruments to the state, such as market or community, in realizing policy objectives. In this sense social democracy comes to be seen less as a fixed political programme and more a flexible means of achieving community and social objectives as these become possible in changing times (Gamble and Wright, 1999).

Networks and governance

Consequently both the established Left and Right appear to share the view that, in many respects, the modern state is an enabling rather than an owning state. The exercise of public authority in nation states increasingly has to take account of other authoritative agencies, including private and international ones. Many domestic organizations, private and public, other than the government, are critical for social steerage. One consequence of this perspective is the more general usage of the term 'governance' rather than 'government' to describe the processes of social and political coordination in territorial states, to cover the whole process of governing (Pierre and Peters, 2000: 1). Although the state retains considerable power and authority, the focus is much less on state hierarchy and more on 'horizontal' forms of partnership. 'Sharing power' in this contemporary view is more likely to produce flexible and innovative responses to the external global environment than rigid demarcations between government and the market. Moreover, the capacity for governments to steer and coordinate society are regarded as enhanced by closer links to other social groups, and by the recognition of the democratic benefits that are gained by the participation of other parts of civil society in governance, rather than by sharp formal differences between state and society.

The idea that the modern state is more authoritative if it is an enabler and 'networker' finds echo in the notion of a state's 'social embededdness'. This produces 'infrastructural power' (Mann, 1988) in which the state has the capacity not only to reach out into civil society and to have its policies implemented, but also is open to the support and influence of civil society groups. This social embeddedness provides a state strength greater than that apparently enjoyed by despotic or absolutist rulers, who generally lacked the means of successful policy execution. Moreover, the approach acknowledges that the state is not a single, unified and coherent agent acting according to a single rationality (such as a capitalist state or a military state) but is a 'polymorphous' state with multiple identities. It does not 'crystallize' into a simple capitalist, militarist, patriarchical, or whatever, form, but is all of these.

A key feature is that the local, national, international, and global levels are embedded in each other and structure each other. Rather than state and society opposing and confronting each other in a zero-sum game, the more they overlap the stronger they are (as in early twentieth-century Britain). The greater the isolation between state and society/economy (for example, tsarist Russia) the weaker each becomes (Mann, 1993: 2; Hobson, 2000: 197).

State power is greatest in this view, not when used against society but when it cooperates with it (Mann, 1993). The key to the modern state, therefore, is not the power of legal violence or surveillance (Giddens, 1985) but the capability to link with powerful social forces. The strongest states – Britain and Prussia in the nineteenth century and at the turn of the twentieth – are those embedded within dominant classes. State bureaucratic power stems not simply from the technical capabilities of its officials but from their ability to reflect and express the national cohesion of dominant classes and their multiple interests.

Hence, perhaps, the popularity of 'policy network' and 'policy community' approaches by academic observers recently in seeking to explain public policy processes. It suggests, as a metaphor, a rather secretive maze of public and private interconnections in public decision-making sectors, which blur state and society differences, and which over time become regularized and patterned, and are bounded and distinguished from other such policy networks. These groups include experts and interest group representatives, as well as public servants, businesspeople and politicians, who form relatively common interests, ideas and values, sometimes known as 'epistemic communities'. However, it is not clear whether the notion of 'network' simply provides a useful analogy and description rather than actually explaining much, which may require other theories of state decision-making. Nor does it tend to predict the emergence of radical or ideological governments, or to fully recognize that state officials are not simply members of interest groups but possess state responsibilities and powers not enjoyed by more private associations (John, 1998, 2001).

The resurgence of 'New Right' thinking not only influenced governments but also political science, particularly the resurgence in rational choice theories of public policy in the 1980s and 1990s. Using economic models, particularly ideas of choice and the maximization of individual interests (sometimes suggestively rather than purporting to be wholly empirical), rational public choice theory utilizes game-playing theories, for example, to show that interest groups need to offer more than collective or moral objectives to attract and keep members (they need to avoid 'freeloading' through the provision of more selective and instrumental pay-offs, such as cheap car insurance). State bureaucrats in these models can be seen as increasing the size of welfare states through individual efforts to expand their standing and influence (and pay) through larger departments and budgets. Dunleavy (1991) also uses a model based on individual interests to demonstrate how senior state officials may prefer to opt for smaller budgets and departments by welcoming proposals to split strategic and higher policy roles from more mundane operational tasks. The latter generally provide the administrative and routine bulk of a government department while the former is viewed as offering more interesting and less burdensome work.

Notions of 'governance' and the 'enabling state' none the less may significantly underplay state ambitions. There is considerable evidence in fields from health care to financial services that, in a number of countries, previously informal, 'insider', or professionally dominated forms of occupational or sectoral self-regulation, have given way to the demands of democratic politics, with the state insisting on greater formality of regulatory arrangement and accountability (Moran, 1999; 2003). Moreover, media scrutiny and competition based on 'scandal', and the raised popular sensitivity to 'risk' (either real or perceived) experienced collectively and over which an individual has little control (such as a terrorist attack), increases pressure on governments 'to do something' about dodgy doctors, incompetent teachers, financial scams, or whatever. In such cases the 'devolved state' soon gives way to highly interventionist ministerial intervention (Beck, 1992; Thompson, 2001).

The regulatory state

The changes in the relationship between the state and society, and particularly between the state and the economy, that we discussed above, including in the context of New Right policies, have led in recent years to the increased use of the description 'the regulatory state' – which refers to the development and enforcement of systems of rules, often legally codified and enforced, to order or to modify socially valued behaviour, usually through the establishment of an independent or institutionally distinct regulator as a formal instrument of government. As with traffic regulations, the overall purpose is to improve conduct rather than to sanction offences, although regulators usually undertake both tasks. Regulation conjures up a mechanical act of steering, as in cybernetics, with an overall governor (the regulator) in receipt of information about the condition of the system and its relationship with the external environment. As such regulation in social life generally seeks an ordering between competing interests, such as shareholders, consumers, employees and the wider public, which constantly evolves. This can involve the regulator having powers to ban, supervise, licence or to monitor. As Clarke (2000) has noted, regulation involves the constitution of a form of authority to achieve order in an area of life that is displaying tendencies to disorder, perversity or excess.

The growth of regulatory authority and instruments marks a key change in the perception of the role of government towards the economy. Outside of the US and particularly in Europe, throughout much of the twentieth century, government was associated with substitution for market failure, through the means of public ownership of enterprises (as with nationalized industries, such as utilities) and through high taxation and public expenditure policies. However, regulation and other recent market-based reforms are associated more with the failure of government than the market, and the need for government involvement with business to be concerned with assisting markets rather than substituting for them, including through the adoption of competition and 'anti-monopoly' policies. Protecting the consumer and minority investors from fraud and other 'insider' risks through regulation, including increasingly of corporate governance, has also become an important state strategy. Moreover, innovative policy in the use of costing, investment and other techniques (in replicating incentives and other market conditions) have enabled regulatory approaches to become more sophisticated and successful in those sectors, such as the utility companies, where competition has been difficult to introduce.

In the US, the independent regulatory agency has been around for some time. During the 1930s its growth was aimed primarily at eliminating the 'rigging' of markets by monopolists and fraudsters in particular sectors, and was often supported by much of business. Since the 1960s, however, American regulation has taken on more of a social dimension (as has occurred elsewhere) involving conditions across a whole economy, and usually responding to revolutions in expectations of rights, legal entitlements and protections. The issue here is less that of market uncompetitiveness than of the social consequences of market failure. These involve factors external to the functioning of markets, such as race and gender equality, or health and safety. The difficulties in regulating such large numbers of firms on a case-by-case basis led to the adoption of very specific regulations of universal applicability. The result has been an over-legalism and control – and conflict – that has led to repeated crises in US regulatory systems.

The growth of independent public regulators, at arm's length from politicians, does not guarantee either the end of ministerial intervention or tension in government-regulator relationships. Where the sector is politically sensitive, or where there is clash between the 'expert' regulator (say, looking for cost-cutting in the power supply industry on behalf of the consumer) and the 'politician' (seeking to promote higher pricing conditions to support the expensive investment needed in, say, nuclear reactors), the differences can remain deep-seated.

The reasons for the extension of government-backed and legally supported regulatory bodies are various (Ogus, 1992; Moran, 2002a). They are seen as more effective and efficient operators than government, while increasing transparency, customer protection, quality control and technical standardization. This decentralization is ideologically attractive to market-orientated politicians, and is also persuasive to those on the Left who seek forms of 'social steering' without incurring large amounts of public expenditure. It helps to differentiate governmental responsibility for the provision of a service from its production, a feature of the 'new state management' since the 1980s.

There appear to be structural factors at work encouraging more state-directed regulation than ever before, particularly as this takes the form of statutory supervision by the state or its agencies, and the increasing formal and codified requirements imposed upon a variety of business and commercial bodies. The challenges of competitive and increasingly global markets, and the rise of democratic politics and the media, and the greater propensity for consumers and others to be assertive and to mobilize, are helping to create forms of 'regulatory state' (Moran, 1999; 2003) and a decline in trust afforded to professional practitioners and their associations of all kinds, almost irrespective of country and the political colouring of governments.

As we have noted, this does not necessarily eliminate detailed ministerial intervention, especially in countries such as the UK which have a long historical tradition of strong central governmental decision-making, nor does it overcome the more informal processes of policy formation that exist within the administration of most states. On the other hand, a longstanding concern is whether regulatory agencies are able to remain fully independent from those they regulate, or whether they tend to be 'captured' by their constituencies, not least because successful regulation depends on at least some level of assent and help from those being regulated (Braithwaite and Drahos, 2000). And because of the emphasis on professional expertise, the staff of regulatory agencies may be drawn widely from within the newly regulated sector. This may provide the regulator with improved, often informal, knowledge, but it may lead to over-sympathetic attitudes to those they regulate. A persisting issue in regulatory matters is whether it is possible to find the appropriate conditions for the exercise of 'smart regulation' (Braithwaite and Drahos, 2000; Braithwaite, 2002).

Regulation has shown a distinct tendency to increase with industrialization and globalization. In large part, regulation has developed to tame the worst hazards of capitalism and to protect workers and consumers from the risks and dangers to health and wallet that follow from the profit-maximization behaviour of some entrepreneurs. Democratic governments, also aware that consumer confidence drives economies, have felt increasingly obliged to respond to the concerns of their citizenry, especially as affluence has fuelled fears of financial and other risks in societies that are increasingly complex and differentiated. Individuals rely on government, media and now regulators to provide knowledge once available in more local and intimate forms (Beck, 1992). People, who are now more educated and assertive, need to know that their money, health, food and environment are reasonably safe, and that the goods and services that they procure adhere to at least elemental standards. They expect to be protected from cowboys and sharks – *caveat emptor* ('buyer beware') is no longer sufficient. Political environments are increasingly imbued with a raised sensitivity to both risks and rights, and regulation is regarded as responding to each.

Regulation can have a number of objects, such as competition, fair prices, securing a service, customer safety and protection, the maintenance and raising of standards, quality assurance, and so on. But an overriding aim is to formally generate processes of accountability and transparency that produce trust. Trust in the product or service, and trust in the provider. For long, higher education and the other professions have enjoyed a form of confidence and working autonomy (monitored by professional associations) that has been based on long periods of training and the gaining of expertise, on state recognition for their control of markets (and for them keeping out the cowboys), for eschewing the principle of commercial exploitation, and from a deep-rooted conviction that the patient or student benefited from a close, if paternalistic, relationship in which due deference was paid to professional knowledge and standing. Customer 'knowledge', and consumer wants and desires, were regarded as unreliable and probably misinformed. Professionally assessed 'client' needs were primary and should lead rather than follow public expenditure levels. Professionalism was seen as an alternative to the bracing winds of market forces.

But this rather cosy state of affairs has been rudely shattered. Intellectual and social criticism of professional expertise has grown with the publication of scandals by a mass media more intent than before in rooting out such stories (Thompson, 2001), automatic deference has declined, and the state is increasingly looked upon to ensure adequate levels and standards of provision at costs that both consumers and the public purse can afford. Higher education and the other professions have been located much closer to business. And, inevitably, this has involved the formal generation of information and other data for consumers. Transparency not intimacy has become the basis of public confidence and trust. The notion of what constitutes a service has shifted from the exercise of professional judgement to satisfying consumers. Moreover, professional autonomy, granted to ensure expert knowledge and adequate standards, has been questioned as delivering complacency, arrogance and an unwillingness to continually learn.

This is not to say that self- or professional or private regulation is over. It still helps to de-politicize sensitive areas of social life for governments as well as helping social steerage in reasonably cost effective and informed ways. But it does mean that professions and their associations are increasingly subject to greater intrusion into their working practices, including state-sponsored regulatory monitoring, in return for the public money that is disbursed to them. The state is in the background to guard the public interest. They do this by insisting on greater public accountability and a relationship that comes close to reconstituting professional associations as officially approved governmental bodies.

In some cases, the relationships between regulators and the regulated can be close and genuinely cooperative, although in others it can turn nastily adversarial. In the UK the belief obtains that general principles and methodologies lead to the best forms of regulation, although in the US, as we have seen, there is greater commitment to more detailed and legally binding approaches. A further difference is that while consideration of the American regulatory state often assumes that it is too strong and too hierarchical, in Britain and the rest of Europe the notion of a regulatory state is regarded as a softer exercise of government authority. Command structures, in this latter view, give way in the regulatory state to looser ensembles of semi-autonomous bodies (Moran, 2002a).

An important question that needs to be answered is whether increases or decreases in regulation flow from the growth of globalization (Gummett, 1996). Provisionally, it would appear that global competition leads to states reducing or severely modifying market regulation. Yet such actions are accompanied generally by forms of re-regulation, such as new regulatory regimes for customer protection. Notions of governance and regulation reflect a decline in the nation state's dominance, and its increased dependence on other societal actors. In this there is recognition that the nation state is seeking to come to terms with global economic neoliberalism and the growth of regional and worldwide suprastate authorities.

This approach – in which domestic and international structure and agency are co-reinforcing and act as pools of both constraint and possibilities – emphasizes the two-faced concept of the state, looking inward and outward. It raises the issues of the relationships between national and international state structures, and the related matter of the power or otherwise of the state in the face of an increasingly international order and globalizing economy. These are matters to which we now turn.

Chapter 6

Globalization

What is globalization?
'Geographical' interpretations
The impact of globalization
Globalization: the end of the nation state?
Globalization: something old or something new?
Globalization and national policies
Social/cultural change
Can globalization be rolled back?

From around the sixteenth century international trade became an important factor in the development of cities and the modern state. We have already noted in previous chapters capitalism's general disregard of (or attempts to circumvent) national and state limitations. From its beginning capitalism was internationalist in its development if not necessarily always global (in the sense that trade occurred between nations, although the reach was not extensive; nor did communications take place instantaneously in the de-territorialized manner of many of today's financial transactions made possible by modern satellites and electronics). The extension of trade propelled market relations over wider areas and, through taxation, it started to provide the funds to the state for military expenditure. From the middle of the nineteenth century, however, the weakening hold of the economic policies of national protectionism through trade barriers (although by no means its elimination), and the growing influence of free trade thinking (alongside growing industrialization), ensured that international trade really took off. Seen as a key to wealth, countries turned to bilateral and multilateral 'most favoured nation' agreements – favourable trade agreements with one country automatically being extended to others – as part of a general desire to reduce tariffs.

The massive development of trade during the second part of the nineteenth century and up to the First World War was mainly the consequence of industrialization, particularly of transport and communications. But industrialization led also to growing demands for raw materials:

For the first time mass trade in basic commodities, not just in luxuries, became profitable. The number of areas engaged in trade

137

rose rapidly: by 1913 155 areas were registered as participating in international trade, while the figure for the early nineteenth century was probably less than half that. An extensive international trading system was thus a reality by the early twentieth century. (Held *et al.*, 1999: 155)

Between 1913 and 1997 exports as a percentage of gross national product rose from 6.0 to 21.1 in France, from 2.1 to 11.0 in Japan, and from 4.1 to 11.4 in the US, for example (see Held *et al.*, 1999: 180). The expansion of international trade was matched by, and indeed stimulated, the growth of a European and then nascent global financial order for organizing credit and capital markets. The creation of unified currencies under central control was a major factor in the formation of nation states, while the need to wage war and to avoid the costs of transporting money also led to the creation of monetary institutions and currency exchanges, such as the Bank of England, and key financial centres, such Antwerp and London. Generally, however, international credit flows followed the expansion of empires, which meant that London, and British banks, became leaders in international finance in the period up to 1914. Domestic financial markets became articulated with emerging global markets, and while there were few governmental restrictions, the operation of a global gold standard system regulated the values of major currencies.

Although the first important companies to perform across continents were the great trading companies of the sixteenth to eighteenth centuries, such as the East India companies of the Dutch and the British, it was not until the late nineteenth century that multinational companies of the kind that we might recognize today began to emerge. Predominantly drawn from the US to begin with – largely as a consequence of the permissive approach to them of the federal US government – they were quite different from the earlier trading companies in that their foreign direct investments abroad were increasingly associated with international chains of distribution and production, initially in mining and agricultural concerns, and then in primary products such as oil. Developments in transport and communications allowed much wider spans of control and coordination, although there were still significant variances in the level of effective control over international assets exercised by corporate headquarters (Held *et al.*, 1999: 240).

During the twentieth century, after a protectionist 'recession' in the mid-decades and particularly since the 1960s, with the growth of highly effective global systems of communication sustained by developments in satellites and information technologies, the integration of the worldwide economy has deepened significantly. The internal transactions of the large multinational corporations that dominate the global economy often have a value that outweighs the transactions of a number of nation states. Alongside changes in culture (such as the growth of tourism and the extension of western media and lifestyles), and in politics (for example, the creation of political 'blocs' and alliances of states), the world appears a smaller place. And globalization, particularly the rising power of transnational corporate interests, appears to some to threaten severely the sovereignty and powers of the nation state, hollowing out its authority, and preventing it reconstructing itself as a legitimate body (Camilleri and Falk, 1992). Before considering this issue, however, we need to understand what are the processes of globalization.

What is globalization?

The term 'globalization' appears everywhere. There hardly passes a day without some reference to globalization in the newspapers and it also appears everywhere in academic journals and books, too (like this one!). Yet it is invoked to explain a myriad of phenomena, some with only very loose connections to each other. Clearly the term refers to a process – to a journey or direction – although some see it as a description of an end state. The destination presumably is some form of 'global society' or 'global age', but there is considerable controversy as to its key features and its causes, or indeed whether the outcome is inevitable or similar for all locations and spheres of life.

A further problem is that globalization is seen by some as a form of explanation for a wide array of circumstances, while for others it is a process that itself requires explanation (by, say, theories of capitalism, or the constant creation of new forms of technology). It is increasingly clear, however, that the processes of globalization do not provide standard or similar outcomes across the world, but are shaped and adapted by a variety of local structures and cultures. Indeed the competition between indigenous capitalisms and cultures (not homogeneity) spurs on the diffusion of innovation and its worldwide adaptations, which is a key source of globalization. Some appear to doubt that globalization has a material substance at all, referring to it as a narrative, or ideology, or even a performance (see Urry, 2003, Chapter 1, for a review). As Urry has noted recently, globalization does not have one centre, nor is it a unified process. Rather it is often chaotic and complex, and models drawn from the physical and natural sciences, such as chaos and complexity theory, may best be employed to understand the phenomenon.

Of course, for many, globalization is primarily an economic phenomenon – it refers to the increasing worldwide integration of economies over recent decades and is associated with the triumph of liberal capitalism as the dominant economic mode. Territory means less than it did. These days, for example, the financial markets operate on a 24-hours-a-day basis, and financial centres open as the sun rises around the globe. When an investment order is phoned from Germany to bankers in, say, New York, the transaction occurs straight away, irrespective of the location of offices and the vast distance between them. Moreover, an investment decision in Washington could have potential reverberations in Wollongong. In this sense, globalization is different to internationalization. Internationalization refers to exchanges between nation states – across borders – and has occurred over the centuries. It is not new. Globalization, however, refers to exchanges that transcend borders and which often occur instantaneously and electronically, and is new.

Economists, however, are not always in agreement on the extent to which the global economy is characterized by the uninterrupted mobility of goods and capital (it is apparent that many categories of labour are clearly not globally mobile), although generally they all recognize that financial investment freedom has rather undermined the economic authority of the nation state, and has resulted in convergence of both economies and polities towards a neoliberal model around the world. There can also be found disagreement on the extent to which capitalist economies possess optimal, equilibrating and self-reproducing characteristics through the market itself (what we might term the 'Adam Smith' approach), or whether they require state intervention and regulation to correct flaws and failures, as well as needing the cultural attitudes instilled through education, religion and the media to provide the necessary work and family disciplines to overcome the excesses of consumerism. The latter view clearly envisages a stronger and clearer role for the nation state than the former, which inclines more to systems of capitalist autopoiesis (self-organizing and self-reproducing), without the need for much state intervention.

The view that capitalism requires state intervention to maintain its equilibrium is not new, of course; it has been a strong feature of Keynesian and social democratic interpretations of national economies. At the global level, Stiglitz (2002) has championed the theory of market failure and its policy implications, and has argued that global economic institutions such as the International Monetary Fund (IMF) and the World Bank have inappropriately adopted the same liberal macroeconomic model and prescriptions for all countries, including the developing ones, where more and better regulated economies are needed.

As Hay and Marsh (2000) have noted, in some approaches there is a common focus on globalization as 'flows' – of capital (financial and physical), people, information, culture, and so on. These move along various global forms of 'highway' and terrain, or 'scapes' (Appadurai, 1990), which create new patterns of inequality of access between people and their locations. Structurally there is increasing difference between the accelerating density of global networks and the less networked, less dense, local and national levels (Urry, 2003; Castells, 1996). Yet the consequences are not uniform. The patterns are fluid and irregular, and globalization is marked by intricate connections and disorder (Urry, 2003). Globalizing processes also are different and distinctive in different sectors and contexts (Braithwaite and Drahos, 2000).

Others regard globalization as a discourse or an idea, or even an ideology, so that it is the very conversation about globalization, rather than world markets directly, that influences national politicians, so that globalization is portrayed as inevitable. Social democratic leaders are regarded as using globalization as an excuse to avoid radical redistributive policies ('there is no alternative'), while neoliberals use it to argue for more market-based innovation – such as flexible labour markets and freedom of capital – and for avoiding interference from trade unions and from national or EU politicians and officials (Fukuyama, 1992; Ohmae, 1992; Kreiger, 1999; Hay and Marsh, 2000).

Everyone then, it seems, 'knows' that the modern world is not like it was and that the 'globe' has become a key referent for most of its inhabitants. Yet quite what this process is, and to what end state it is leading, is not particularly clear and is subject to a range of interpretations, as we have noted already. Perhaps it refers to technological change, especially the growth of electronic forms of communication, as much as to the development of world economic integration? Langhorne (2001) appears to take this line. He suggests that globalization is the latest stage in a long process of technological progress that has enabled humans to operate around the world without reference to nationality, government authority, time or physical environment. He delineates three stages in this advance. The first lasted longest and resulted from the accumulated effects of applying the steam engine to land and sea transport, and from the invention and implementation globally of the electric telegraph (the first transborder telephone connection occurred in 1891 and the international airmail commenced in 1918). The second stage, the start of which Langhorne locates in the Second World War, derives from the development of rockets and then orbital satellites, which, when combined with the telephone, liberated the latter from its essentially local coverage and generated reliable global communications. Finally, the third stage

following rapidly in the 1970s, applied the computer, itself transformed in speed, volume and efficiency by the evolution of the microchip, as both manager and transmitter of the system. The Internet was the result. (2001: 3)

The outcome, in Langhorne's view, is a communications revolution which has transformed the political and commercial landscape, away from one filled with tall structures, hierarchically arranged internally, territorially defined and communicating with each other only from their apexes, to one which is more horizontal and overlapping.

However, technological advances are a necessary but not a sufficient set of factors for explaining the rapid globalization of the economic order in recent decades. They have been inextricably combined with political actions to open up and stimulate world markets. State decisions to abolish post-war capital controls and allow more autonomy for private market agents in the 1970s were critical in the globalization of the finance sector, for example. Similarly, although states remain the primary source of monies that flow so readily across national borders, a number of currencies have come to be used outside their originating country. In some cases foreign currencies (such as the US dollar) provide stiff competition for domestic currencies as the preferred means for exchange. This competition between national currencies seems to be intensifying and money is effectively becoming 'deterritorialized' (Cohen, 2000). As a consequence, even for stronger currencies, nation states are finding it increasingly difficult to isolate their monies from global flows and the decisions, sometimes speculative, of privately operating currency traders, who are able at times to achieve considerable leverage over national governments, thus diminishing the latter's sovereignty.

Yet a description such as 'globalization' that is used in such an all-encompassing manner is in danger of losing both its descriptive and analytical bite unless we can be clearer and more specific about the phenomenon. What actually is 'globalization' and how does it differ from processes that we would want to describe in other terms, such as 'internationalization'? Does it represent something fundamentally new – a decisive break with the past and as truly epoch-changing – or is it essentially continuous with modernity and capitalism and what has passed before? Is globalization a force for good and the alleviation of hunger and disease and the transposition of greater affluence; or, as in the views of the Seattle protesters at a meeting in 1999 of the World Trade Organization, is it pernicious, species-threatening and a source of increasing inequality and hunger? What are its causes – mono or multi? And does it herald the passing of the nation state and, if so, what forms of governance are to follow?

We can usefully characterize the impact of globalization processes at three levels: economic, political and cultural.

Economic

Economically, globalization refers to more than free trade or trade liberalization, but to the development of a world market, powered by global corporations, in which local economic and political actors are increasingly losing influence, and where these worldwide companies are characterized by globally coordinated business strategies (production, distribution and retailing) and accelerated flows of commodities. Held *et al.* (1999) describe as 'hyperglobalists' those who argue that global markets and the 'denationalization' of economies are part of an economic logic – a neoliberal theory of progress – in which national governments are little more than transmission belts for global capital, and with liberal democracy and western consumer culture increasingly the norm. 'Hyperglobalists', perhaps counter-intuitively, are not necessarily opposed normatively to powerful and independent governments, at least not for international purposes. They can sometimes espouse the need for a stronger nation state (rather than, say, a European 'super state') to take advantage of global markets. This seems to be at the base of much Conservative opposition to the euro in the UK (Gamble and Kelly, 2002), which is regarded as a regional protectionist measure seeking to inhibit global competitiveness, to the UK's disadvantage as a worldwide open trading economy.

These and other strong adherents of the globalization thesis hold the view that globalization is historically unprecedented, recasting world stratification, global governance, and the nation state in quite novel ways. The nation state does not wither away, because it can engage in a range of adjustment strategies, but it can no longer modulate exchange and interest rates, while the mobility and worldwide location options for the multinational corporations restricts governments' abilities to raise taxes, increase social expenditure, and generally manage their economies as they would wish. The primary role of the state becomes that of accommodating the structure of the domestic economy to the imperatives of international competitiveness.

Other, more sceptical, approaches argue that economic internationalization is not that new, that multinational corporations do not dominate world trade and that they tend to operate regionally rather than globally, and that nation states are still the most powerful actors, both in terms of their domestic economies and in relation to international economic agreements and most international schemes of governance and regulation (Hirst and Thompson, 1996; see also Dearlove, 2000, for a useful summary). Through elections they remain the critical agencies of popular representation. Nor is there empirical substantiation indicating that nation states are inhibited overmuch in their public expenditure policies as there is no clear correlation between a country's openness to foreign direct investment and social spending. Indeed multinational companies often welcome high public investment in education and training, for example, particularly if they are part of the high technology or knowledge-based industries. We shall examine some of these claims later in the chapter.

In some of its economic and technological versions globalization is linked with the systemic tendency of capitalism to destroy value and recreate it through innovation (Schumpeter, 1942; Baumol, 2002). Gibbons (2004) notes that globalization puts firms and other organizations under competitive pressure to innovate, which, increasingly in knowledge-based economies, stimulates new research practices. In this sense globalization is the result of the processes of imitation, adaptation and diffusion of 'solutions' to problems of many kinds – whether these be new technologies, organizational forms, or modes of working – as these are taken up by one firm after another, and in one country after another. It is because these solutions are increasingly more numerous and may arise from almost any quarter that globalization poses a threat to the existing practices of many companies, and therefore intensifies competition between them.

In this formulation, intensified competition and innovation both follow from the processes of globalization and help to sustain them. Globalization intensifies competition which, in turn, stimulates innovation. As a competitive threat can now arise from many different sources, firms continue to innovate because they know that, if they do not do so, their very existence might be threatened by others who do innovate. However, much innovation and economic development is dependent less on original discoveries and more on the timely take up, modification, and marketing of solutions or innovations that already exist but that need to be adapted to local environments. Innovation, in this view then, remains a local phenomenon and reminds us that globalization turns on differences in the sentiments, cultures and institutions of regions, nations, and localities. Innovations are adapted differently and locally, retaining the impetus for competition and therefore continued globalization. Globalization is not measured by a diffusion of a uniform set of market institutions or homogeneity throughout the world, but by the continued recreation of many specific and local capitalisms.

These developments are reflected in the rise of the 'competition state' (Jessop, 2002) which seeks to secure economic growth within home territories through comparative advantage for the capitals operating within them, whether these are domestically owned or not, by encouraging innovation, competitiveness and the research conditions for knowledge-based commercialization.

A form of economic globalization can also be found on the Left, however. In this approach, Marxist class conflict and exploitation associated with the capitalist mode of production goes global, and global capitalism produces inequalities between as well as within nation states. That is, current forms of globalization are capitalist, characterized by the dominance of transnational corporations, a transnational capitalist class, and a cultural ideology of consumerism. As with earlier such analyses of national capitalism, global capitalism inevitably produces the conditions of both national and international inequality that generates opposition to the system in the form of resources, purposes, competing ideologies, and organizational capabilities. Social movements, the drive for worldwide forms of democracy, and the universalistic ideology of human rights, are such oppositional manifestations. Increasing class polarization and ecological unsustainability are predicted to produce regular and intensifying crises in capitalist globalization that are likely to result eventually in more socialist, egalitarian and cooperative forms of globalization than currently prevail (Sklair, 2002).

Yet such prognostications seem far from being realized, and the complexities and unintended consequences of globalization make hard and fast predictions highly problematic. It is difficult not to view such analyses as an attempt to resurrect and to apply Marxist and similar socialist explanations at the global level, although, particularly with the fall of east European communism, their inadequacy appears well substantiated. Moreover, globalization may not simply enhance large transnational corporations but may also spawn novel economic organizations that are able to forge global positions rapidly. These (smaller) firms have a networked and decentralized character, based on the new technology, and do not go global but 'are born global'. Found particularly in Asia, such companies have a less interventionist command and control structure than is traditional, with head office more a coordinator, and where linkage and leverage are the key market drivers. This suggests that the globalized business environment may be more pluralist, diverse and dynamic than is often supposed (Mathews, 2002).

A variant of the economic approach fuses economic liberalism with the technology revolution identified by Langhorne (above). It regards information technology and the networks that it generates, rather than simply economics, as the key to the global 'information age' (Castells, 1996, 1998, 2000a). Global financial capitalism (increasingly the predominant mode), in this view is structured around a network of financial flows made possible by the new information technology paradigm. Expansive, dynamic, and innovative, networks – sets of interconnected nodes, so that, for example, stock exchange markets form the nodes of the network of global financial flows – are regarded as particularly appropriate for a world where work has become flexible, culture deconstructed, politics decentralized, and social organization characterized by the supercession of space and the destruction of time.

The impact of the new technology on politics, power and the nation state is considerable in the view of Castells. Politics becomes obsessed with media flows of signs and symbols, while the privileged instruments of power are seen as residing in the 'switches' connecting the networks (for example, financial flows taking control of media empires that then influence political processes). As networks are multiple, the interoperating codes and switches are the key elements in shaping and steering dominant processes and functions, that is, in guiding society as a whole, while pivotal power-holders are the 'switchers' who help connect the different networks. They control the information and the flows of messages and images between networks, and their operations ensure that the global networks of wealth, power and information take away much of the sovereignty of the modern nation state. Desperately seeking to influence these global flows, all that the nation state succeeds in doing is losing touch with its more territorially bound constituents. It induces a separation of the politics of representation from the politics of intervention (Castells, 1996: 354).

Yet this account surely exaggerates the importance or determinism of technology and the inability of actors, including nation states, to respond and to adapt. Nor is it clear that information, rather than knowledge and its changing epistemic and cognitive structures, is as important a source of power as Castells argues.

Political

At the political level, therefore, globalization generally refers to the decline in the sovereignty and importance of the nation state, to increased inter-state collaboration, and to the decline of socialism and the worldwide acceptance of liberal democracy. As Beck notes, 'globalization' is the blanket term to describe 'the processes through which sovereign national states are criss-crossed and undermined by transnational actors with varying prospects of power, orientations, identities and networks' (1997: 11).

Undoubtedly states are required more than they have ever been to cooperate internationally, not only to find effective and acceptable ways of regulating economic globalization, but also to cope with worldwide issues such as the environment, illegal immigrants, crime, and human rights. The United Nations and its agencies, and global economic institutions such as the WTO and the IMF, are key organizations. Moreover, these connections between governments are increasingly dense and occur, not only at all levels of government, but in a wide range of regional and international meetings, where representatives of non-governmental international organizations are also to be found in plentiful supply.

An important variant to this approach at the political level, however, is offered by Shaw (2000) who argues that globalization is a purposeful, humanly constructed set of processes to help realize groups' interests and values through increased global connectedness, and not simply the consequence of forces (economic, technological) over which we have little control. This can be seen particularly with the creation of 'the global state'.

In this view, notions of economic and cultural globalization as undermining the nation state are incomplete without consideration of the specifically political transformations that also directly influence these processes. These involve the reconstitution, rather than the straightforward debilitation, of state forms and inter-state relations. The imperial systems of both the West and the communist East, which integrated large sections of the political globe within their respective confines during the immediate post-1945 decades, and which were based on military protection and common security systems within each, and common understandings on deterrence and mutually assured destruction between them, were important steps in the Cold War after 1945 in moving the globe towards greater interconnectedness and producing more complex global concentrations of state power. It resulted in previous autonomous nation states becoming incorporated into 'blocs' for military and other purposes and, in the case of the more advanced West, led to the creation of more sophisticated and specialized global economic institutions for regulating the world economy. Even the latent cooperation of the Cold War period helped establish universalistic norms of human rights, as part of negotiations over détente and reductions in arms, that had dramatic outcomes for national independence after the fall of east European communism post-1989.

One outcome for Shaw has been the consolidation of a global western 'state-conglomerate', an integrated authoritative organization of violence that incorporates legally defined states into inter-state organizations such as in NATO (North Atlantic Treaty Organization), but which is stronger than simple military alliances. It makes the notion of an individual nation state engaging in war outside the constraints of the 'bloc' increasingly remote. Moreover, this emerging 'global state' is part of an increasingly complex globalization of authority, with the extension of both national forms of state alongside global institutions that mediate and curtail notions of national sovereignty, including through the promulgation of international personhood norms and rights. The EU, too, may be regarded as a regional example of these developments, but without constituting a 'new state' given its lack of military and foreign policy powers.

The value of this approach is that globalization is also regarded as a political order or regime, and not simply as an economic phenomenon. Consequently it emphasises the purposeful actions and agency of individuals and groups (and states), and does not portray them as rather helpless vessels in the face of overwhelming worldwide economic or technological processes. Rather than conceiving of the state as an object increasingly assailed by global economic flows – which leads to questions of whether the state can survive or is headed for oblivion – the state is regarded as much more interdependent and implicated with globalization. Historically, as we have seen in previous chapters, both the state and global capital have developed together, not necessarily in harmony, but often symbiotically and tied together in a mutuality of interests. As a result, states make of globalization what they will, both in its advance and, occasionally, in its regulation and control (see also Clark, 1999).

Cultural

At the final, cultural level, globalization describes the increasingly pervasive influence of western consumption culture, diffused through new entertainment and other media, such as television, pop music, cinema and tourism, so that people everywhere start to exhibit identical lifestyles and tastes, and also similar attitudes with the growth of universalistic concepts of the self and personal identity. People, in this view, are simply more aware, of themselves as citizens of the world, and of alternatives to the status quo and to conventional forms of authority and morality. They are, to follow Giddens (1990), more questioning and 'reflexive'. Benyon and Dunkerley (2000) suggest that cultural globalization, especially the spread of western ideas, images and consumerism, can be viewed in one of two ways: as either liberating and transforming social relationships in a most progressive manner, or as destroying local culture and its vitality.

However, the globalization of culture not only extends western consumption culture, as found in Hollywood-produced films and fast food outlets, for example, but also generates adverse reactions to it, as, say, with certain Islamic groups. Interestingly, Robertson (1992) denies that globalization necessarily leads to cultural sameness or the blanketing of western- or American-dominated values. It is possible to distinguish between the objective process of the diffusion of western artefacts and beliefs from how individuals actually interpret and respond to them. Individuals and localities are capable of responding differently to the processes of globalization, in some cases by reinforcing their distinctive culture and beliefs, while in others by embracing the newer forms. Although there is a sense of the 'globe' as a primary identifying referent for increasing numbers of people, considerable variations in interpretations and responses are as likely to result in a more differentiated and 'loose-fit' world. The path of globalization is not linear or predetermined and the future of the world is contingent and increasingly risky.

Held *et al.* (1999) link the cultural to the economic by pointing to the critical role of the new media technologies in the development of cultural globalization, but argue that it is the globalization of the corporate infrastructure in which these are located, rather than the technologies themselves, which is important. The multi-and trans-national media and culture industries are the motors for the spread of the principal agents of cultural globalization, predominantly media-delivered entertainment.

Yet it is clear that technology, and political and commercial decisions, are important and linked in reinforcing globalization. The new technologies, however, are critical in allowing individuals and groups to communicate and identify in circumstances where territorial boundaries seem less significant than before. And, moving on to consider explanations of globalization, it is this notion of de-territorialization that takes us on to examine what we might term some of the 'geographical' interpretations of globalization, not least the notion of 'space–time compression'.

'Geographical' interpretations

A common theme in the many disparate accounts of globalization is that the growth of globe-circling communication and information technologies has profoundly altered the relationships between time and space and conduced a world as a more compressed place. We no longer measure space by distance, but rather by time. It takes, for example, in our conceptions, eleven hours to fly to Singapore from London, rather than it being 10,000 kilometres. It takes even less time, of course, to connect the two locations by telephone, computer or fax. Instantaneous communication across the world levels out spatial differences in location and territoriality. Consequently globalization may be regarded as a spatial concept, as referring to a historical process that transforms the spatial organization of social relations and transactions, generating transcontinental or interregional networks of interactions and the exercise of power (Held *et al.*, 1999).

Harvey (1989) is perhaps the most significant theorist who has utilized the notion of time–space compression as means of formulating what we might term a social geography of late capitalism. It refers to the ability of capitalism to speed up its transactions and the spread of its markets, and, with the help of new technologies, to overcome the dysfunctionality and crises that beset capitalism around the 1970s, through the global reorganization of production, consumption and exchange. This involves greater communicative rapidity, fragmentation, and time–space compression in the productive sphere to meet the challenges of international competition and perpetual fiscal crises of the state. Flexible work practices, such as outsourcing, job sharing, casualization, and just-in-time inventories are also key factors in capitalist global reorganization, and which are made easier to implement and manage with new communication and information technologies.

A major consequence of this global capitalist reorganization is the growth of urbanization and large, 'global' cities (such as New York, London and Tokyo). These urban concentrations reduce production costs, and provide outlets for profitable investment in finance and the built environment, and for the generation of land rents. Global cities thus come to possess a range of attributes for capitalist accumulation as a site for both mobile capital and migrating labour, and become located within a stratified world hierarchy of cities.

Within the field of urban studies, these approaches are criticised for an overemphasis on a 'logic of capital' model, and for ignoring the social construction of global urban living by local inhabitants. Rather, the 'local' is not simply a 'space' free from the 'global' but is constituted by it, as part of a critical interplay with the situational and contingent subjectivity of actors, not as an outcome of a generalized or universalistic logic (Smith, 2001). Yet these urban geographers have helped to stimulate some of the more compelling accounts of globalization.

One of the best, based on the 'geography' of time–space compression and the decline of territoriality, is to be found in Scholte (2000). Scholte defines globalization as the growth of 'supraterritoriality', or the spread of de-territorialized relations between people. This involves the spread of 'transworld' or 'transborder' social spaces, a trend that he believes is relatively recent, and quickening since the 1960s. Particularly, the decline of state territorialism means that countries start to lose their pride of place above other kinds of territorial realms. As with culture, however, people may react adversely to globalization processes and emphasize instead more local political or economic identities. Global and territorial spaces thus coexist and interrelate in complex fashions.

Scholte claims that social connections are becoming more detached from territorial logics as the world becomes a single space. Telephone calls, electronic finance, and the depletion of the stratospheric ozone are examples of phenomena that operate largely regardless of fixed territorial locations, distance or borders. In this view, supraterritoriality is generated by a combination of (a) the emergence of global consciousness, spurred by the extension of rational knowledge; (b) the growth in international, especially finance, capitalism, operating worldwide production, marketing and distribution strategies; (c) technological innovations, especially in communications and data processing; and d) the development of regulatory frameworks, involving both nation states but increasingly suprastate institutions.

The development of global communications leads to the growth of global organizations. Some of these supraterritorial bodies have governance roles, that is, authoritative worldwide organizational and communicative functions (such as the World Bank and the International Monetary Fund). Many corporations and civic bodies also become involved in emerging systems of governance, seeking to pursue transworld rules, norms and regulation, such as in the field of technical standards or human rights. The consequence is an increasing sense of global identity in which the world is conceived less as a collection of territorial states and more as one place or one planet.

A problem with the time and space compression approach, and similar accounts that define globalization in terms of processes that 'stretch connectedness' (see also Held *et al.*, 1999: 15; and Delanty, 2000), is that it is not clear whether the processes of globalization will lead to outcomes that are distinctive (that is, have definite characteristics of globality) from what passed before. Spatial reorganization obviously has important consequences, but quite what these are in terms of individual psychology and even institutional rearrangement, is not yet clear. Nor is it certain that these processes are the primary causal agents, as opposed to, say, changes in regulation, politics, or capitalism.

Moreover, how far most people perceive their social space in this 'deterritorialized' way, apart from time spent holidaying abroad, is not apparent. The sharp-suited corporate business traveller, increasingly unable to distinguish one airport or hotel from another, may feel forever located in global space, but it is at least arguable that ordinary mortals are likely to remain preoccupied with more territorially concrete and immediate concerns. Similarly, while Scholte locates the beginnings of globalization effectively as recently as four decades ago, for some the contemporary world is less a disjunction that a continuation of trends going back many centuries. Robertson (1992) identifies five phases of globalization in Europe, starting in 1400, while Held *et al.* (1999) see cultural globalization as only the most recent sign of a set of long-standing historical processes. Globalization, at least in its early and 'proto' forms, in these views, precedes capitalism and modernity, rather than being their successor.

The impact of globalization

None the less, the current impact of globalization is much more widespread and multidimensional than it has ever been. Scholte describes the dynamics of contemporary globalization as involving several of the core forces of social life: rationalist knowledge, capitalist production, automated technology, and bureaucratic governance. None of these factors or causes of globalization is, by itself, primary; rather, all are closely interrelated. Rationalist knowledge – the ways of explaining and interpreting the world – sustains globalization by focusing on the planet as a single place, as the space of *homo sapiens*, rather than on gods or other transcendental entities, and by encouraging the view that knowledge is more widely gained by seeing the world as a whole. Rationalist analysis, however, should be seen as closely tied to the other key factors that underpin supraterritoriality, such as capitalism, with the dependency of its mode of production on rationalism, technologies, bureaucracy and law, and also the state, which has helped to stimulate the national and transnational regulatory frameworks that now underpin globalization. Rationalist, utilitarian and instrumental epistemology increasingly frustrates the territorial geography and hindrances of nation-state borders. In this sense rationalism is a more powerful and enduring influence than the sentiments of nationalism (Albrow, 1996).

Scholte is clear, however, that supraterritoriality develops rather than debilitates capitalism. In his view the growth of transworld spaces has encouraged several major extensions of capitalist activity, including into global and electronic finance, information industries, and consumerism. Moreover, the expansion of transworld spaces has encouraged major shifts in the organization of capitalism, including the rise of offshore centres, transborder companies, corporate mergers and acquisitions, and oligopoly. Similarly, consumer capitalism is sustained by globalization: most of the principal consumerist articles ('brands') are transworld products; many objects of consumerist desire have emerged directly from the technologies of globalization (mass tourism and air travel, for example); and global contexts have played a pivotal role in generating the hedonistic desires on which consumerism thrives (worldwide advertising operations that utilize supraterritorial mass media, for example). Indeed, as globalization helps generate consumer capitalist accumulation (rather than its commercial and industrial forms), the failure of regimes, such as the recently disbanded Soviet Union, to secure such consumables for their increasingly 'worldly' populations becomes a source of potential instability.

The dynamics of capitalist surplus production have clearly played a crucial part in the development of globalization, not least by constantly extending the reach of capitalism into more and wider domains. Money, as a 'universal commodity', considerably aids accumulation through its considerable characteristics of mobility and storage, and, as we have seen, money has been a major facilitator of supraterritoriality.

Sholte suggests that capitalism has stimulated globalization in four main ways. First, companies have seen global markets as providing new opportunities for profitability in ever-competitive economies and for raising corporate scale. Second, supraterritorial accounting enables transworld pricing strategies to maximize profits. Third, global sourcing allows supply and production activities to be located in a more efficacious way for profitability, such as manufacturing operations in low-cost areas, such as China, while the threat to relocate can stimulate forms of assistance from national governments (and support from their own workers) that would otherwise have been lacking, in the form of grants, lower taxation or reduced wages. And finally, capitalism has further stimulated globalization as the entities that constitute supraterritorial space have themselves generated opportunities for accumulation in their own right, particularly in the finance, information and communication sectors. Telecommunications companies, for example, periodically have been able to generate high profits, as the returns to governments from auctions and sales of spectrum bands have testified.

However, globalization has also required the human capability to technologically innovate, particularly in the fields of transport, communications and data-processing. Compressed time–space, often substantially detached from territorial logic, has depended on innovations that have not only produced what Albrow (1996) describes as the 'social technology' of the global age through enhanced and speedy information exchange, but also the requirement for increased standardization and regulation. It is the latter that enables the applicability of technology in both productive and ubiquitous ways.

Globalization: the end of the nation state?

We have noted earlier that while strong proponents of the globalization thesis tend to see it undermining or 'hollowing out' the authority of the nation state, sceptics such as Hirst and Thompson (1996) take a rather different view. Or so it appears. They argue that globalization is not historically unprecedented – at best it is heightened internationalism – while states still possess important regulatory powers. Similarly, they see the world as dividing up into large regional blocs, rather than into one world, with culture becoming more fragmented than westernized. Hirst (1997) elsewhere also claims that the state still matters in an era of globalism. Indeed he suggests that 'globalization remains more myth than reality'. In his view most so-called multinational companies are predominantly national and still dependent on national social and political solutions. Nor can one detect much sign of truly multinational managerial elites; companies, he maintains, actually benefit from distinct national managerial styles (but see Sklair, 2001, for research with a different conclusion). More particularly, nation states retain a crucial role in most international schemes of governance and regulation. While they may 'pool sovereignty' it is a mistake to assume that nation states have ever been all-powerful. Today they play crucial legitimating roles in international regulation and, through elections, are critical agencies of representation.

We should be clear that Hirst and Thompson set out to challenge what they describe as 'an ideal-typical construction' or 'the strong version' of the thesis of economic globalization. This would not appear to rule out a position that may accommodate at least some elements of the globalization propositions. In such a context, therefore, there are a number of reasons for agreeing with Hirst and Thompson and suggesting that multinational corporations and global capital generally may have less influence and impact on governments than the more enthusiastic proponents of the globalization thesis often claim. Levels of taxation and social expenditure, for example, may reflect more a government's domestic economic policies and electoral concerns, and awareness of the relative immobility of labour and parts of business, than the influence of worldwide capital. Economic growth recently in Eire, for example, may be best explained by a mix of domestic factors, including an industrial policy and a social partnership approach, apparently at odds with the requirements of globalization (Smith, 2002).

There would appear to be a number of policy options for countries wishing to compete effectively in the global economy. These include social democratic corporatism, based on Accords with trade unions, in which wage restraint is exchanged for labour-friendly welfare measures, and for spending on externalities or infrastructure seen as benefiting the economy and allowing change to occur without too much protest and with adequate compensation to the displaced (Garrett, 1998). In some northern and central European countries the systems of social protection created throughout most of the last century have not been dismantled. Social corporatism, inclusive electoral arrangements producing coalitions, and federalism are among the factors that give those opposed to global neo-liberalism the opportunities to exercise vetoes and other brakes or 'leverage points' on 'pro-globalization' policies. This compares with polities in the US or the UK, for example, where fewer such opportunities occur (Swank, 2002).

National governments appear not to be too cowed by the threat of mobile global capital making exits if they do not lower social spending and taxes. *The Economist*, for example, has noted that governments around the world are now collecting slightly more in taxes – not just in absolute terms, but as a proportion of their bigger economies – than they did ten years ago (2001). Two of the most open (to capital) countries in the world, Denmark and Sweden, have some of the highest levels of taxation (as a percentage of Gross Domestic Product), at well over 50 per cent. Nation states retain juridical and other restraints upon their citizens that can hardly be matched by multinational corporations, no matter how large or globe-circling they may be. Moreover, if relatively high levels of social expenditure help improve or maintain high productivity and training, there is no necessary reason why multinational companies should object, or leave.

Similarly, while there may be benefits for multinational companies in globally dispersing their operations on cost grounds, there are also potential negatives, particularly for companies that require high levels of research and development, and which can suffer lack of synergy and applications if research and development becomes geographically remote from existing production processes. Agricultural and manufacturing companies particularly may find it less easy to relocate their operations than multimedia and other firms specializing in the manipulation of freely moving symbols and signs. Global capital may be less mobile than is thought.

Analyses of foreign direct investment (FDI) flows indicate that in high technology and knowledge-intensive sectors, multinational companies are attracted more by knowledge-intensive labour than by low-cost employees, and exhibit the desire for already well-established local subsidiaries to seek vertical or horizontal integration in their current domiciles (Dunning, 2000). The outcome is that the growth of intra-firm trade now exceeds that between firms. Companies and other investors look for locations that have available cost-effective and reasonably skilled labour, a good physical infrastructure, an enterprise-oriented political regime, and a host of market-supporting facilities and services that reduce distance-related transaction costs (which are falling rapidly, especially in free trade areas such as the EU).

However, Hirst and Thompson come close to underplaying the global changes that have occurred, even if they offer a useful corrective to more extreme 'the state is dead' theories. We have seen Scholte's description of the sheer density and integration of contemporary global capitalism that makes it clearly much different from the looseness of international trade flows of an earlier period. Held (1991) also suggests that there is a fundamental difference with what has passed before: nowadays there exist extensive webs of transnational relations, instantaneous electronic communications, a vast array of international regimes and organizations, and the development of a global military order.

Held *et al.* (1999) expand on these themes. On trade, for example, they indicate that around 20 per cent of world output is now traded, which is unprecedented. Moreover, trade globalization is integrated to the extent that markets for traded goods function at a worldwide level, which entails a system of regulated exchange of goods and services between regions. It transforms national economies to the extent that production is conditioned increasingly by global competition. Economic activity between regional blocs, in comparison with intra-regional activity, is also comparatively strong enough to sustain the globalization thesis: more accurately it might be best to describe regionalism as part of the process of globalization, in which the old 'North–South' distinctions are giving way to a new architecture of relations, as perhaps best testified by the manufacturing successes since the Second World War of a number of East Asian 'tiger economies'.

However, again as a corrective to globalist super-enthusiasm, we need to ensure that we do not conclude too much from the evidence for global economic integration. For example, many multinational corporations are less globally placeless than nationally situated. Although such companies were predominantly American in the 1960s, the flow of direct foreign investment by European and Japanese companies into the US since has resulted in the amount of US capital held by foreigners being larger than the amount of foreign capital held by Americans. Multinational companies are headquartered in a number of countries. Some would describe them more as 'national firms that operate internationally' (Dearlove and Saunders, 2000: 676) as they all have identifiable home bases where the really important corporate strategic decisions are taken, and which means that they are at least potentially subject to national regulation. In fact, these days, it may be questionable to over-compartmentalize multinationals when all large firms have to be internationalist in orientation and operations. Such a focus may be redolent of an earlier era when economic activity was regarded as mainly nationally based, with multinationals a clear exception (Brown, 2001: 173). There is evidence, too, that national governments can influence the competitive success of firms, not least in improving education and fostering innovation, through the use of its purchasing power on strategic grounds, and in encouraging industry 'clusters' (Porter, 1990).

Moreover, there are freedoms of manoeuvre for governments that are often overlooked. Governments are well aware that while capital may be increasingly mobile and global, labour is not. Workers and employees are very place-bounded. Even the increased migration of populations, especially in times of wars and economic prosperity in the West, makes them not so much footloose as anxious to obtain security and a stable environment for work (Castles and Miller, 1993). This means that most populations are available for fairly high levels of taxation if a government so chooses (presumably having taken electoral considerations into account) because most people will not flee the country under any circumstances. Democratic constraints are likely to loom larger in government calculations on these matters than the possible impact of policies on global corporations. Moreover, considerable amounts of trade still occur within national boundaries, not least because contractual compliance procedures and remedies are easier to obtain domestically than when operating abroad. For these and other reasons many parts of business welcome the continued administrative and legal functions of nation states, despite increased reassurance and protection for international trade from the growth and regulatory activities of supranational bodies such as the European Union.

However, globalization clearly constrains governments. We have noted already the diminished loss of currency sovereignty for national states, while the global integration of financial markets means that where a country's exchange rate is fixed, actions to promote expansionary monetary policies will lead to capital outflows unless interest rates rise sufficiently as an 'inducement' to speculators, but with potential deleterious consequences for the domestic economy. Trade integration across the world also means that too high a level of public expenditure on the welfare state, for example, is likely to lead to high inflation and interest rates, again stagnating output and employment prospects. Yet the impact of global competitive pressures on government policies is often quite pedestrian, and labour and political institutional impediments can be quite formidable (Garrett, 2000).

Consequently, rather than large international companies and nation states being in an 'either/or' relationship, they may best be seen as partners seeking a larger market share of investment and economic activity, and who engage in a mutual 'diplomacy' to achieve the best terms (Brown, 2001: 74). States want high-tech and forward-looking companies to set up in their countries; companies want states to provide skilled workers, good labour and trade conditions, and easy access to domestic and other markets (for example, in other states of the EU).

Globalization: something old or something new?

The question that we might pose, therefore, is whether we are witnessing with globalization simply the continued development of capitalism and modernity, or something quite different. Since their inception nation states have been required to adapt to ever changing circumstance – what is so different now? It could be argued, too, that the study of social and political development is always about both continuity and change, and globalization is no different. Indeed, some have pointed to the flows of international exchange a century ago as indicating that globalization has speeded up but not transformed contemporary exchanges between nation states. Before considering the social/cultural implications of globalization, it is to the question of whether globalization is a fundamental break with the past or not that we now turn.

In *The Times* (London) of 31 October 2000 it was reported that

> diehard Chinese Communists have decided that globalization, the new buzzword of the modern economy, is old hat. Karl Marx and Friedrich Engels, they say, invented the concept more than 150 years ago.

Consequently it appeared that Chinese academicians and officials felt that there is no inherent contradiction between China's market reforms – the embrace of global trade – and the continued worship of Marxism. Marx and Engels, in this view, long ago had seen globalization as the inevitable outcome of increased global production and worldwide networks in capitalism and, as a result, the contemporary Chinese gurus felt globalization would not 'alter the destiny of capitalism'. Instead of thwarting Marxist predictions about the eventual demise of capitalism globalization was a predicted stage in capitalism on the way to a thoroughgoing socialist society. Indeed its worldwide scope merely indicated the improved eventual global prospects for socialism and that states were crucial for the development of globalization processes. (These views are quite similar to some of those found on the Left in the West – see, for example, Sklair, 2002.)

Such arguments, articulated as China prepared to join that apotheosis of globalization, the World Trade Organization, obviously serve as a convenient political position for those within China seeking to rebut the view that communism is no longer on the agenda now that China has welcomed foreign capital and market reforms, such as the creation of stock markets. Rather, globalization is regarded in this interpretation as one more step along the dialectical path mapped by Marx, and does not change the nature of capitalism, particularly its exploitative dynamic. However, despite its ideological convenience, how credible is the view that globalization is capitalism (or modernity, or industrial society) writ larger? Has globalization changed things much?

One problem with the official Chinese account above is that Marx and Engels never got around to mentioning the word 'globalization' (although no doubt they may have recognized it if they had seen it). Another difficulty is that, these days, globalization is seen as wider than just economics and as encompassing, for example, broader cultural phenomena. A major objection, too, might be that it is only in the last three to four decades that globalization has emerged in a potentially epoch-changing and possibly quite unpredictable manner. While some development of supraterritorial circumstances can be traced back for several centuries, large-scale acceleration of globalization has occurred chiefly through recent decades.

Scholte notes, for example, that while it is possible to discern quite large international sales for some companies a hundred years or so ago, they did not take place in the context of a tightly coordinated transworld marketing strategy. Certainly it is only in recent years that we have seen the growth of suprastate monies and the ability of corporations to use the new global communications infrastructure to tightly control and coordinate their worldwide spread of offices and strategies.

None the less, it is worth considering further the views of those who still would wish to locate globalization within classically developed accounts of capitalism and modernity, as well as those who regard it as heralding quite different forms. This raises the issue of how contemporary commentators are able to recognize fundamental change – being so close to the action in comparison with later historians – and whether the analytical and conceptual tools of modern social science are a hindrance to locating epochal transformation.

Martin Albrow (1996) could be described as a 'supertransformationalist' as he argues that globalization involves a comprehensive social transformation that takes us into a new era, which he describes as the 'global age'. In his view modernity has been supplanted by globality in at least five major ways: the global environmental consequences of aggregate human activities; the loss of security where weaponry has global destructiveness; the globality of communication systems; the rise of a global economy; and the reflexivity of globalism, where people and groups of all kinds refer to the globe as the frame for their beliefs. When combined these developments pose a major threat to modernity and the nation state as individuals become ever more ready to cross physical and conceptual boundaries.

This view is at variance to those of theorists who accept that globalization results in major change but who are reluctant to recognize this as involving a critical epoch leap. Rather, 'transformationalists' such as Giddens, and others, such as Robertson (1992), see globalization as the inherent thrust of modernity towards greater connectedness worldwide. Giddens (1990: 64) believes

> Globalization can thus be defined as the intensification of worldwide social relations which links distant localities in such a way that local happenings are shaped by events occurring many miles away and vice versa.

For Robertson globalization is above all a cultural process in which the unity of the world is driven by global consciousness and which is a process that has been continuing for centuries.

These latter interpretations, therefore, see globalization as the result of institutional processes inherent in modernity: capitalism, industrialism, and state control of the means of violence and of information. But it does create major change by contributing to the de-traditionalization of social life and the growth of what Giddens describes as reflexivity, which is the ability and willingness to subject taken-for-granted assumptions to critical reasoning. Globalization sustains and extends reflexivity, as cultural diversity is no longer as geographically bounded as it once was. The result is a new form of global politics that he calls 'life politics'. Where fate becomes a matter of choice, new concerns arise about what kind of world and what kind of lives we are creating for ourselves, as expressed, for example, in feminism or ecological politics. Such movements recognize that the responses have to be transnational rather than national.

It is clear that Giddens regards globalization as the consequence of many causes, unlike, say, Harvey (1989) who sees it as economically determined. Indeed Harvey, much more in the 'sceptics' camp, would prefer to describe the changes in contemporary capitalism as more of a move from 'Fordism' to 'post-Fordism' than as a move to a global age. For him globalization is one aspect of this fundamental economic shift in relations of production, away from Keynesianism and corporatism towards a more flexible, and less costly, form of capital accumulation (see also Lasch and Urry, 1987, and their similar account of 'disorganized capitalism').

Globalization, for Harvey, particularly of finance capital, is one of the strategies adopted to escape the rigidities of Fordism-Keynesianism, which was organized around nation-state regulation. Insecure employment, the decline of manufacturing, and more niche specialization are other features. The result is that globalization successfully empowers capitalism in relation to a weakened state. The state becomes reduced to an entrepreneurial role in its regulation of capitalist activities, predominantly in helping to provide or stimulate the right investment climate in increased competition with other national economies. But it remains a capitalist state.

Both Giddens and Harvey, however, share the view that globalization is best understood as some form of continuation of modernity, although the former is less economistic than the latter. This position contrasts with that of Albrow who prefers to see modernity as a passing stage of history with the global age as the start of a new epoch. However, in his view, modernity and its models have exercised such a grip on intellectuals that they seek to assimilate all subsequent social transformation into it. They fail to recognize a new historical period when it lies right under their nose, and even though globalization is seen as involving profound change.

In large part this reluctance to move away from modernism is explained by the rationalistic and universalizing characteristics of reason and scientific enquiry. Globalization may be regarded as a logical and perhaps inevitable consequence of rationalist, modernist knowledge and its accumulation. After all, as Albrow observes, reason knows no territorial limits and its appeal is to principles which are unbounded by time and space.

Globalization and the extension of the principle of rationality, however, mean that the state is no longer rooted in the nation but globally, with the state (as a universalizing, objective force) increasingly the site for a host of transnational practices. For Albrow this results in the state no longer belonging to a particular set of people at a particular time, although it may have originated with them in mind. The state in the global age is 'uprooted', with the origin of its rules multi-local and polycentrically administered. Consequently, there is vastly increased potential for social groups to constitute collective action outside the frame of nation-state society.

These propositions probably exaggerate the extent and implications of globalization, and also underestimate the activist jurisdictions of nation states. Moreover, the extent of general public support for 'progressive social movements' based around the environment and human rights, for example, is probably less than claimed. Nationalist, 'anti-foreigner' and other 'reactionary' forms of political protest can retain considerable vigour, while those who are not participants in new, cosmopolitan social movements – and who are silent because they have private lives to live – may be substantial in number.

Both Scholte and Held may be classified as amongst those as viewing globalization as more than capitalism writ large, but who are not persuaded that we are now entering a quite different type of society. And while the nation state has lost much of its sovereignty it remains important in both the promulgation of globalization and in adaptations to it. Held *et al.* suggest that the forms and modalities of the state have differed with globalization, and that the costs and benefits of policy choices have changed, and the outcome is more one of multi-layered governance. Giddens, too, sees the nation state as retaining its importance, not least because the world's territory lies under the legitimate control of nation states. However, he points out that the modern state has always been involved in a dialectic in which it trades control over practices in its territory for more global influence by joining with other states. None the less, increasingly there seems loss of state autonomy and a growing perception by states of the need for a greater degree of cooperation.

It is difficult to know, with hindsight, when change, even when large-scale, constitutes a phenomenon so transforming that previous intellectual categories no longer apply. However, it could be regarded as not especially disabling to retain existing models provided they capture and adequately explain major social change. We can then leave to others the issue as to whether the change is of sufficient magnitude to warrant the description of it as 'epochal'.

Globalization and national policies

It is questionable whether nation states were ever so powerful as the 'death of the nation state' theorists allow (Dearlove, 2000). The British state, for example, never controlled the economy to the extent that the 'hyperglobalists' suggest. Nor can we ignore domestic levers for state policies, or the requirements of electoral politics. National policies between countries can differ considerably, despite similar globalizing environments. In parts of Asia, too, can be found forms of 'state-led capitalism', while neoliberal models are by no means ubiquitous in the face of globalizing pressures. More corporatist political systems can be found in central and northern Europe (Swank, 2002).

A more useful approach than asking whether globalization implies the eventual death of the nation state is to investigate the policy impacts of globalization, for example on state regulatory regimes. The policy implications of globalization for national governments remain inadequately researched, although there are signs that this situation may be changing in the UK (Gummett, 1996). These globalizing implications are likely to be found in both the private and public sectors. In asking whether national healthcare policies are being globalized, for example, which might appear on the face of it to be an unlikely area for such enquiry, Moran and Wood (1996) helpfully distinguish four ways in which such a change might take place. One would be through the greater influence of international expert communities on national policies, while a second would lie in the increased movement of practitioners and patients across territorial boundaries. Third, the market, and possibly its regulation, for healthcare products, such as drugs, may be becoming more global. Finally, healthcare policy could be becoming more influenced by wider global economic policies, such as, for instance, the view that more 'user-pays' policies are necessary to achieve broader governmental policies of reducing public expenditure and enhancing economic competitiveness globally.

Moran and Wood find the case for the globalization of healthcare policy as 'not proven', with evidence for it in some dimensions, but not in others. But the value of their analysis lies more with the kind of schema adopted, which allows globalization to be formulated with operational dimensions that allow some form of empirical testability of claims for its implications for nation-state policies and their relative 'independence' from wider global forces. Their work may point to the need for further 'policy network' or 'policy community' research, particularly on global gatherings of experts and professionals (so-called 'epistemic communities'), if we are to get a more soundly based handle on the wider implications of globalization for the nation state. Comparative analysis of different policy sectors would be especially helpful, given that different agents and styles are likely to be found within them.

Social/cultural change

Recent years have seen a revived 'cultural turn' in political sociology, which argues that attention should shift again from formal politics at the level of the nation state, and especially its relationship to class, to politics as an inherent possibility in all social relations. Although the state remains important, it is displaced as the centre of political activity. In this view, the 'new politics' is increasingly characterized by social movements and media representations that operate outside the formal institutions of state bureaucracies, political parties and interest groups (Nash, 2000).

There is no doubt that since the 1960s we have witnessed in a number of advanced countries the growth of new social movements and forms of direct action – including against globalization. These movements are broader and less nationally integrated than traditional interest groups and have been concerned more with consumer and 'cause' issues than with the economic producer matters associated with class, citizenship and the state. The Women's Movement and the Green Movement are two examples of groups that have been associated with the informal, the personal and the anti-hierarchical, as opposed to the formal organization and bureaucratization of conventional sector and voluntary associations. Often they are peopled by the 'new middle class' in the professional, knowledge-based, public services, such as education, social work and administration, where a high level of work autonomy and self-direction can be the norm, and who can display extraordinary disdain for materialist values.

Globalization has a strong influence here too, as many of these social movements function transnationally, constituted by new cultural identities and issues, such as gender, sexual orientation and ecology, which cross national boundaries. Moreover, much of the lobbying of such groups is aimed at supraterritorial or international bodies, such as the European Union or the United Nations.

This approach is considerably influenced by the work of Foucault (1977). As we shall see in more detail in later chapters, for Foucault power is not dependent on institutions, nor possessed by agents, such as classes or bureaucracies. Rather, it hardly seems to be the product of any human volition or responsibility at all. Power is seen as productive of subjectivity or identity – such as feelings of being criminalized, or as mentally ill – and is socially ubiquitous. The state does not deliberately set out to create these feelings or perceptions, by exercising power over others, but it does take advantage of them. In this way, politics is associated as much with the meanings and interpretations that actors give events and practices as with structures and formal institutional arrangements. It is cultural and involves the manipulation of symbols and signs, including the repression of 'legitimate' or alternative options. The nation state, as a consequence, find itself increasingly marginalized as a site for the resolution of such issues, which largely takes place elsewhere.

There is little doubt that cultural fragmentation and new social identities have resulted in forms of political action occurring outside the purview of the nation state. But much action also is focused on securing advance or redress from those structures that predominantly possess the means to act, in some cases because they control the legitimate means of violence, and that is the state. As Albrow (1996) has remarked, without the state there is an ever-present danger that violence lodges 'in cliques, mafias, mercenaries and murderers'. Globalization does generate movements that seek to mobilize on issues which nation states have not always considered especially salient, but often the result is to bring pressure to bear on national governments who become, at least in some cases, increasingly aware of global issues. It is only when some of these groups see the nation state as part of the problem that the nation state becomes seriously challenged.

Perhaps the key to answering the issue of whether supraterritoriality and globalization spell the end of the nation state is to recognize that adaptability is not the same as weakness, and that changing institutional configurations do not necessarily lead to a loss of state power. State power may be less a matter of being able to impose its will on society and more to do with the capability for increasing adaptability to domestic and global environments (Pierre and Peters, 2000). This is particularly the case following pro-market liberal reform in the last decades of the last century in a number of countries.

Can globalization be rolled back?

A persistent theme in the literature on globalization is the sense of a seemingly unstoppable and inevitable process. In part this stems from a view that its major proponents, especially in the field of transnational corporate business, are powerful interests who are likely to be more influential on key decision-makers and on reconfiguring the world than its detractors. But it also stems from a view that globalization is a natural 'rolling out' of modernity and capitalism, and that it possesses characteristics of rationalism that generate systemic tendencies to universalism. Even those who see it as a new historical period and as indicating a major social transformation, such as Albrow, remark on its increasingly enveloping features. However, it may be possible to moderate this perspective and to suggest that, economically at least, the integration of the world economy does have potential limitations.

The governments of nation states, for example, are not as powerless as is sometimes assumed and, with their electorates, are capable of being persuaded by anti-globalists and other protesters to at least slow and possibly even reverse recent globalization. The street protests at the Seattle meeting of the World Trade Organization in 1999 and subsequently were only one sign of increasing public disquiet at the policies of globalization's supraterritorial agencies, such as the International Monetary Fund and the World Bank. Both companies and governments recently seem more apologetic about the possible deleterious effects of globalization than merely asserting that poverty and its alleviation is best served by further world economic integration and market liberalization.

Restrictions on international trade, purportedly to protect labour and the environment, are increasingly likely if anti-globalization protests increase in influence. Yet it is difficult to know how sustainable such a backlash may be, not least because many such protesters take pride in being 'anti-hierarchical' in their approach to organization, while often displaying disparate priorities in their policies. Global social movements often appear uncertain on how to regard the nation state. Does the state's regulatory and legal frameworks pose dangers for groups seeking global forms of democracy based, not on existing state and legal institutions, but on bottom-up civic association, or should national and international state frameworks be utilized and cooperated with in order to obtain the instruments without which change may be unrealizable (Baker, 2002)? The nation state is sufficiently strong for new, 'civil society' approaches to 'global democracy', based on human rights and ecological sustainability, and demands for more direct forms of global corporate and government accountability, to face considerable difficulties without enlisting state support.

We pick up on these issues, and the development of supranational forms of governance, in the next chapter.

Chapter 7

Suprastate Governance

Realism
International regimes
Global regulation
Human rights, international law and national
    sovereignty
Cosmopolitan law
Global democracy

In previous chapters we examined the development of the nation state and democracy, and recognized that, from the beginning, the international order was a critical factor in these processes. The competition of the inter-state system in the period of the absolutist rulers helped the build-up of central administration, more efficient and better-based tax collection, and standing armies that were essential ingredients in the formation of the modern state.

By the first part of the twentieth century, a model of largely autonomous development by relatively isolated nation states looked increasingly untenable in the face of an expanding international economy. Apart from economic flows, large-scale movements of people around the globe, not least in the form of migration to the US, added to growing internationalization (although today far more restrictive immigration policies apply; see Woods, 2000). Gradually, too, pressures grew for the harmonization of standards and rules for trading, the results of which became reflected in international agreements, some established by governments but also a number generated by private interests. Institutionalized arrangements to promote and regulate the growth of international transport and communications infrastructures, regarded as vital for trade relations, were also developed, often privately and relatively autonomously from national governments.

In the first decades of the twentieth century, liberal internationalist views became particularly influential, especially in Britain (such as with the Fabians), and in the US. The approach was comprised of two components: a desire to encourage national self-determination and liberal democracy, which, it was thought, would help to prevent the essentially pacific tendencies of ordinary people being ignored by unrepresentative and warlike elites; and the construction of an international institutional

166

structure, such as a 'League of Nations' (Brown, 2001: 22–3). The aim was to do away with the Westphalian concept of nation states enjoying untrammelled independence, including the right to wage war, and to replace it with some form of 'collective security', or mutual defence and assurance, by all nations. An attack on one would mean an attack on all.

McGrew (2002), in pointing to the re-emergence of liberal internationalism in recent years, and as part of a useful outline of its key elements, describes it as the 'means for using reason and morality to overcome the tendency of national states to wage war'. He also suggests that liberal internationalism can be regarded as advocating aspects of liberal pluralist democracy at the international level, albeit without the requirements of electoral politics (2002: 267–89). Liberal internationalism seeks to re-interpret a new world order in terms of cooperative and collaborative – norm- rather than interest-based – action by states through bodies such as the United Nations. Yet, in the aftermath of the popular support for the Second World War, and the inability of the international structure to prevent it, liberal internationalism gave way in the post-war years to more 'realist' notions of international relations. These were regarded as essentially the struggle between self-interested nation states and therefore incorrigible to normative international structures.

Realism

As the name implies the 'realism' version of the international order was seen to be more 'realistic' than 'utopian' liberal internationalism. 'Realists' argued that the 'flawed' or 'fallen' nature of mankind meant that states were largely impervious to collective moral suasion. States inevitably pursue their own interests and power resources. The international order, therefore, tends to be characterized by the actions of nation states as rational egoists. It was essentially 'anarchic' (it lacked a controlling worldwide formal source of authority as found in the domestic sphere), which meant that states had to look out for themselves and their security as nobody else would (Carr, 1939; Morgenthau, 1948).

The most influential theorist in this tradition has been Waltz (1959), who offered what has been called a 'neo-realism' approach, the term 'neo' being applied predominantly because – rather than just focusing on the interplay of states – he emphasized the self-reproducing and constraining system of inter-state relations. States really had little option – if they wished to survive – in accepting the realities of the international system. Patterns of international relations endure over the centuries, the outcome of the compelling nature of the international 'self-help' system. States are forever preoccupied with their security and continuously monitor their position in the world to take steps to preserve it, if necessary through alliances that restore an essential balance of power. The situation is rather like a market. Although capabilities and powers among states change, their basic functions are similar. The result tends to be emulation of the leading states by the others to ensure that the former do not build up too powerful a position. For example, if a new form of military administration is seen as particularly effective, then it will be copied by other states (as followed the warfare success of the Prussians' organization of military administration in the late nineteenth century).

The theory of the state in neo-realism is somewhat problematic. In fact, rather like the rational choice and pluralist perspectives used in the post-1945 years to account for domestic politics, the state is never really theorized at all and is treated as a form of 'black box', with states as ricocheting billiard balls on the international pool table. As Hobson (2000) has pointed out, the state would appear to be strong and autonomous over domestic social forces in one reading, to enable it to adjust successfully to the exigencies of the inter-state system. Yet, in emphasizing anarchy and the compelling requirements of the international system, 'Walzian' theory offers a view of the state that is remarkably weak in the international sense. States appear to have little scope to change much; rather, the needs of survival compel them to follow the herd.

Neo-liberals, however, have criticized the self-help views of neo-realism in suggesting that states are able to realize that cooperation internationally can confer major advantages, and that competitive self-preservation is not the only option (Keohane 1984/1989; Axelrod 1984). A so-called 'English Constructivist School' has also argued that anarchy is not the only condition for the international system but that norm-governed relations can emerge – often created by the states themselves – in which states recognize acceptable values and proper ways of behaving (Bull, 1977/1995; Dunne, 1995). The notion of 'embeddedness' is sometimes used in these approaches to indicate that norms and values become institutionalized, patterned and routine, and become valued in their own right, irrespective of the original reasons and interests that lay in their foundation, such as the power play of a hegemonic nation (Imber, 2002). However, while international cooperation may add to overall system advantages, as the neo-liberals and constructivists maintain, neo-realists are more concerned with the relative advantages to each particular state from their various actions, which is likely to make states focus on the gains of cooperation to them in comparison with other states. Consequently, neo-realists generally see alliances as temporary and expedient.

International regimes

The future of the nation state came under increasing scrutiny throughout the twentieth century. On the one hand there were those known as international functionalists who felt that the idea of national sovereignty had had its day. Instead the growing array of technical, functional or specialist international organizations, such as the IMF, offered more hope of a peaceful and cooperative world than, say, liberal internationalist ideas of a world government (Mitrany, 1943/1966). It was a view that rather curiously echoed internationally the arguments that prevailed in the US domestically in the New Deal years that we outlined in Chapter 5 for the growth of independent and technically competent economic regulators. Yet Mitrany and others offer a basically apolitical interpretation of the decline of the nation state. They overlook the persisting strength of territoriality, the perceived need for national security and defence, the power of affective nationalist sentiments, and popular support for national representational assemblies, all of which point to the continuance of the nation state. On the other hand, 'integrationists', associated particularly with the European Commission of the European Union, have argued for the greater integration of states, perhaps as a precursor for regional or even world federalism. Integrationism and supranationalism are regarded as particularly effective responses to the challenges of a globalizing world, especially the need to manage global economic liberalism and the rise of the multinational companies.

Increased worldwide economic integration is regarded as a prime cause of the growth of international 'regimes', such as the World Trade Organization (WTO). Regimes have been defined as a set of 'implicit or explicit principles, norms, rules and decision-making procedures around which actors' expectations converge' (Krasner, 1983: 2). Generally underwritten or initiated by a hegemonic power, such as the US in the post-1945 years, international cooperative and authoritative institutions have been established because they are regarded as conveying advantages for the states that make up the world community. A hegemonic power is thus virtually a substitute for world government. However, states are still regarded as rational egoists – as in 'neo-realism' – but who come to recognize the benefits to them of international economic regimes, not least as the transactions costs of such regimes are incurred by the hegemonic power. Moreover, the formalization, writing down, and institutionalization of regime rules give these rules a life of their own that comes to be potentially independent of the originating great power.

The growth of supraterritorial organizations and institutions, such as the European Union (EU), the World Trade Organization (WTO), and the International Monetary Fund (IMF), which in part have been formed to both regulate and further the processes of free trade and global economic liberalization, also are seen as diminishing the freedom to act of nation states. Yet powerful nations, such as the US, have been strongly influential in these bodies, as the example of the introduction of a strong intellectual property regime (which favoured US interests) as part of the WTO processes testifies (Braithwaite and Drahos, 2000).

The key to the rapid and extensive globalization of intellectual property regulation over the last decade or more lies with it being tied to issues of trade. This has ensured a compliance through the WTO (which has juridical authority and enforcement mechanisms) that would have been much more difficult to achieve if it had not been linked to trade. It also enabled the US – as the prime information economy and the main net exporter of intellectual property – to use the prospect of denial of access to its large domestic trade market to countries dependent on the US to overcome their initial objections and to secure agreement within the WTO.

The use of coercion to obtain 'non-reciprocal coordination' – so that even net importers of intellectual capital, such as Australia, felt obliged to support the US proposals so that they would not lose US support for their own interests in agricultural trade – demonstrated the bilateral and other trade-offs, the linkages, that pave the way for wider multilateral agreements. The use of the WTO (as opposed to the more ineffectual World Intellectual Property Organization) to make intellectual property a trade matter also indicates the willingness and ability of strong countries such as the US, or those in the EU, to 'shift global forums' to where they may be best placed to obtain their preferences.

There is no doubt that the eventual agreement in the WTO on intellectual property in 1994 reflected the interests of the major US corporations, who have a significant comparative human capital advantage in their ownership of abstract objects. These corporations have resources and a political clout denied to even most nations, particularly for lobbying and the preparation and analysis of technical and complex cases. The example illustrates how misleading it may be to define the causes of global regulatory and other change within such multilateral frameworks as the outcome of 'globalization' or even 'worldwide democracy'. Such organizations can effectively mask, under rules of formal equality, the very real interplay of national and large corporate interests and often the success of the most powerful and dominant of these.

None the less there is evidence that these global economic organizations are influenced also by criticism from the developing world and elsewhere. Increasingly their loans are predicated on social safety nets, and recognition that public sector deficits may be needed to protect a basic standard of provision of food, health, education and employment.

Moreover, intellectual property regimes that provide lengthy periods of protection for pharmaceutical giants are recognized as leading to severe problems for some countries with major AIDS/HIV epidemics and has led to moves to relax such measures, to help the supply of cheap medicines, in the wake of concerted opposition from the developing world and its supporters to perceived over-restrictive patent protections.

Weaker nations generally have much more difficulty none the less in exercising their interests in these transnational organizations and feel increasingly supplanted by the willingness of these bodies to consult more readily with a host of non-governmental organizations (NGOs). O'Brien *et al.* (2000) argue, on the basis of detailed research, that institutions such as the IMF and the WTO are moving beyond their inter-state mandates to deal with a wide range of global civic society actors and representatives of social movements. Although not influencing the policies of these bodies much, yet broadening their agendas to include social issues more regularly, this increasingly institutionalized participation by NGOs undermines the nation state's claim to be the sole legitimate representative of the public interest in its country. Many developing countries, and especially weaker nations in the southern hemisphere, oppose such widening consultation and representation to unelected NGOs on these grounds. But these examples of global governance may be considered a further indication of the operation of globalization at the political level, and which incorporates increasingly growing numbers of international social groups in key multilateral institutions.

Pierre and Peters (2000) suggest, however, that the growth of transnational economic and other regimes may lead to an underestimation of the power of nation states. Although undoubtedly it has led to changes of operation and a 'pooling' of sovereignty for states, it is not unusual historically for states to have to respond through international and domestic alliances to major shifts in their external environments. Indeed, it is often nation states themselves that have sought greater international liberalization of private capital, and associated supranational governance processes, as conferring benefits on their own economies. They suggest that 'linkages upward towards trans-national governance institutions and downward towards sub-national government should be more thought of as state strategies to reassert control and not as proof of states surrendering to competing models of governance' (2000: 16).

Global regulation

Regulation is perhaps the key to the development of supraterritoriality in its more institutionalized forms and in a manner that indicates a continuing role for the nation state. Although global regulation has quickened in recent decades it has a long history. Examples of trade and financial regulation across countries can be found in the medieval period, as merchants and their bodies and networks formulated practices and customs that enabled their markets to function and develop effectively. Legal notions of property, contract, currency, and credit, for example, were essential in providing a sound and reasonably secure basis for the expansion of international trade. In Europe, these developments were considerably aided by the rediscovery and the reinterpretation of Roman private law, which provided many of the foundation concepts for regulatory regimes over succeeding centuries. This had a codified and systematic jurisprudence – conceptual depth, technical detail, and a capacity to solve new problems – that proved invaluable in formulating ideas and frameworks that aided the spread of international commerce, and which were quickly exploited by the merchant classes.

As with other forms of social processes, legal and rule-like arrangements are necessary to regulate, standardize, 'make fair', and to promulgate the processes of globalization, and these procedures are increasingly developed through regional and transworld institutions created by states. The mid-nineteenth century witnessed the emergence of cross-border regulatory and rule-based regimes as international trade accelerated. The movement to standardize negotiable financial instruments (securities and other bonds and shares) internationally began in the second half of the nineteenth century, as did the establishment of specialist international organizations with the purpose of creating a worldwide commercial law. Initially legal instruments such as standard contracts were formulated by private trade associations. Only in the twentieth century have international governmental organizations sought to standardize and regulate the variety of privately ordered contract law.

It was the post-Second World War international agreements at Bretton Woods that created an international monetary system administered by international organizational bodies such as the IMF and the World Bank. The incursion into state sovereignty was considerable and marked a shift away from the tacit, convention-based cooperation of central bankers to a sweeping, rule-based, multilateral cooperation of states (Braithwaite and Drahos, 2000). Although much of the Bretton Woods regime broke down in the crisis-ridden 1970s, for example in favour of floating currencies, the last two decades of the twentieth century have seen the further establishment of global regulatory frameworks.

From their study of seventeen different sectors or domains, Braithwaite and Drahos (2000) found that transparency was the principle that has most consistently been strengthened over recent years in negotiations on regulatory regimes (while that of national sovereignty has weakened most). They trace this to the shift in contemporary capitalism from an industrial to an informational base, and the move from an intimate and clubbable form of capitalist relationships and organization to a more impersonal one based on the risk analysis of company prospects as indicated by public information that has been properly accounted. This form of capitalism is constituted by a legal commodification of knowledge and is increasingly transnational. Global regulatory regimes are increasingly confronted by abstract objects, such as patents, which have become one of the most important forms of property, as much as physical goods or tangible services.

However, although many of these suprastate bodies have acquired a degree of autonomy from national governments, national states continue to have considerable and decisive inputs. Forms of transnational private sector governance through associative and voluntary 'self-regulation' have often been supported by states, too. State policies have in many instances encouraged supraterritorial developments – not least in support of business's desire for regulated and wider and more open markets, and in the recognition that rule compliance is sometimes best secured over all nation states by some form of supraterritorial decision and monitoring, rather than through inter-state argument.

However, states are not the only bodies able to provide the legal and institutional bases for the growth of supraterritoriality. A variety of sub-state, suprastate and market entities have also contributed the elements of governance required. The forces of capitalism, rationalism, and technology have encouraged state and other regulators to facilitate supraterritoriality and the spread of global relations through standardization. Supraterritorial connections are obviously reinforced when the parties involved follow the same rules and routines, and much of this standardization involves the harmonization of the technologies that have underpinned globalization. Bodies such as the WTO, and free trade areas such as the European Union (EU), have helped further globalization through: technical and procedural standardization; liberalization of crossborder movements for investment, goods and services; guarantees of property rights for global capital; and legalization of global organizations and activities.

European Union

It is analytically useful to think of the European Union, if not as a state, then as a powerful regulatory organization 'owned' by a number of states. Modern states are regarded as fulfilling three main functions: redistribution (tax and welfare), stabilization (macroeconomic policies, but also welfare again), and regulation (promoting efficiency in markets and socially correcting for market failure). The development of the regulatory state is constituted by the rise of the third function, generally as a replacement or diminution of the first two. At the EU level, however, the growth of regulation may be regarded as less the loss of confidence in redistribution and Keynesian policies, than the lack of the budgetary and bureaucratic resources to undertake such functions. Rather, notions such as 'subsidiarity' allow the growth of regulation at the EU level, but with its costs picked up nationally.

The EU is the most ambitious example in the contemporary world of multinational governance. The use of qualified majority voting on some issues (which may become extended as a consequence of impending revisions to its Treaties and constitution following the recommendations of a special Convention) means that a country may find directives passing into law which it opposes, which raises issues of accountability to national electorates and assemblies. Moreover, following the Single European Act of 1986, the express purpose of the EU is to eliminate all the obstacles preventing a level and competitive market place. This has major implications for national governments because such a goal removes many of the social and economic instruments that they have traditionally employed, including finance, currency, subsidies and taxation.

The regulatory function of the EU aims to correct various forms of 'market failure': monopoly power, negative externalities (adverse consequences of an economic activity that affects other parties but without it being reflected in market prices), failures of information, or insufficient provision of public goods such as law and order or environmental protection (Majone, 1996). The US federal government has long been seen as a classic regulatory state and as an exemplar for European regulators in new fields of regulation such as environmental protection, nuclear safety, consumer product safety, and the regulation of new technologies. Although there are few regulatory functions specified in the founding Treaty of Rome, the scale of EU regulation has been large, partly because, as we have noted, such policy-making is not particularly limited by the lack of budgetary resources (which are small in the EU). However, regulation requires institutions to implement, sustain and monitor regulation and it is arguable that the EU has lacked these. The establishment of the European Central Bank, however, does provide an example of institutional regulation (Moran, 2002b).

Majone suggests that both governmental and non-governmental groups may have an interest in specific European regulations. For example, multinational export-orientated industries are interested in having consistent regulations across countries, and also benefit from a consequential regional cohesiveness in dealing with other major trading blocs, such as the US. International regulatory failure rather than market failure tends to drive supranational regulation, as this makes it easier to check whether individual countries are compliant in observing cooperative agreements, and to impose sanctions if necessary, which would be more difficult for an individual member state. Supranational agencies (generally insulated from the electoral cycle) can sometimes also be a useful scapegoat for both individual governments and companies when difficult decisions have to be made, such as refusals of subsidies for loss-making operations.

Yet it is not always easy to reconcile the specialist expertise required for a regulatory body with issues of legitimacy and proper accountability. For some, partisan or majoritarian politics are not suited to the complex and highly technical tasks of large-scale economic management, while Keynesian welfare state interventions of command and control are largely discredited. As we saw in the US, the regulatory mode is seen to be more effective, and this requires experts and functional agencies (Majone, 1996). In the UK a recent government drive for 'greater democratic oversight' of boards and agencies at local level – such as for hospitals and schools – reflects a view that such specific agencies can ignore the wider views of communities (or at least local politicians) in their efforts to be more efficient and up-to-date. Yet reintroducing partisan politics through more elected bodies in areas of specific functions may not only encourage petty parochialism and resistance to change, but actually obscure attempts to make such services more accountable to their clients through effective survey and managerial methods. Responsive and effective health or education services may not be best achieved through partisan democratic control of specialist boards and agencies. However, at the EU level, the notion of the so-called 'democratic deficit' that, in considerable part, flows from the regulatory and technical aspects of many of its functions is regarded as a significant issue that requires addressing urgently. It has led to the establishment of a Convention to reconsider the EU's general constitutional arrangements, but it is by no means clear that, for example, greater involvement in EU decision-making by the elected politicians of the European Assembly would improve its policy-making.

It is important to recognize that the steady development of regulatory functions in the EU has more generally followed from the everyday routines of 'low politics' engaged in by the suprastatist European Commission, the administrative arm of the EU, than from the high-profile decisions of national leaders made in Council meetings. The Commission and its officials have generally been regarded as more 'federalist' or 'integrationist' than the intergovernmental Councils. Despite periods when the Council of Ministers and the European Council were relatively becalmed in taking forward the process of economic integration in Europe (mainly in the 1970s and early 1980s), transnational regulation and standardization continued at bureaucratic level. Indeed, it's very 'technical' nature meant that when matters required referral to the Council of member states' ministers, they were often nodded through (Major, 2000: 284).

Moreover, the EU has not hesitated to include private organizations within the sphere of governance, particularly European-wide, industry-based, standards-setting organizations. Since the Maastricht Treaty (1993) the EU has accumulated competencies in virtually every area that national governments have controlled, now often backed up by the decisions of the European Court of Justice, whose supremacy has become accepted by the legal systems of all member states. This helps to ensure that the development of the internal market could not be compromised too much by variations in strictly non-tariff areas, such as education, and social and environmental protection. The result is a multilayered system of governance, a 'suprastate' rather than an 'inter-state' organization, with decisions that help determine member government objectives at both national and European levels. It has been estimated that some 80 per cent of economic and social legislation and perhaps 50 per cent of all other legislation passed at the national level within the EU now emanates from Brussels (Edwards, 1996: 143).

It is not only large multinational companies taking a global or European view that lobby the EU; environmental and other groups with wider perspectives and issues than contained by the nation state have seen benefits from European-level solutions and representation. Nor is this process likely to falter with the processes of globalization. As Keating and Hooghe (1996: 218) note, increasingly

> Policy-making retreats into complex networks that do not correspond to formal institutions; and new and rediscovered forms of identity emerge at the subnational level and even the supranational. Perhaps the most important loss has been that of an arena where the needs of economic competitiveness and those of social integration can be reconciled.

As to why nation states are willing to lose or to 'pool' their individual sovereignties, it may, as Pierre and Peters (2000) suggest, be their most logical response to a globalizing world where the aim is to find new forms of cooperation and modalities of influence. Moreover, integrating sovereignty with other states may not simply be a 'zero-sum game' (you lose to the extent that someone else gains), but one where losses of national sovereignty are more than compensated for by the increase in a wider sovereignty. The speed with which the ex-communist European states, and others, have sought entry to the EU, indicates that hanging on to sovereignty (even though recently gained) is regarded as less important than gaining access to markets, especially if joining also enhances democratic credentials and respectability, despite the poor economic terms often offered to the new joiners.

The case of the EU is an example of how the issues of nation state sovereignty, globalization, and supranationality remain in tension and flux. The European Monetary Union (EMU), for example, illustrates the divided views on the EU's relationship to globalization. It is seen by some as the internalization of economic globalization and neo-liberalization, through seeking the freer movement of capital and open trading, while others see it as a means of standing firm against a US-powered globalization that is regarded as malign (Dyson, 2002). These divisions are reflected within the British Conservative Party. 'New Right' thinking towards the European Union in the UK has generally been antagonistic to it on the grounds that the EU is dominated by corporatist and social democratic ideologies and interests that threaten the labour market and other reforms instigated under the Thatcher governments. This hostility is likely to be reinforced if Britain joins the European Monetary Union and abolishes its currency in favour of the euro.

Yet, although this position is sometimes defended on nationalist grounds, a considerable body of Conservative party opinion has opposed too close an integration with the EU on global market grounds. That is, the EU is seen to be inward-looking, and a defensive and restrictive organization that is ill-suited to advancing the interests and economic prospects of a liberal and long-established trading nation. In these circumstances national sovereignty and a strong state is required to ensure that Britain has the capability to take full advantage of an increasingly global world economy based on multilateral trade agreements as found within the WTO (Gamble and Kelley, 2002).

The 'neo-realist' school of International Relations, however, regards the EU as a site for the interplay of state interests and underplays the federal and supranational role of, for example, the European Commission. The EU, in this view, is a particular location and institutional configuration for the normal pursuit of state interests through diplomacy and bargaining. Nation states are the dominant force within the EU and intergovernmentality is likely to be its primary mode of decision-making and agreement. Even European directives vary widely in their national interpretations, applications, and compliance. Others, however, point to the increased role and influence of Commission officials since the late 1970s, and the superordinating legal authority of the European Court of Justice, as a sign of weakening state sovereignty and growing integration (Paterson and Blomberg, 1999).

However, intergovernmentality by itself does not necessary imply that the sovereignty of nation states is generally maintained despite membership of the EU. Although the Council of Ministers is made up of nation state representatives it possesses major legal powers to formulate and to implement policies with very little further action or even scrutiny at the level of national parliaments. Its regulations have a legal status irrespective of subsequent bargaining by member states. Moreover, following the Treaty of Maastricht in 1993, national citizens of member countries are also citizens of the EU, with EU passports. They are able to travel freely to other member states and to take up residence, and also to engage politically in that territory.

The enlargement of the EU to take in countries from the former Soviet bloc and elsewhere, and the implications for the EU budget and decision-making processes, are not likely to resolve the national/supranational tugs and flows that characterize the EU. It provides an example of multilayered governance, where so-called 'national' interests are forged within a wider transnational context and set of constraints. The EU lacks key state functions in defence and foreign affairs (despite recent steps to start to overcome this), and efforts to widen the scope of the EU to significant, non-directly economic matters are likely to run into considerable opposition from multinational corporations, who are happy with the 'common market' policies of the EU but have little appetite for the growth of a strong European state. These inter- and supra-national flows, and debates over 'big' or 'small' forms of global governance and regulation, are likely also to characterize political debates in wider global forums.

Outside the EU, there have been concerted attempts in other parts of the world to establish regional organizations or associations, particularly in Asia and the Pacific, but also in the Americas, although none matches the close legal, economic, and political integration of the EU. Although these developments have accelerated since the ending of the Cold War, their purposes appear primarily economic rather than based on collective military security. In Asia, for example, countries have used the prospect of regional cooperation as a means of tying China to multilateral trade agreements, not least to help offset its increasing economic power as a cheap exporter of manufacturing goods.

This is not to deny that globalization has changed some of the characteristics of states. Clearly it has contributed to the 'pooling' or 'sharing' of national sovereignties and has facilitated moves towards more multilayered governance, particularly in respect of regulatory competences, as well as encouraging private regulatory bodies, such as those of civic associations and companies. All continue to share, however, the bureaucratic structures and principles characteristic of the nation state's governance.

Nor is it likely that a global financial system, for example, will lead to a global financial regulator, as this would be too threatening to nation states, and would lack the political consensus needed for implementation, in the face of the benefits that appear to follow for companies currently from regulatory competition between different national regimes.

Globalization has also generated in some parts of the world what Ohmae (1992) calls a 'borderless world' in which national state boundaries are losing economic significance. Rather, the 'region state' – geographical units such as Hong Kong and the nearby stretch of southern China, or the Kansai region in Japan, or Spain's Catalonia – are becoming more important. These may lie within or across the borders of a nation state, and they are defined by being the right size and scale to be natural business units in the global economy. None the less, decisional units other than the nation state, such as the European Union, or these 'regional states', lack what Axford (1995) describes as expressive, as opposed to instrumentalist, characteristics. That is, people tend to have a sense of belonging to their country whereas these other levels generally lack such identities and emotions. One result is that citizens often still focus on the national state for their demands and supports.

Human rights, international law and national sovereignty

Developments in international law increasingly focus on individual and human rights, and wider social issues, as well as those of states. We see the emergence of a vast body of rules and law which are beginning to alter the basis of coexistence and cooperation in the global order and which challenge sovereign statehood. Gradually trade agreements, and aid or loan programmes, contain democratic and human rights requirements and obligations, while the protection of basic humanitarian values transcends the claims of nation states, and can lead to military interventions on behalf of the 'world community' by bodies such as NATO, as occurred in the states of the old Yugoslavian Federation in the 1990s.

As we remarked in previous chapters, there is an increasing role for international law to constrain national sovereignty and a tendency for rights to become post-national, as a further sign of the erosion of the nation state, and again one encouraged by the supraterritorial consequences of globalization. For some these developments are breaking the nexus between citizenship and the nation state. Rather, citizenship is 'post-national' and belongs to individuals as part of 'universal personhood' rather than 'national belonging' (Soysal, 1994: 1; also 2000).

Global bodies, such as the UN and international courts of justice, help sustain such notions and overcome state reluctance, leading to the greater integration of foreigners, including migrants, into citizenship schemes. However, while citizenship rights are formally universal – in principle they are granted to citizens on the grounds that they are human beings – in modern times they have been guaranteed by nation states. There are now multiple statuses in western liberal democracies in relation to citizen rights, including those that have certain rights without citizenship, such as those of guest workers and refugees.

Thus, while the large-scale growth of supraterritorial spaces has extended capitalism's position as the dominant structure of production, the state has lost some predominance as a site of governance. Hirst (1997) is right, none the less, to emphasize that the nation state remains a major part of the new world order. It has, for example, attracted new powers in areas such as surveillance, and environmental and customer protection, as the result of globalization. But nation states do find it increasing difficult to control the global spaces that affect their jurisdictions, particularly capital and financial flows, and also to respond to the rise of transborder movements associated with gender, religion and ecology. Post-sovereign states have tended to become arenas of collaboration and competition between a complex array of territorial and supraterritorial interests. Departmental ministers can often find more in common with their functional counterparts abroad than with national ministerial colleagues.

States, then, remain an important entity through which the issues of supraterritoriality can be formulated and resolved, even if they no longer possess the independence and sovereignty of the nation state of previous years. As we noted above, globalization is a rather chaotic and multidirectional, multilevel set of processes that have differential effects in sectors and localities. Homogeneity and uniformity are not necessarily its key consequences and national cultures and institutions retain significant influences in determining policy and other responses to these processes. Intergovernmental bodies, such as the Council of the European Union, are key arenas in both advancing multilateralism and national state interests. Whereas international relations are interterritorial relations, global relations are supraterritorial. The former features crossborder exchanges over distance, while the latter is characterized by transborder exchanges without distance. Consequently, the processes of globalization are not ones of simply bringing to an end the territorial; sometimes the sentiments of nationalism at state level can be a reaction to the perception of too much supraterritoriality. After all, even supraterritorial phenomena have to touch ground sometimes and when they land they do so in territorial spaces run by nation states.

As we noted above the issue of whether supraterritoriality and globalization mark the end of the nation state is to note that adaptability is not the same as weakness, and that changing institutional terms do not necessarily lead to a diminution of state power. State power may be less a matter of dominating society and more to do with the capability for adjusting to new conditions in domestic and global environments (Pierre and Peters, 2000). This is particularly the case following liberalization recently in a number of countries.

Cosmopolitan law

The idea of cosmopolitan law (or global law) has been developed to refer to a form of law that differs from that internal to nation states, and also to that operating as agreements between territories. However, it is still created by states as limitations, rights and responsibilities that surpass the assertions of individual nations and which generally aim to articulate and to defend basic humanitarian values, particularly as these collide with national law (Held, 1996; Held *et al.*, 1999). State sovereignty is not accepted as the sole principle for the direction of political arrangements within or between states, which must operate according to universal standards. Perhaps the best-known examples of such law lies in the application of such universal humanitarian standards to war crimes or crimes against humanity, such as the recent trial of Slobodan Milosevic at the International Court of Justice at the Hague. Environmental protection law, however, can also fit within the category of global law. Increasingly we find that customary or informal sentiments as to what constitutes human rights or civilized behaviour are becoming more formal and are being codified and incorporated within international agreements. The Weberian notion that states are defined by their legitimate monopoly of the right to engage in warfare on behalf of their inhabitants is clearly checked and bounded by such law; no longer can might be right, even in warfare.

The Nuremburg Tribunal trials of German and other defeated leaders at the end of the Second World War, and also those tribunals that were used to try Japanese leaders in Tokyo, introduced international rules that defended basic human values even in the face of state laws. Individuals, whenever they had a moral choice, were expected to disavow governmental orders if they violated basic universal rights. Increasingly in recent years we have seen a strong move away from the idea that such notions of international humanitarian law were simply an inter-state mode, to one where international criminal and other courts can promulgate law and establish rules. However, not every state has been willing to subscribe to all of these developments, as the unwillingness of the US and some other countries to sign up to the International Criminal Justice Court testifies. Such countries not only feel that their state sovereignty may be compromised but that such arenas are easily used for wider political purposes, such as the arraigning of top US government officials.

Global democracy

There is considerable interest in the notion of 'democratizing globalization' and theorists, particularly David Held (2002), have argued that the notion of 'cosmopolitanism' is relevant here too. The starting-point is the vast panoply of transnational bodies that have developed to deal with the collective policy issues of globalization and its consequences. Global interconnectedness, and the growth of supranational agencies and multilayers of governance, is seen as generating many 'overlapping communities of fate' across countries, rather than the silo-like national political communities we have been accustomed to. This results in disjunctures between globalization and the nation state, with many political issues now capable for resolution only outside the state, and with traditional processes of accountability similarly shifted 'upward'. The result is the need for 'a cosmopolitan framework of accountability and regulation' and the objective of securing 'a common framework of standards and political action, given shape and form by a common framework of institutional arrangements' (Held, 2002: 308).

Box 7.1 Features of cosmopolitan democracy

1. The people govern through communities, associations, states, international organizations, and all are subject to cosmopolitan democratic law
2. The form of global governance is *heterarchy* – a divided authority system subject to cosmopolitan democratic law.
3. The key democratization instruments are constitutional and institutional reconstruction, intensification of globalization and regionalization, new social movements, and possible global crises.
4. The traditions of democratic thought are liberal democratic theory and developmental democracy, participatory democracy, and civic republicanism.
5. Its ethic of global governance is 'democratic autonomy'.
6. The mode of political transformation is reconstruction of global governance.

Source: Adapted from Held *et al.* (1999: 448).

These provide the basis, and are seen to offer real prospects, for what has been termed 'cosmopolitan democracy' (Held, 1996; Delanty, 2000). What is required is the development of independent political resources and institutions, particularly mechanisms for accountability, at regional and global levels as a complement to those in local and national political systems. For example, the EU and the UN would require parliamentary forms of decision-making for ensuring greater popular involvement in the determination of those decisions which are global in character and where, because of this, the jurisdiction of suprastate bodies would be superordinate to the powers of nation states. This would also allow more effective cosmopolitan 'peacekeeping' operations to be undertaken under the auspices of bodies such as the UN in the context of the decline in 'old' war-making between states and the development of stateless and insurgent 'new wars' (Kaldor, 2001). None the less, local, national, regional and global democratic structures would be essentially complementary and specifically defined.

However, whether nation states are prepared to concede such authority, and whether global democracy might meaningfully be 'a stretch too far', are at best open questions. Furthermore, national governments have appeared anxious to respond to the democratic and other concerns raised by globalization, and there have been successes for the anti-globalizers. Governments appear more willing to seek wider access to debt relief in many poorer parts of the world, for example, while some businesses have acceded to demands that wage and other conditions in their supplying, mostly poorer countries, become 'fairer' or less 'exploitative'. Moreover, anti-globalists have proved adept at using the technologies and methods of globalization to good effect; their use of the internet and related information and communication technologies is often better, quicker and more effective than their corporate and governmental targets. These 'concessions' may help to underpin state legitimacy in the face of globalizing processes.

'Cosmopolitanism', however, refers not only to political arrangements in these views but also constitutes a new form of self, and which is a product of international and global relations. Global person is a cosmopolitan. Although cosmopolitanism is not a new concept, within the context of globalization it assumes a new form of subjectivity in which individuals feel attached to a 'world culture'. It follows from the erosion of national identity by globalization and offers the hope of an end to nationalism and ethnic wars. The less parochial world citizen should be more tolerant than its national counterpart and be an amalgam of the best of all the world's culture (Kanter, 1995; Strange, 1996; Tomlinson, 1999; Held *et al.*, 1999; Pollock *et al.*, 2000). In these understandings of the term, cosmopolitanism is being used as a kind of utopian vision – the ideals of cosmopolitanism have not been achieved but such a prospect is one to which we might aspire. However, here we find one of its major difficulties as a concept, its lack of specificity. No doubt because it functions as an ideal image, writers such as Pollock *et al.* (2000) suggest that it is indefinable. In fact, it is a very non-cosmopolitan action to try to define cosmopolitanism.

Consequently cosmopolitanism seems a rather spectral phenomenon. Underlying the emergence of this new, idealized type of citizen who inhabits the flows of the post-national world is the idea that the Westphalian settlement has well and truly run its course. Western nations are no longer sacrosanct, and the permeability of borders and the slow death of sovereignty have given rise to a new form of subjectivity. Yet, as we noted in the previous chapter, we are a long way from being able to pronounce the end of the nation state. Not only is the nation state still the fundamental governmental mechanism of world capitalism, but it is still held to be accountable for international exploitation (however much politicians seek to shuffle it off to the vague world of 'globalization').

We have yet to see, too, studies that actually set out to measure cosmopolitan attitudes and to ascertain whether, in fact, this new form of subjectivity is so different from the old. The suspicion is that it will be shown to be scarcely different: what passes for cosmopolitanism is often the rather (politically) trivial, such as enjoyment of the world cuisines or of the many global forms of music. The reaction to the events of 11 September 2001 did not suggest that many westerners were that interested in understanding other cultures. As we noted in our earlier discussion of Chinese rationalities (see Chapter 3), the forms of person-hood that underlie the political practices of different parts of the world are deeply ingrained and anthropologically varied. It seems *prima facie* unlikely that a new form of self can be ushered in over the period of a few short few years just because more individuals can travel more widely and extensively. While it is important to more fully comprehend the kinds of changes increased global mobility might be causing to the subjectivity of those westerners who are rich enough to engage in it, the range of such experience remains still substantially limited.

In the notions of global democracy articulated by Held, not only nation states but also global civil society and the social movements that help to comprise it are subject to a wider framework of cosmopolitan democratic law. As Baker (2002) points out, if such law is going to be effective and to be regarded as legitimate it requires sovereign institutions at worldwide level, which themselves will be constrained by such law. Although civil society is regarded as a key instrument for achieving democratic global governance, it must also be an object of such an order. This may be regarded as at variance with those who regard global civil society as organized and operating outside the forces of the state and even of international law. Such cosmopolitans, who place their hopes for global democracy in global social movements rather than in the frameworks of state-supported global law, and in transnational political institutions, see state and legal structures as relegated to the hinterland, for they act essentially as brakes on progress for achieving global democracy. They question how Held, and others committed to 'stretching the state and the law globally', explain which instruments will achieve global democracy if they are not found in global civil society, rather than in the existing frameworks that remain predominantly the creation of nation states and which are likely to act negatively on the progress of transnational democracy.

However, it is not clear how, without the powers of national and international state institutions, global civil society groups can achieve their goals. Moreover, if they are successful, as groups that are predominantly western in composition and orientation, their outlooks and influence may increase inequalities between nations and threaten the equal sovereignty of nations as expressed in prevailing interpretations of state-backed international law.

These issues highlight a further set of questions: to whom are the anti-globalization protesters, or even non-governmental organizations such as Oxfam, accountable? Will the imposition of new labour standards on factories in developing countries result in their workers losing their jobs as a result of declining competitiveness? Will the alleviation of debt relief in some countries, if not all, where corruption and inefficiency prevail, lead to greater economic misery in the longer term with the withdrawal of levers (like those provided by bodies such as the World Trade Organization or the International Monetary Fund) that might have promoted anti-corruption structural reform?

Clearly nation states and supraterritorial and other trans- and inter- national bodies will be central agencies in determining the pace of the progress or the regress of globalization and its democratic forms into the first decades of the new millennium.

Chapter 8

The Liberal State

So far we have focused on the state's historical emergence, current powers, and future prospects in the context of globalization. We have recognized democracy as a major variable that has facilitated the emergence and development of the modern state. At this point, we need to enlarge our discussion of liberalism, which we have dealt with only sporadically; liberalism, like democracy, will be seen to coexist with the western or 'modern' form of the state. It is important to understand liberalism as directly related to the state and its functions: in particular, this chapter will focus on how liberalism provided the possibilities for a regeneration of the state in the late eighteenth and early nineteenth centuries, and how continuing transformations in liberal thought can be mapped onto transformations in the state, and especially in the relationship between the state and civil society.

The major task is to analyse this relationship from the late eighteenth century onwards. The focus initially will be on three themes. First, the nation state's dependence on liberalism and its rejection of other, historically earlier, mentalities of government, such as the police state, will be stressed. Second, the twentieth-century 'triumph' of liberalism over other, 'non-democratic' mentalities of government will be examined. Third, the peculiar relationship between liberalism and individualism will be explored, with specific reference to the forms of personal identity which emerged in the heyday of liberalism. In all of these settings, the focus will be on how the state's form and functions were transformed by liberalism.

Then we shall build on our discussion of liberalism to discuss the latest incarnation of this political rationality, neo-liberalism. Our discussion will begin with a rough attempt at definition, which focuses on neo-liberalism as a specific, timebound version of liberalism that invents a new understanding of the market and its significance for the rest of society. The importance of a number of precursors to neo-liberalism – commonly regarded as failures – such as Nazism and Keynesianism, will be stressed. In developing our discussion of the theoretical base of neo-liberalism, we shall spend some time discussing the *Ordoliberalen*, the Chicago School, and the ideas of von Hayek. We shall try to understand how this doctrine – economic, political and social – was put into practice in a number of states around the world from the 1970s. Following Nikolas Rose, we argue that these practical neo-liberal programmes of government focused on three problem areas: the downgrading and 'economizing' of (often informal and tacit) professional knowledge; the reorganization of governmental departments and the devolving of powers to a rapidly proliferating number of quangos, such as regulatory agencies; and the invention of a new type of citizenship in which activity and entrepreneurialism were extended to every conceivable area of life.

Precursors to liberalism: from Machiavelli to *raison d'état*

While we can track the emergence of liberalism as a political philosophy at least back as far as John Locke (1632–1704) in the seventeenth century, liberalism as a political programme has a much more recent history. Roughly, we might say that this latter form of liberalism did not become established until the beginning of the nineteenth century. Its emergence must be understood as a critique of *raison d'état*, which in its turn was closely associated with *polizeiwissenschaft*. So we need to proceed more slowly here, and describe the political systems against which political liberalism contrasted itself and which it aimed (successfully) to supplant.

We can start with Niccolò Machiavelli's *The Prince* (1513), a text written for the Medici family in Florence, and intended as a guidebook for the maintenance of political power. This text, destined to be read and reread over the centuries, and regarded as more or less scandalous at various points (Foucault, 1978, discusses the strength of anti-Machiavellianism at the end of the sixteenth century, for example), is of course famous for advising the prince to do whatever is necessary to maintain power, and to worry less about being loved than being feared. Yet what is interesting for our purposes about *The Prince* is that Machiavelli's theorization of power begins and ends with one individual: the sovereign. The sovereign's relation to his territory is both crucial yet always tenuous. By contrast, little more than a hundred years later when Thomas Hobbes produces his *Leviathan* (1651), the theorization of power has moved to an abstract, non-human and potentially eternal entity, the (sovereign) state.

For Hobbes, as we noted in Chapter 3, the state is an unpleasant necessity to mitigate the selfishness of civilized humans who do not live under the law, and who otherwise would engage in a war of all against all (see van Krieken, 2002). Hobbes's characterization of the impersonal nature of the state dovetails with an emerging conception of the state as having an autonomous (and especially non-religious) rationality (the pope called it 'the devil's reason'). As early as the sixteenth century we can trace the emergence of this (at first scandalous, because secular and even atheist) notion of *raison d'état* ('reason of state'), which served as a proto-philosophy for the absolutist state whose birth we discussed in Chapter 2. The notion of the so-called 'rational state' – typically a highly centralized absolutist state, of which the paradigm case was Prussia – attracted a highly developed political philosophy known as *Polizeiwissenschaft* (or the science of police), the aim of which was the exhaustive disciplinary regulation of social, cultural, economic and political life (Pasquino, 1978; Tribe, 1984). *Raison d'état* is about the maintenance of the power of the state (which is potentially eternal), rather than of the power of the prince (which is limited to one human lifetime). While Hobbes's text is the most famous example of the literature which begins to theorize this eternal state as the most important unit of politics, such a notion can also be seen in German, French and Italian contexts (Chemnitz, 1647; La Perriere, 1567; Botero, 1589; Palazzo, 1606).

An excellent discussion of the philosophical elements of these police states is given by Oestreich (1982), which especially stresses the neo-stoic development of a fiercely militaristic and highly regulatory system of government. Neo-stoicism equipped the individual citizen with a mental and physical toughness, and in accustoming the citizen to privation, made him ready for warfare – a vital accomplishment in sixteenth- and seventh-century Europe. Of course, these sorts of skills proved vital in the development of more recent states: Elias's *The Germans* (1996) is an account of how late nineteenth-/early twentieth-century aristocratic ethics of toughness, aggression, and readiness for battle eventually made their way down into the middle and lower classes. As Elias tells the story, this is the fundamental ethical moment in the evolution of Nazism – something we shall return to later in the chapter.

As Dean (1999: 84–9) points out, neo-stoicism is vital because it turns a focus on self-government – now seen as essential throughout the citizen body. Self-government or self-mastery, the ultimate aim of neo-stoicism, becomes required both for the government of the household and the government of the state. We thus have a three-level theory of government (self, family, state) that enables politics to be conceived of in a radically new and more comprehensive fashion. The anti-Machiavellian literature moves from a model in which politics/government is simply the relation between the prince and the state, to one in which politics/government is about macro-, meso- and micro-levels of the social body.

Dean (1999: 86) also draws our attention to the fact that we must conceive of *raison d'état* as existing within Machiavelli's 'moral universe' (see also Skinner, 1978): *raison d'état* is a notion that emerges in the critiques of Machiavelli (see especially Budé (1547), and the work of Justus Lipsius). None the less, the emergence of *raison d'état* marks a discontinuity in the history of government, 'a rupture ... with divine, natural or even human law' (Dean, 1999: 87). Not least of its achievements was its ability to offer a new way of visualizing government outside of previously prevailing Christian notions, a vital move in an era torn apart by religious wars (see Hunter, 2001, who provides a more detailed context for these shifts, but is perhaps less keen than Foucault to see these as constituting discontinuities in notions of sovereign power). Foucault (1978, 1981) also discusses the models of government that precede *raison d'état*.

Police

Hobbes himself is aware of the importance of discipline and self-discipline in the social contract, commenting in *De Cive* that 'man is made fit for Society not by nature, but by training' (1642: 25). As we have seen already, the series of doctrines we call *raison d'état* implied a model of government in which self-discipline was tantamount. If we follow this concern with discipline and order a little further, we come across a notion known as 'police' (especially in Germany, where it is *Polizei*). This is a term that is used in continental Europe as early as the thirteenth century (Dean, 1999: 90), but was sufficiently important in the seventeenth and eighteenth centuries to be the object of a 'science' of ordering (*Polizeiwissenschaft*). It is easy for this term to be confusing to an Anglophone audience used to 'police' as a fairly narrow concept, but it covers a much larger range of problems and concerns than the term now designates: *Polizei* may be translated better as 'policy'. The term 'police' was not current in Britain in the seventeenth and eighteenth centuries, but it began to be used with more frequency after 1790, although to refer specifically to the organized police force.

But what exactly is 'police'? Von Justi's definition captures its mood eloquently:

> The purpose of policing is to ensure the good fortune of the state through the wisdom of its regulations, and to augment its forces and its power to the limits of its capability. The science of policing consists, therefore, in regulating everything that relates to the present condition of society, in strengthening and improving it, in seeing that all things contribute to the welfare of the members that compose it. The aim of policing is to make everything that composes the state serve to strengthen and increase its power, and likewise serve the public welfare. (Justi, 1768, cited in Donzelot, 1979: 7)

We can take two points from this definition: first, we can see evidence for the 'regulation mania' (Oestreich, 1982: 157) that was so characteristic of police states. Second, we must not lose sight of the fact that *Polizeiwissenschaft* was not fundamentally conceived of as a negative science: rather, its focus lay on the increased production, the maximization, of health, wealth, happiness, and anything else that might make the state strong. The science of order was fundamentally a science of the state. As we have discussed in Chapter 2, the historical emergence of the absolutist state needs to be traced back to the ways in which the *Stände* (or estates) broke down the feudal simplicity of government, as the relationship between a sovereign and his territory, and allowed government to become multilayered and 'civilized'. The science of police is the maturation of this process. It is important that we remember that this 'civilization' is not just a process of 'big politics' (at the state, or inter-state, levels), but that it also operates at the level of the civilizing of the warrior citizen (Elias, 1982). We shall elaborate on this notion of the civilizing process below.

A third point we need to make is that although police and absolutism existed simultaneously, these two differ in their degree of centralization. Police was not seen as emerging only from the state, but was intended to be a notion that suffused everyday life (Knemeyer, 1980; Raeff, 1983).

Information-gathering and the emergence of 'population'

Cesare Beccaria is rather typical of political theorists during this period. For Beccaria (1970), it is only possible to arrive at a healthy state with an efficient police, and an efficient police can only be guaranteed if we can obtain an appropriate knowledge base. Beccaria, then, enunciates the need for a statistics, or a science of the state. As this call is taken up, by the mid-eighteenth century, we may say that the population has been 'discovered'. A variety of (mostly amateur) investigations into the quality and habits of the inhabitants of various territories had revealed this entity, the population, which required a new approach to government (for a detailed discussion of this amateur fact-collecting in the nineteenth century, see Hacking, 1986). The population emerges as the state is understood as a *demographic* phenomenon, one that no longer can be governed in the manner of the feudal governing of the family. There is a sharp discontinuity between models of government that have a domestic or familial orientation, and those that target 'population'; the latter is the object of 'bio-politics' (Foucault, 1979: 139). Bio-politics is the attempt to govern the various processes of life itself: birth, morbidity, mortality.

The government of the family was the key to the philosophy of government in the early modern state. Just as the king was head of the state, so each father was head of his household, the structures at the macro- and the micro-levels mirroring each other (Foucault, 1981). However, the discovery of the problem of population allowed the problem of the government of the state to be conceptualized anew – henceforth, it became possible to understand government as targeting a variety of *layers* of society, such as the young, the criminal, the indigent, and so forth. The moment of the discovery of population relegated the family to merely an instrument of government, rather than its target. Governing a state came to be no longer simply a matter of governing a territory (and incidentally governing the inhabitants of that territory through family structures that mimicked the pastoral power of the king); it came to be about governing the population and the 'social, cultural, environmental, economic and geographic conditions under which humans live, procreate, become ill, maintain health or become healthy, and die' (Dean, 1999: 99).

To a certain extent the problem of population, and the information about the population that slowly began to be produced, highlighted the failure of the police state. Studies of the population focused on its pathologies: its criminality, its madness, its divorce rates, its illness, its poverty and so forth. However, the population also came to be understood as an entity with its own rhythms and logic. Just as in the sixteenth century the state came to be understood as having its own internal, autonomous rationality, so too, in the eighteenth century, the population came to be understood as a kind of living organism with its own specific laws and characteristics. This was the moment at which the separation of the state and 'civil society' became necessary, empirically, theoretically, politically and ethically, and it seems that the major spur to this separation was the 'technicality' of population studies. Of course, this notional separation is one of the foundation stones of liberalism and of modern statecraft. Population, then, sounded the death-knell for *raison d'état* and *Polizeiwissenschaft*, since these were doctrines that amalgamated order and the social. Liberalism, the (by now) fully-fledged political philosophy, had been reinvented also as a way of governing. Crucially it ordered the social while appearing to maintain a strict separation between state governing processes and the autonomy of civil society.

Liberalism as a governmentality

Foucault (1978) describes 'governmentality' as a mentality or rationality of governing, and urges us to view liberalism in this light – that is, as a series of mundane, daily practices of social ordering – rather than as an idealized philosophy. A point worth stressing here is that Foucault's approach is rather different to classical state theory. For the latter, the state is the precondition of government – that is, government flows from the state. By contrast, Foucault views the state as a result of practices of government. In this way, we can see just how vital it is for us to have a firm understanding of liberalism if we wish to understand the form and functions of the state.

The task is to understand liberalism as a fine mesh of governmental activities: a convenient label for a series of practices that can be seen in families, in personal relations, in the workplace, in institutions, in internal statecraft and in international relations. We can sum up liberalism as the permanent problematization of government: whereas *Polizeiwissenschaft* did not shirk from governing (or trying to govern) every area of life, liberalism engaged in an almost neurotic worrying about whether government would do more harm than good. Liberalism can be seen as a direct critique of *raison d'état*, in that the latter was a doctrine of absolute rule, whereas the former was a doctrine of limitation and restraint.

Of course, the political philosophy of liberalism, emphasizing as it did personal freedom, equality, and the rights of rational man, was always likely to corrode the doctrines of *raison d'état* and the police state. However, the emerging economic liberal tradition, most closely associated with Adam Smith (1776), made it clear that certain areas of life were inappropriate realms for governmental intervention – most obviously the economy and civil society, but potentially many others. Hence liberalism engages with an ongoing process of reviewing the value of governing, and tends towards *laissez-faire* unless absolutely necessary. Smith's economic liberalism can also be seen as a critique of the versions of the 'analyses of wealth' known as cameralism and mercantilism, and involving state protectionism. To the extent that *Polizeiwissenschaft* was closely associated with such economic strategies, Smith's work is a direct refutation of police. Incidentally, Dean (1999: 92) argues, with the help of Small (1909), that mercantilism was considerably more than a mere economic doctrine but was 'the theory and practice of governmental management'. Dean (1999: 115) develops Small's argument about protectionism to suggest that Smith does not inaugurate a new economic science so much as a new science of government, in that Smith's primary concern is not so much governing (or not governing) the economy as governing the social *through* the economy. Smith, as we have seen in earlier chapters, theorized the 'hidden hand' of the economy, an unknowable motor for economic developments that we regulated at our peril; but by analogy, liberalism is able to see that more than just the economy might benefit from being granted a certain autonomy from government.

It is hard to overestimate the importance of this new way of seeing how the art of government might best work; as a point of departure, it allowed the emergence of a new politics which could cross from left to right and back again. While the lineage of Smith's approach to new right policies is well documented, it is also worth reminding ourselves that other political perspectives, from revolutionary socialist through to anarchist, have made use of this watershed in the conceptualization of the limits of governing. The young Marx, for example, made an almost direct link from Smith's work to his theorization of the state and civil society as inimical to each other, with the former parasitical upon the latter, which is by nature virtuous. Similar understandings can be teased out of thinkers from diverse intellectual traditions such as Thomas Paine and William Godwin. Here we must remember the discovery of the population that we noted earlier, which in its liberal problematization turns into the issue of the government of the social (Donzelot, 1979). There is a continuation here of the *Polizeiwissenschaft* themes of the maximization of the individual citizen's contribution to the strength of the state, yet there are subtle differences in the liberal incarnation. Not least of these differences is the necessity for government to be internalized within the citizen, rather than externally imposed: in this way, liberal government of the social can still be said to be free, in that citizens 'choose' forms of social ordering (such as social insurance – Ewald, 1991) of their own free will.

Competing rationalities of government

Liberalism generally saw off its predecessor governmentalities, but during the nineteenth and twentieth centuries, a number of alternative models of government emerged. Foucault (1981) argues that the modern western constellation of governmental possibilities is framed by two trends, the attempt to govern at the individual level (what he calls the 'pastoral' model or the 'shepherd game', as the good shepherd guards his sheep and as God guards his flock), and the attempt to govern at the level of a community (what he calls the 'city game'). The fusion of these two models (governing *omnes et singulatim*) is characteristic of liberalism, but Foucault is clear that this coupling is somewhat 'demonic' – so it should not surprise us that it gave rise to other forms of government less palatable to most modern sensibilities than liberalism. As has already been foreshadowed, both Marxism and anarchism are also built on the fundamental liberal premise of the separation of state and the social, even though they all make use of the permeability of that boundary to postulate governing *through* society.

Mitchell Dean makes a useful distinction between three levels of 'illiberality' that, just as with liberalism proper, have their origins in the coupling of shepherd and city games (individual and community) and are predicated on the notion of bio-politics (governing the very processes of life itself, such as birth and death). He distinguishes non-liberal practices that are embedded in liberal rationalities; non-liberal practices that somehow achieve levels of legitimacy within liberal rationalities; and 'proper' non-liberalism (Dean 1999:134). State racism and eugenics are examples of the first two. Yet it is the third that is of most interest to us. Nazism is the most striking example here. Nazism is characterized by Dean, citing Peukert (1993), as a variation of liberalism, in which 'mass wellbeing' becomes transmogrified into 'mass annihilation'. Yet, as we have already seen, although this is a kind of 'pathological' liberalism, any reader of Weber would recognize the potential for this sort of configuration of state violence, since the monopoly of legitimate state force is the foundation of modern political systems, and, in that sense, is thus 'available' for pathological distortion. Peukert is especially forceful in implicating the human sciences in the governmental system of Nazism, since they produce an ever more closely defined and harsher set of norms (of blood, of race, of *Volk*, of 'fitness for life') which lead to a genocide focused within German society and without. In this reading, the similarities between liberalism and Nazism are quite striking, in that the human sciences also provided the techniques for the liberal attempt to govern through social life, and govern through constituting the citizen as a self-governing entity (as we discuss in more detail below).

However, in the West, it is socialism, rather than Nazism, that has provided the most consistent challenge and alternative to liberalism. Bobbio (1990) argues that a similar symbiotic relationship has existed between socialism and democracy as between liberalism and democracy: although these pairings often are troubled, in general both liberals and socialists believe their political systems are congruent with democracy. The major politico-philosophical difference between liberalism and socialism lies respectively in the insistence upon or rejection of private property as the key to freedom (Bobbio, 1990: 74). While liberals regard economic freedom as predicated on the right to private property, the socialist critique sees collective ownership as the only route to (economic and especially social) freedom; for socialism, then, the liberal defence of property reveals it to be an ideology of the ruling class. However, as a series of governmental strategies, the differences between liberal and socialist governments (or perhaps we should say 'social governments' and include the social democracies of, for example, Scandinavia) have often been difficult to spot. Certainly, we might notice the principles of *laissez-faire* more or less strongly emphasized, a stronger or weaker welfare system, and more or less state ownership of utilities. However, the similarities outweigh the differences. Virtually all those elements that we have described as characteristic of liberalism can be seen in socialism. It would seem that there is a case for characterizing socialism as a variant of liberalism.

Forms of self: liberal techniques of government

As we have already suggested, it would be a mistake to take at face value the notion that liberalism is about 'governing less'. Rose (1990) has argued that the nineteenth-century liberal states engaged in an endless process of inventing appropriate techniques of government, which focused on equipping citizens with the wherewithal to govern themselves, to maximize their own happiness, wealth, health, and so forth. We are reminded of the aims of the police state: yet the crucial difference between *raison d'état* and liberalism lay in the locus of control – while *raison d'état* worked with a notion of a citizenry who needed to be externally (corporeally) regulated to be happy, liberalism worked with a notion of a citizenry who needed to be taught how to guarantee their own happiness.

It should not surprise us, then, to find that education is one of the major sites of this new political rationality. Liberal thought comes to prioritize education as the technique by which citizens can be retrained (specifically, they can be divested of the morality of their class and their ancestors, and they can learn the life skills necessary for self-actualization). Education became an important battleground for government in the nineteenth century: on the one hand, it appeared that a lack of education might endanger the individual and the state (mostly through the correlation that began to be made between lack of education and crime, but also through studies which suggested that the best-educated nations were the most successful in the international arena, whether success is measured by military or commercial criteria); on the other hand, there was the worry that mass education might be a prelude to mass revolution (Jones and Williamson, 1979). However, slowly the force of the former argument began to overpower the latter, and most of the advanced liberal democracies of the West moved towards compulsory mass education – for example, in England and in Australia in the 1870s, in the USA from 1852 (first in Massachusetts), in Prussia in 1868 and in France in 1882. Two points are worth noting here in passing. First, the state slowly assumed control of a variegated edifice that had been in the main constructed by philanthropists and the religious orders; the evolution of a compulsory education system is no purposeful state design, but a rather contingent series of shifts, acquisitions, and moments of short-term strategy (on this point, see Hunter, 1994). This gives us quite a different perspective from the conspiracy theorists in the history of education, who imagine the school to be a much more consciously constructed entity, purpose-built for the enslavement of the population (Bowles and Gintis, 1976; Bourdieu and Passeron, 1990). It is also a different perspective from that which sees the school as the historical means for working-class self-actualization, but an instrument that has been corrupted (Green, 1990).

The second point is that we should not forget the philosophical difficulty for liberalism of compulsory schooling. Liberals, of course, worry about any forms of compulsion in the realm of civil society, and so it was a peculiar set of arguments which, in a sense, deferred freedom to a moment after compulsion: you can be free, the argument ran, but only after we have forced you to learn the skills which will enable you to be free. Liberalism is full of such paradoxes, yet once the arguments in the field of education had been made, it became easier and easier to transfer them to other realms, such that freedom became the result of a series of (more or less) authoritarian practices, rather than the natural state of the human being (for a more detailed discussion on liberal freedom, see Brown, 1996; Rose, 1999). Areas such as public health and welfare were similarly colonized by liberal governments, with the dual focus of a compulsory health, or welfare, and the tactic of equipping citizens with enough know-how that they could manage their own affairs in these domains.

Expertise: governing through social life

Such liberal tactics mean that we must take with a pinch of salt the liberal political philosophy that sharply demarcates public and private life, the state and civil society. Liberalism as a political practice is not a doctrine that necessarily respects these boundaries, not least because they have become so entangled in our societies. The big institutions such as the school, the hospital, the workhouse, and the prison, have required professional experts, increasingly employed by the state, to operate them successfully, and to inculcate moral norms. For example, it is clear that much hope was invested in the schools as places where (lower-class) children could be removed from the malign influences of their home life and be taught a new morality. While in the early part of the nineteenth century this sort of transformatory education was in the main accomplished by the teacher (especially the model of the teacher as a friend and mentor as articulated in Britain by Matthew Arnold and others), from the beginning of the twentieth century, psychological experts were adding their skills to this programme of social re-engineering. Rose (1999) has reconstructed the story of the incursion of psychological thought, and the growth of psychological expertise, not only in the school, but also in industrial relations, and in warfare. Rose's thesis is that psychology is one of the primary governmental techniques of liberalism: it designates appropriate norms of conduct, and then works with individuals to ensure they can achieve those norms. Importantly, Rose argues that psychological techniques quickly made their way down into the most private of realms, including relationship counselling and other forms of personal therapy. Elsewhere, Rose (1993) has discussed how, after the fall of the Berlin Wall, the rapidly liberalizing states of eastern Europe enthusiastically embraced these techniques, being especially keen on the development of psychologies of the workplace, of the environment, of personal relationships, and of individual self-motivation.

Rose calls this 'the gentle reshaping of desires'. Once again, we see that liberalism as a political practice is far from antagonistic towards the idea of governing or ordering almost every element of life. The crucial difference between liberalism and the political practices it supplanted lies in liberalism's attempts to govern the mind or soul of the citizen. Foucault (1977) stresses how important the English social reformer Jeremy Bentham's ideas were in the emergence of this attempt to reshape desires: Bentham, of course, famously devised the panopticon in 1791, a design for a building (typically a prison) which functioned as a kind of surveillance machine. The ever-present possibility of surveillance was designed to engender self-government in the unfortunate prisoner (or patient, or schoolchild, or worker).

We can also take another tack on this issue of the formation of types of liberal persons by using the work of Norbert Elias. To begin, we can remind ourselves that Elias (1996) also has a view on the emergence of Nazism, but one slightly different from the notion discussed above of Nazism as one possible product of the demonic coupling of shepherd and city games – what elsewhere Foucault has referred to as the 'governmentalisation of the state' (1977: 20). Elias constantly links state formation with novel personal ethics – in this regard he follows Weber – and produces an argument which tempers the theory of the development of the state in the Foucaultian governmentality literature. Using the same theoretical framework that allowed him to deal so successfully with the civilizing process in European court society (crudely, the transformation of warriors into gentlemen and the social elevation of women such that the two sexes became 'companions'), Elias first describes the nineteenth-century German aristocratic ethics based around a kind of 'might is right' philosophy. However, this is an ethics that existed alongside enormous reserves of self-control (for example, the drinking games that these classes engaged in meant that they consumed enormous amounts of alcohol, but the maintenance of self-control and personal propriety when drunk was critical – it was one of the markers of the true aristocrat). For Elias, this worship of power is transmitted down throughout German society to the middle and lower classes, but the aristocratic restraint is missing. What emerges is a national cult of the boundless exercise of violence, which found its most eloquent representative in Adolph Hitler. There is a nice symmetry, or perhaps complementarity, about what Foucault and Elias have to say about the emergence of (normal or pathological) liberal states out of absolutism, even though they appear to start from opposite ends (Foucault from the problem of sovereignty and discipline, and Elias from the problem of personal comportment).

Towards neo-liberalism

As we have seen, liberalism has established itself as the prime rationality or ethos of government in the West. It arose as a critique of systems of absolute rule (reason of state, police), and throughout its life it has seen off a variety of competing political rationalities, some of which have arisen from within liberalism itself. It is worth remarking, as Dean (1999: 51) does, that because liberalism can be understood and defined as a critique of overgoverning, it is constantly in the process of self-renewal: it constantly critiques itself and its previous governmental incarnations. It therefore has a reflexive and iterative character, generating new forms as it seeks to distance itself from the past. In this way, we can understand that liberalism at different historical conjunctures has regenerated itself as a critique of the governmental failures of the immediate past.

The early nineteenth-century versions of liberalism found their place, in part, by being non-totalizing – in contrast to notions of 'reason of state'. On the other hand, Keynesian versions of liberalism emerged against the perceived lack of market regulation (by the state, rather than the informal self-regulation of market actors themselves) in Great Depression-era liberalism (and which was followed, for example, in the 1930s US by New Deal social and regulatory interventions); and, in turn, economic rationalist versions of liberalism gained their voice as a critique of Keynesianism's greatest problem, welfare dependency.

Kendall and Wickham (1999) have made a similar theoretical point, arguing that failure is fundamental to liberalism in a way that is just not true for other rationalities of government: failure is always seen as the opportunity for renewal, and the starting point for new projects of social ordering. We concern ourselves, then, with liberalism's capacity for self-renewal, and its ability to transcend its own failures. We concentrate especially on the re-growth known as neo-liberalism. Thus, we need to finesse our earlier discussion of liberalism somewhat. It is common in political sociology to make a distinction between classical liberalism and neo-liberalism, and we intend to explore this distinction and what it adds in terms of political analysis.

What is neo-liberalism?

Our first task must be one of rough definition. What is neo-liberalism? To begin, in making a definition based on historical periodization, we may say that after the Second World War, liberalism took a new turn. This had two major temporal phases. The first phase is sometimes described as 'welfarism' (see, for example, Rose 1993), in which many advanced liberal democracies followed what might be termed a 'Keynesian' path, engaging in a variety of social insurance measures while following a 'mixed economy' strategy. We need to distinguish the various levels of welfare support offered throughout the world. In Europe, for example, Giddens (1998: 6–7) makes a useful distinction between the UK model, which emphasized social services and health; the Scandinavian model, which provided higher benefits from a higher tax base; the middle European models, which had a low commitment to social services, but well-funded benefits in other areas; and the southern European systems, which were similar to the middle European, but less comprehensive and with lower levels of support. The second phase emerged roughly in the 1970s, and is characterized by 'economic rationalism', the disposal of publicly owned national industries to the private sector ('privatization'), the rolling back of the welfare state, the introduction of market-style competition into a range of arenas previously uncontaminated by such an ethos, and enforced state-sponsored inspection of zones such as education and health (which had previously been granted a greater degree of professional autonomy). This second phase is what we term 'neo-liberalism'; however, we should be aware that it is common in the literature to distinguish these forms of liberalism by 'sphere', such as 'economic neo-liberalism', 'social neo-liberalism', 'political neo-liberalism', and so forth.

We can also make a second type of definition in terms of the relationship different forms of liberalism have to the *character* of society. Burchell (1996) has usefully described this turn as away from classical liberalism's conceptualization of society as 'natural' (Adam Smith, in this context, spoke of the 'natural system of liberty'), towards the neo-liberal understanding of the social sphere as one that needs to be actively constructed by government. The *locus classicus* is Hayek (1979), who describes society as an 'artefact'. In classical liberalism, civil society can be seen as a kind of resource for the invigoration of the state; consequently, the themes of the separation of state and civil society and the importance of a *laissez-faire* approach to economy and civil society are enormously important in eighteenth- and early nineteenth-century liberal political philosophy. As we saw earlier in this chapter, the discovery of 'population' and 'the social' is a fundamental moment in the birth of liberalism, but we need to stress that the social under classical liberalism is seen as spontaneous or naturally self-reproducing. There is a long and continuing history to this idea of the naturalness of social relations. A crucial early resource in political philosophy is Hobbes, who distinguishes a natural (although brutish) civil society that the state can and must regulate. The young Marx, of course, generated a new morally charged version of this idea in arguing that a virtuous natural civil society was endangered by a parasitic, artificial state. More recently, Habermas (1987b) has distinguished between system and lifeworld, the latter being the natural site of everyday relations. Further, Habermas suggests that we need to protect the natural virtues of the lifeworld, which are in danger of being strangled by the bureaucratic, artificial system. It is worth remarking that in this regard – in its re-characterization of what is natural and what is constructed – neo-liberalism is remarkably innovative: it is rarely given appropriate credit for its political inventiveness.

The neo-liberal turn is a complete reconsideration of this conception, in that government comes to be seen as the active constitution of the conditions under which civil society might flourish. The conditions include both the introduction of market forces and the attachment of performance targets in social areas such health, education, and so forth, and the associated requirements that individuals take responsibility for their own lives (rather than becoming dependent on state distribution). Interestingly, this emphasis on the need to constitute society artificially can potentially lead to the idea, most famously enunciated by Margaret Thatcher (1987; 1993: 620), that there is no such thing as society. Of course, she meant that there should be no such thing as a dependent, 'welfare' society. She did not resile from the governmental invention and imposition of frameworks that would allow individuals and families to constitute the most auspicious social conditions for themselves.

To a certain extent the philosophical differences between liberalism and neo-liberalism are slight: it is certainly the case that all the elements of neo-liberalism are contained within liberalism – responsibility, self-government, private rather than public ownership, an essentialization of the market, the attention to practices of freedom of the individual, and so forth. It might be accurate to say that it has only been because of socialist and social-democratic versions of liberalism that such notions as 'the welfare state' became embedded in liberal politics at all (certainly the *Ordoliberalen*, who we shall discuss below, regarded Keynesianism as a macroeconomic doctrine as illiberal, to the extent that it failed to understand market pricing mechanisms and intervened in fiscal and monetary matters to the detriment of society). Neo-liberalism, then, at one level, is an emphasis on certain well-established liberal themes. However, as a political practice, neo-liberalism is distinctive: in the neo-liberal political landscape of the 1970s and 1980s, especially in the policy directions of the Reagan and the Thatcher administrations in the US and the UK respectively, but also in Australia and New Zealand, there were stringent attempts to remove the 'nanny' state, to put an end to a perceived culture of welfare dependence, and to reinvigorate the nation by giving free rein to individuals' own entrepreneurial proclivities. While there is an element of reducing the state, what is fundamental to these efforts is that a more authoritative state must now concentrate on providing the conditions under which individual entrepreneurship, self-government, freedom and responsibility can be possible.

In terms of trying to define the differences between liberalism and neo-liberalism, then, we have seen that liberalism, as a doctrine of permanent self-critique, is always likely to generate new governmental rationalities. There is not one neo-liberalism, but many: we could understand Nazism, for example, as a form of neo-liberalism, since it was a response, within the liberal framework, to address the pathologies of the liberal Germany of the 1920s. In the same way, Keynesian policies can be understood as a neo-liberal response to the problems induced by lack of governmental monetary and social intervention in previous incarnations of liberalism. However, in common parlance, the term neo-liberalism is most closely associated with the models of the last thirty years, which focus on a new and reduced role for government as a 'condition provider', and argue that government must take a back seat to market forces. In these models, we see the old paradox of liberalism, in that it has an overt philosophy of social non-intervention, yet it cannot bear to leave civil society alone. Indeed, despite philosophies of 'deregulation', considerable state intervention and re-regulation has occurred, not least in the UK (Moran, 2003).

The post-war Keynesian experiment

As we have already discussed in Chapter 5, the post-Second World War period saw a shift in the style of western governments, whether they were from the left or the right of the political spectrum. State involvement in production and industry increased dramatically, and in Britain and elsewhere, the extraordinary conditions of the war economy were built upon as (especially, but not exclusively) heavy industry was taken into public ownership. The lessons of the war economy and of the inter-war Great Depression were that it might be possible and desirable to plan and manage economic demand to a much greater extent than was typically understood under classical liberal systems.

Allied to this planned economy were a number of social interventionist measures, including the provision of public housing, public health and welfare services, social security, and public education schemes. We stress that this change should be neither underestimated (it is clearly a renewal of and innovation within liberal ethics) nor overestimated (governmental intervention was limited to exchange mechanisms, while private capital was still the driving force behind production). All of this came together in what is sometimes called the 'mixed economy', in which an attempt was made to reach a consensus between capital and organized labour, around the goals of full employment (or at least low unemployment), low inflation, steady economic growth and a trade surplus. Keynesianism was an attempt to use fiscal and monetary instruments to help establish a mutually supportive relationship between economy and society.

John Maynard Keynes developed his macroeconomic theories in the 1920s and 1930s – a crucial indicator of his developing work is Keynes (1926) – in the context of liberal failure: the depressed western economies. There is an interesting point here about differing possible 'liberal' reactions to failure: Nazism and the planned economies of Keynesianism both began from the same economic problem, but generated radically different 'liberal' solutions.

The argument that economic management could and should be used to promote the wellbeing of the social was one that was eventually taken up enthusiastically, and, of course, periodically revived (for example, by Mauroy's French socialist government of 1981–4). Rose (1999) cites Tomlinson (1981) and Schott (1982) in expressing a certain scepticism about whether British economic policy was ever Keynesian; and he cites Weir and Skocpol (1985) in noting that Sweden and the US were perhaps more enthusiastically Keynesian than Britain ever was. As a macroeconomic theory, Keynesianism did not especially concern itself with the supply side of the economy, but with the 'social end' of economic strategy, seeking to manage demand through fiscal and monetary policy. The Beveridge Report (1942) generated a way of dovetailing macroeconomics with policies of social insurance (out of this report came governmental provision of health services, housing, accident insurance, workers' compensation, education, and so on), and was taken up in the post-war welfare state in Britain. Similar models were constructed elsewhere in Europe, especially in France. Another prominent strategy that fell by the wayside was corporatism, although it continued to flourish in parts of northern and central Europe. In Britain, Marshall's (1949/1963) lecture on citizenship draws our attention to the fact that this watershed in liberal government was understood as acting in concert with a clearly specified moral agent, the citizen, with its inherent rights and duties.

While Keynesianism is a critique of liberalism, and sees society as a realm that needs to be constructed, it is not yet neo-liberalism. We can pick up again on this point about the 'artificiality' of the social in this post-war welfare version of liberalism: as Dean points out, the hybrid, constructed citizen who emerges from Keynes/Beveridge/Marshall is 'the social subject with its needs, the prudential subject with its responsibilities, the economic subject with its interests, and the juridical subject with its rights' (Dean, 1999: 151). However, while Keynesianism can be regarded as a clear starting point for neo-liberalism, the emerging versions of neo-liberalism, contemporaneous with Keynesianism, such as those associated with the German *Ordoliberalen* or with the Chicago School, do, of course, set their critical sights on Keynes, and generate contrasting political philosophies, which we move on to discuss in the next section.

The *Ordoliberalen* and the Chicago School

The German *Ordoliberalen* (so-called because of their association with the journal *Ordo*) generated a series of novel propositions that proved vital in the regeneration of liberalism. These thinkers, mostly jurists and economists, were working from the 1920s in Germany, but were mostly in exile under Hitler's rule. Returning to Germany at the end of the war, they played a major part in the rebuilding of West Germany. In essence, they suggested that a variety of failures of liberalism – including the Depression and the Third Reich – were a result of the lack of the appropriate cultural, legal and social frameworks that would guarantee the correct working of the market. The *Ordoliberalen* were far removed from Adam Smith's natural system of liberty: for them, the market was understood as an artificial game of competitive liberty. This game was not to be guaranteed by market intervention, but by intervention into the vital conditions for the market-game: the rule of law, the surrounding culture, and the institutional frameworks. While they saw an analogy between the necessary competitiveness of the market and of social and cultural life (the latter should emulate the former), they none the less advocated policies of social assistance. As Gordon (1991: 42) summarizes, 'the major problem of social politics ... is not the anti-social effects of the economic market, but the anti-competitive effects of society'. Juridical and institutional interventionism was the order (pun intended) of the day, an interventionism that, it was hoped, would suffuse society with the appropriate competitive spirit: this, Rüstow (1980) calls *Vitalpolitik*:

> He [Rüstow] proposes that the whole ensemble of individual life be structured as the pursuit of a range of different enterprises: a person's relation to his or her self, his or her professional activity, family, personal property, environment, etc., are all to be given the ethos and structure of the enterprise-form. This 'vital policy' will foster a process of 'creation of ethical and cultural values' within society. (Gordon, 1991: 42)

This emerging philosophy has many of the elements of what we now recognize as neo-liberalism. To the modern sensibility, it is perhaps jarring to see a mixture of market-led policies and social insurance: but this should serve to remind us that 'purer' forms of neo-liberalism have never quite purged themselves of social government, and that there is a direct line of descent between the *Ordoliberalen* and the 'There is no alternative' (TINA) neo-liberalism of Margaret Thatcher and Keith Joseph.

The Chicago School theorists, the most prominent of whom was Gary C. Becker (see, for example, Becker, 1964, 1976), took a more radical approach to the relationship of the market and the social. While the *Ordoliberalen* aimed to govern the social to preserve and strengthen the economic, the Chicago neo-liberals, who established a number of strong links with their German colleagues, proposed that the social become a *form* of the economic. While the *Ordoliberalen* regarded the market as a rather fragile entity, for the Chicago economists, by contrast, the market was so robust that its rationality could be extended to the social – including crime, family life, work life, and so forth, as we mentioned briefly in Chapter 5. The Chicago economists' work can be seen as a reaction to the 'overgovernment' of the New Deal and the US wartime economy, but it was also profoundly influenced by the behaviourism that was in vogue in the US in the social sciences of the 1950s and 1960s (see Chapter 4). The starting point for their radical reconceptualization of the social lay in the idea that all rational behaviour is about deciding which resources are best devoted to which ends. Once all rational human behaviour has been understood as economic behaviour, government becomes nothing more or less than economic government.

The rational economic actor's choice is his/her defining characteristic, allowing *homo economicus* to supplant the theorizations of 'man' that had been developed in anthropology, sociology, psychology, criminology, and so on. As Gordon (1991: 43) makes clear, this is a reactivation of the Scottish Enlightenment's economic agent; yet it is also a rewriting of what Adam Smith and his like-minded theorists had in mind, since the behaviourist element in the Chicago characterisation allows *homo economicus* to be manipulable – 'perpetually responsive to modifications in his environment' (*ibid.*). In addition, Becker and his colleagues construct the notion of entrepreneurship as a model for the permanent project of self-development, a notion that is crucial for later neo-liberalism. The Chicago School suggested that the individual needed to conceptualize his or her skills and aptitudes in the language of the market, as human capital, which can be put to work to earn revenue (wages). A skill or aptitude is a 'quasi-machine for the production of a value' (Gordon, 1991: 44), while activities such as education come to be understood as investment in the (long-term project of the) self. Life, for the Chicago School, is an enterprise.

This latter notion has clearly been vital in contemporary neo-liberal politics, as the emphasis has shifted away from Keynesian safety-net provision to individual responsibility for one's own life projects. For example, in governmental interventions into education, we have seen the stimulation of 'lifelong learning' (it is no longer acceptable to imagine one is finished with education). Meanwhile, in health provision, the move towards private health cover has been associated with an educative function that stresses self-management and preventative health practices. Even at the level of popular culture, as any frequenter of airport bookshops will attest, the notions of self-help and self-development have made fortunes for a huge number of lifestyle gurus who have outlined the magnificent possibilities for the individual who 'takes control' (and, once again, it seems impossible – or culturally idiosyncratic – to argue that one does not want to be developed).

For neo-liberals, this notion of life as a project solves the problem of the possible descent of economic man into selfishness, greed, and acquisition for its own sake; a solution just as neat as the one Weber identified for his proto-capitalist Protestants. As Gordon argues, this right to permanent retraining has become enshrined in neo-liberal-inspired legislation, but has usually been played out via a

> technical content [which] has relied heavily on the contributions of the 'new psychological culture', that cornucopia of techniques of the self which symbiotize aptitude with self-awareness and performance with self-realization (not to mention self-presentation). What some cultural critics diagnose as the triumph of auto-consuming narcissism can perhaps be more adequately understood as a part of the managerialization of personal identity and personal relations which accompanies the capitalization of the meaning of life. (Gordon, 1991: 44)

We have dwelt a while on these early moves in neo-liberalism, since they enunciate some of the fundamentals of its later ethos and practice. First, they establish the artificiality of the social; second, they understand the market as the source of liberty, and a true description (in the case of the Chicago School) of other areas of life, especially the social; third, they stress the importance of the manipulation of the frameworks (*Ordoliberalen*) or the stimuli (Chicago School) that surround the market; finally, they construct a new notion of self, in which actors can be seen as fundamentally economic, while their aptitudes and skills can be understood as human capital. As for the state: it has moved from being 'social' to being 'enabling' (Rose, 1999: 142).

Hayek

In his 1944 book, *The Road to Serfdom*, Friedrich Hayek launched his highly influential critique of state intervention. Nazi Germany and the Stalinist Soviet Union were pilloried as examples of whither excessive state control could lead. In addition, however, other somewhat milder versions of liberal interventionism – especially Keynesianism – were attacked. Hayek's notion of freedom is important here: it is somewhat different to that presented in the works of the *Ordoliberalen*, in that freedom is an artefact of civilization. Within Hayek's framework, there are three 'levels', nature, culture and reason, and it is within the second of these that freedom is to be found. The three levels are built upon each other, and concern the realm of instincts, the realm of civilization that tamed nature, and the world of abstract rules such as the law. In this conceptualization, civilization is a precondition for reason, and, as we have seen, for freedom. Freedom for Hayek is a matter of the submission of the individual to discipline, and to this extent he echoes Hobbes. As Dean (1999: 157) points out, Hayek's negative (freedom is freedom from the will of others) and anti-naturalist position on freedom brings him into conflict with his *Ordoliberalen* compatriots and their 'constructivist' approach to the origins of freedom. Hayek (1976: 17) suggests that this erroneous approach has its beginnings in utilitarianism. Finally, freedom has a role to play in the future of civilization: although it is a product of civilization, freedom is at the same time the condition of civilization's evolution. In stressing this role for freedom, Hayek is keen to downplay the possibility that any kind of cultural evolution is possible through central (governmental) planning. This critique promotes the possibilities of freedom in an individualistic culture as against the proven failures of Soviet command economies and Nazi authoritarianism.

As for the market, again Hayek is subtly different from other neo-liberal theorists. The market is not understood as a natural phenomenon, but nor is it the result of a contrived governmental policy. It is rather something like a 'spontaneous social order' (Dean, 1999: 157), arrived at through the rules of conduct established in cultural evolution. While there may be a need for a conditioning of the market's social and political framework, the market itself is 'culture' rather than 'reason', and thus is not sensibly regulated at the level of government.

Neo-liberalism in action

The Conservative government in the UK, led by Margaret Thatcher from 1979, provides us with a good example of neo-liberalism in action. The Thatcher government's policies were, of course, informed by the sorts of political philosophies we have discussed above, but especially by Hayek, as well as by Milton Friedman (see, for example, Friedman and Friedman, 1980; Friedman, 1962), who was perhaps the most important popularizer of notions of economic monetarism as well as an intellectual guru for many of the Cabinet. Our difficulty in discussing the Thatcher government is that we need to be mindful of a difference between neo-liberalism and neo-conservatism, especially since

Thatcher's administration, like Reagan's in the US, was a potent mixture of the two. The neo-conservative elements in 'Thatcherism' (a strong commitment to anti-immigration, the protectionism seen in an anti-EEC attitude, a desire to return to 'family' morality, criticisms of the 1960s' counter-culture, and similar) were certainly visible in some of Thatcher's immediate predecessors in the British Conservative party (for example, in 'Powellism', or in Edward Heath's appeal to the notion of 'Selsdon Man'), and in this chapter we have little to say about neo-conservatism. It certainly did not seem to be an especially innovative theme, unlike neo-liberalism, which has been taken up by political parties across the political spectrum.

Thatcher's neo-liberal approach can be characterized by following Rose (1996), who suggests three propositions on the character of what he terms 'advanced liberalism'. We shall take these three in turn. First, Rose argues that neo-liberalism entails a 'new relation between expertise and politics' (1996: 54). Under classical liberalism, the human and social sciences played an important role in providing the necessary expertise for welfare, for example, to operate. To a certain extent, the human science experts (sociologists, criminologists, psychologists) had a professional autonomy that was unchallenged. While these 'expert machines', as Rose calls them, did not lose their powers, they became much more highly regulated, especially by means of 'market tests' – for Rose, the three most crucial elements of this neo-liberal regulation are budget disciplines, accounting, and audit (see especially Power, 1994). We can add benchmarking to Rose's list, a procedure that introduces an economic-style competition into realms such as social services and education (see Larner and Le Heron, 2002). The neo-liberal move, then, is to introduce a market mentality into areas previously 'protected' by autonomous expert knowledge. In terms of the Conservative (and later Labour) governments' practical imposition of these sorts of practices, we can point to the introduction of such devices as the publication of league tables showing schools', universities' and hospitals' performances in servicing their clientele, and in such budgetary innovations which force these experts (hospital administrators, school principals, social service managers) to invent their own budget priorities within increasingly stringent allocations. These latter tactics have been analysed by Miller (1992) as 'governing at a distance': liberal governing in such situations is not so much about a face-to-face confrontation between governor and governed, as the attempt to set goals and activities which the governed must work towards. The individual, in what Miller terms 'calculative regimes', is given responsibility for his or her own conduct; the general framework is known to all the participants in the 'calculative regime', and to a certain extent the actors are free to get to the (economic) ends any way they choose. In Thatcher's version of neo-liberalism, it is this element of 'choice' that was a crucial political principle: hospitals, for example, were given greater 'choice' over what they did with their (shrinking) budgets, and provided they met certain basic requirements, were set free to 'entrepreneurialize' their activities. In such ways, expertise became indissolubly linked to the demands of the market.

The second characteristic theme of neo-liberalism in action identified by Rose is 'a new pluralization of social technologies' (1996: 56). This refers especially to the proliferation of a whole new series of quangos (quasi-autonomous non-governmental organizations) which work to 'de-state' government. Thus the old monolithic welfare state is now a plethora of para-organizations; the utilities are privatized and, in some cases, broken up into a myriad of providers; entities like the national rail system are transformed into a number of private companies on the basis of geography as well as function. While elements of these strategies are concerned with the movement away from the supposed inefficiencies of large bureaucratic organizations and towards smaller, more responsive units, and from public ownership, for so long unused to saving money, to the more market-responsive private sector, we should also note that this proliferation of organizations is linked to a supposed 'democratizing' function, as attempts are made to include local stakeholders and community representatives. Thus, companies, schools, utilities, and hospitals are permeated by community, parent, user, client, and patient groups, usually through formal 'board' mechanisms. In the university, similarly, there has been a transformation away from an organization which saw itself as distant from the community (necessarily so, since its ethical role was to lead in the production of ideas and the future of society), to one in which responsiveness to students, community, industry, and other sectors of the education system, are guaranteed by these groups having formal representation on boards of governors, and in other ways.

The third element of neo-liberalism in Rose's schema is 'a new specification of the subject of government' (1996: 57). Here, Rose's reference to the 'subject' is to the individual with his and her rights and responsibilities. In short, Rose's diagnosis is that an increased burden of responsibility for self-actualization, self-fulfilment and self-securitization is required of the individual under neo-liberalism. First, the monolithic 'society', with its associations of the provision of all to the passive member, is sidestepped in favour of notions such as 'community', or 'family', or 'local environment'. These latter bonds signify the importance of the individual taking a more active role in the direction of his or her life. The individual, then, is enjoined to throw off the shackles of the nanny state, and live a life of freedom through responsibility and choice. One must now take care of one's own health provision, for example, choosing and paying for the policy which best suits one's needs; the element of freedom comes here, but also in the notion that one is free to choose hospitals, doctors, and so on. All of this is made possible by cuts in personal income tax levels, so that money in the pocket is relayed directly to the services required rather than to an inefficient, bloated central government. These shifts occur across a number of areas which had previously been regarded as best looked after by the state: education, health, insurance, and so forth, are all made increasingly private rather than public spheres. A new range of concerns is also generated: for example, individuals are encouraged to take a greater role in home security, financial planning, and health and fitness. This increased range of areas of life about which one should be concerned is referred to by O'Malley (1992) as the 'new prudentialism'.

There is plenty of evidence for how this third tendency identified by Rose was played out under British Conservative governments in the 1980s and 1990s. Cuts in income taxation levels, aside from being standard election-winning strategies, have had an important ideological component, in that individuals are less paying for services indirectly, as 'collective consumers'; instead, they engage in a number of private contracts. Certainly, there is plenty of evidence in the new buzzwords of the times that something has changed in terms of how the individual must perceive him or herself. Rose's own examples mention the linguistic shifts from the 'unemployed person' to the 'jobseeker', and from the 'homeless person' to the 'rough sleeper' (1996: 59), both changes of nomenclature bringing with them visions of activity rather than passivity, and even containing elements of lifestyle choice.

We are now in a position to see just why we need to separate the concepts of neo-liberalism and neo-conservatism: the three trends we have characterized as distinctively neo-liberal have scarcely been reversed by the Labour or Democratic governments that succeeded Thatcher/Major or Reagan/Bush. Both Tony Blair's and Bill Clinton's administrations maintained the emphasis on small government, choice, accountability of public and private institutions, and the raft of innovations which stemmed from neo-liberal political programmes. This is one of the reasons why neo-liberal concepts such as choice, freedom, and small government now seem so uncontroversial: there are very few intellectual alternatives.

Many of the political and social critiques of neo-liberalism that were mounted in the 1970s and beyond also failed to understand the intellectual innovation of neo-liberalism, but importantly, they tended to conflate it with neo-conservatism, and to focus on aspects such as racism, the return to Victorian values, increased militarism, an emphasis on strong policing and law and order policies, and similar, which are not strictly part of the neo-liberal reinvention. One example where neo-liberalism and neo-conservatism can be easily mixed-up is in a field like drug policy. The notion of harm minimization, for example, which has been taken up in many different national contexts, seems on the surface a classic neo-liberal idea. The provision of drug education and medical help is shifted to a local level; drug users themselves are confronted with 'choices' and given help to make themselves more responsible about the impact of their drug use upon themselves, their families and their community; a number of quangos, and paralegal and welfare groups are invented to relay and mediate expertise; and the composition of these expert groups is strongly oriented towards representation from a number of relevant stakeholders. This is a long way from the sorts of 'social control' attacks on drug use that were common in the period 1945–70.

However, in the main, the worries about such schemes from the political Right stem not from the neo-liberal perspective – after all, harm minimization is a good example of setting up the conditions under which people can make better choices and be more 'entrepreneurial' about their life decisions – but from a neo-conservative perspective, which tends to be anti-drugs, and to prefer a legal 'crackdown' approach (such as zero-tolerance policing and sentencing) over a (probably more realistic) approach which accepts that drugs cannot be completely eliminated from our society. Again, in this example, we can see that both right and left wings of the political spectrum usually come to agree about the elements of the problem that are neo-liberal (choice, expertise, community involvement), but disagree over morality. In this example, it is important that we are able to disentangle neo-liberalism and neo-conservatism, since it allows us to see just how few alternatives there are to neo-liberalism, in an arena that is so hotly contested politically and morally.

Neo-liberalism and the abrogation of national responsibility

Rather than take a globalized world as a brute fact, we are interested in looking at the ways in which neo-liberalism as a narrative has begun to corrode the notion of a national economy, and thus allowed neo-liberal politicians to sidestep questions of responsibility for economic management; or at least to use globalization as the rationale for the introduction of policies promoting market competitiveness (in the UK, the spectre of globalization has been used since the late 1970s by politicians of both the major parties to engage in major reconstructions of policies and institutions in the search for improved national economic competitiveness). However, while outcomes have not necessarily been benign and social issues have frequently been ignored, a number of contingencies which seem less malign have emerged from the neo-liberal conjuncture: in particular, the downgrading of the importance of the nation state has left a number of gaps that can be filled by alternative politics, with an emphasis on human and animal rights, ecological protest, and so forth, as we shall suggest below.

In much of what we have discussed so far in this book, neo-liberalism as a practice of government has been examined especially in terms of its social and political mission. However, in turning to the question of how neo-liberalism impacts on the question of the continuing salience of the nation state and the move towards a global polity and economy, our question focuses more on neo-liberalism as an economic doctrine. Our first point is that while it has frequently been suggested that globalization (as a kind of inevitable fact of the late modern period) has eliminated or reduced many national-level governmental activities, it is probably more helpful to look at this issue in terms of how neo-liberalism has played a role in a shift from the national to the international economy. In such a perspective, then, globalization can be considered a result of neo-liberalism rather than its cause.

Hindess (1998) argues that a crucial difference between liberal and neo-liberal approaches to the economy centre on the extent to which it can be considered a national or an international entity. For Hindess, the classical liberalism of Adam Smith, and especially of Ricardo, maintains a notion of national economies, reasonably self-contained within the bounds of the nation state. International trade is not untheorized in these doctrines, but it is based on the building blocks of national economies. Not surprisingly, currency and exchange rate fluctuations came to be seen as the essential problem in international trade. Hindess suggests that the collapse of the Bretton Woods system of exchange rate management after 1973 was the last gasp of the classical liberal economic world as advanced by Ricardo. After then, there is a growing consensus that the self-regulating economy is no longer a national phenomenon, it is an international one.

One of the obvious consequences of this view is that national governments can now plead that the economy is not only to be left alone as a matter of policy, but that it is out of reach of national regulation even if such were desirable. In addition, as Hindess argues, in the old liberal economic doctrines, every nation could be a winner, since it would be possible for every national economy to grow. With a single international economy, this is no longer possible: the international economy, when analysed at the national level, will be a game with both winners and losers. This leads to the idea that the only way for national economies in maintaining their security is for them to be as competitive as possible. Additionally, under the liberal system in which the economy was a relatively self-contained element of the nation (which was a mixture of economy, state and civil society), it was possible to understand some elements of life as non-economic; under the neo-liberal understanding, the limits to the economic are no longer so clear cut (since the economy stretches out into the unknown distance of international networks), and it becomes much easier for the sorts of arguments we saw made by Gary S. Becker – that everything is economic.

We can see a complex relationship between neo-liberalism and the international economy, and an assumption that everything is somehow economic (or crucial dependent upon the economic). In this fundamentally economic world, national governments' approaches to their own domestic economies increasingly circle around a *fetishization* of competitiveness and efficiency, in order that the challenges of the yet-to-be-discovered future can be met. Thus neo-liberalism is an important force in the continued development of the international economy, not least because nowadays, politicians often mislay the art of national economic management; and to the extent that everything is now understood as economic (or impinging on the economic), what we might term 'social management' (reinventing education, health care, welfare, and so forth) is now what passes for economic management.

Here we hit upon one of the dangers of the neo-liberal enthusiasm for an international or global economy: the nation state comes to be understood as of decreasing relevance to the new world order. This in turn leads to a certain amount of fatalism about international politics and economic activity. The state, which, since the Treaties of Westphalia in 1648, has been the prime mover in a thoroughly international political world, now seems to be downgraded to a local authority within the 'superstate' – whether this superstate is seen as the global state, or as one of a number of post-national regional economic and political entities, such as the EU.

Conclusion

In this chapter, we have sought to provide an account of liberalism, not so much as a political philosophy, but as a political practice. In constructing this discussion, we were never very far from Foucault's concept of 'governmentality', which refers to the rationalities and mentalities of everyday governmental activities. Our first argument showed that liberalism emerged from a previous governmentality, *raison d'état*, and in fact emerged as a critique of it. While liberalism can be understood as a permanent problematization of government, it should be noted that liberalism rarely ignored governmental problems: rather its solutions made use of the freedom of liberal citizens in a novel and imaginative way. The emergence of liberalism strengthened the state, since it became to be seen less and less as an imposition upon an unwilling populace, and more and more the condition of the freedom of that populace.

Our next section examined some of the threats and challenges to liberalism. First, within the nations in which liberalism gained its ascendancy, and growing out of the same soil, political philosophies such as socialism have sought to question the liberal agenda. Our treatment of these alternative philosophies was, in the main, to treat them as variations upon liberalism. While there are many who would argue with this strategy, so many of the same conditions apply across the political spectrum – the forms of specification of self, the approach to freedom, the value placed on democracy – that this approach has some validity. It enabled us to examine political experiments such as Nazism as variants of liberalism: pathological variants, no doubt, but we also took pains to show how violence and genocide are potentially present (and therefore available for pathology) in the liberal governmentality.

In Chapter 2, we examined political systems outside the West, especially the Soviet Union, China, and the Islamic world. It seems that while liberalism has withstood the challenge from Soviet political rationalities, more problematical are its abilities either to vanquish or to enter into peaceful dialogue with either of Chinese Marxism or Islamic political thought. This conclusion rests on the inseparability of forms of self and forms of political rationality. The Islamic form of self, based on the Qu'ran, and the Chinese form of self, based on Confucianism, are so alien to the West that neither liberalism as a political practice nor the concept of the nation state are likely to have a lasting impact on the political rationality of these last two guardians of non-liberal thought.

Broadly we have stressed how the efficient functioning of liberalism presupposes a citizen equipped to self-actualize or self-maximize, which could require forms of compulsion. Freedom has its price. We spent some time discussing the education system as the major institutional guarantor of this personal freedom, although others, such as welfare, are mentioned.

In developing this theme, we spent some time on the notion of expertise. Rose has drawn our attention to the important role expertise plays in maintaining the liberal social contract, and we followed Rose in outlining how experts constitute norms of behaviour which are filtered back into everyday life, and how these experts are increasingly required to operate growing state institutions. To avoid the impression that the relationship between the state and the individual flows in one direction only, we discussed Elias's work on the vital importance forms of personal comportment have on state formation. Elias has not only shown this in relation to the transformation of the feudal notions of self into the modern introspective and tactful self, he has also tested out his theories in trying to understand how the forms of self found in Nazi Germany were possible. We rehearsed Elias's arguments here, contesting that a form of self which worshipped personal power and strength was transmitted down through German society, but as it made its way into the consciousnesses of the middle and lower classes, the cult of power was stripped of any ethic of limitation. Elias's account dovetails nicely with our earlier account, derived from Dean and Peukert, about Nazism as a perverted variant of the liberal state in which certain features of the 'normal' state were turned inward or translated to different concerns. Ultimately, the intention is to argue that it is not possible to understand fully state formation and forms of specification of subjectivity in isolation from each other.

We also attempted to analyse neo-liberalism as a series of practical programmes of government, rather than merely as a political philosophy. This is difficult, as neo-liberalism has frequently been mixed in the realm of practical or governmental politics with neo-conservatism, or with 'Third Way' politics, or with other forms of social democracy. Giddens (1998:11), for example, conflates neo-liberalism and neo-conservatism, a move that allows him to understand Third Way politics as a distinct turn from the former; from our perspective, Third Way politics are another iteration of neo-liberalism.

What can be casually referred to as neo-liberalism may not strictly deserve that definition. Because neo-liberalism as a political programme first saw the light of day in a number of right-wing governments, it has frequently been misdiagnosed. Neo-liberalism is at heart an economic doctrine: it criticizes Adam Smith's notion of the market as a natural system, and agonizes over the extent to which the market needs to be stimulated and the best conditions under which it will flourish. Ultimately, however, the notion of the market as an analogy for all other areas of life – the heritage of the *Ordoliberalen* and the Chicago School – is what gives neo-liberalism its characteristic flavour. Where classical liberalism sought to govern through society, neo-liberalism seeks to govern by administering society as if it were a market. This has led to a reorganization of the state in neo-liberal perspectives to one that can be more activist in creating the free economy than found in classical liberalism. The neo-liberal perspective has also contributed to the disintegration of the notion of 'national economies'; the economy is understood as tending to expand beyond national boundaries, and consequently, as we saw in Chapter 6, the role of the state in regulating the international economy has become a topic of contention.

Chapter 9

Power, Domination, Culture and Sociality

In our previous discussions of the nature of the state, we have not explicitly considered the concept of power. Yet within political sociology and political philosophy, it is scarcely possible to discuss the state without simultaneously emphasizing power. The concern with power stems, of course, from the commonplace observation that the state is nothing without the ability to enforce taxation, military service, legal codes, and suchlike. In this chapter we shall trace the changing conceptions of power, beginning, as in Chapter 8, with Machiavelli and Hobbes. In these pre-liberal conceptualizations, we shall see that power is understood rather crudely – in particular, a simple notion of power as capacity is developed – yet this elementary characterization of power is one that has proved very resilient, right up to the present.

We shall move on to consider some of the more complex notions of power, especially those linked to the modern liberal state, focusing on decisional and pluralist accounts, radical and Marxist interpretations, concepts inspired by the work of Foucault, and other views found within what is described as the 'new political sociology'. In these last two approaches we note particularly the proposition that politics and power are inherent in all social relations, and not simply found in state or other large and 'official' organizations. For these theorists, while the state remains important, it is displaced as the centre of political activity. The related emphasis on culture as a sphere of governance will be examined, as will the notion of power as productive of forms of self (in contrast to the Weberian emphasis on domination and contestation in subjectivity). To this end, an analysis of forms of subjectivity based on the politics of gender and sexuality will be explored.

Machiavelli and anti-Machiavellianism

We can start with Machiavelli, even though power is hardly mentioned explicitly by him. For Machiavelli (1513), writing in the sixteenth century, power is conceptualized simply in terms of the prince's ability to govern: power is definable in terms of sovereignty. However, we can be more specific about the limits of this power: it is power over a territory, and (consequently) over the people who are in that territory. What is important for Machiavelli is the notion of power as external to the state. It is wielded over the territory and the people by a sovereign who is 'above' or outside them. Sovereign power has a certain analogy with divine power in its externality and transcendence. Because the prince is external to his territory, Machiavelli comes to characterize power, first, as the prince's capacity, and second, as the strength of the external bond between the prince and his territory and people. The guarantee of this bond is not through any especially subtle procedures: at root, power and force are virtual synonyms.

In the so-called 'anti-Machiavellian' literature, which begins almost immediately after *The Prince* appears, a subtle shift emerges. Rather than continuing the Machiavellian emphasis on force and territory, authors such as La Perrière (1567) stress a new complexity for government. First, La Perrière's notion of 'governor' is considerably wider than that of 'prince', and allows him to theorize power as connected to multiple agents, and to be internal and immanent rather than external and transcendent to the state. The objects of government, and hence of power, can be a prince's subjects, but can also be a father's family, a teacher's pupils, a priest's parish. This move allows power to be understood as much more widespread, rather than being the prerogative of the prince, and to be exercised within a territory, rather than simply being exercised to guarantee the bond between a territory and its external ruler. In this way, La Perrière and his contemporaries move us from an external, transcendent sense of power characteristic of Machiavelli's writings, to a notion of power as internal to, and constitutive of, the state. Within a hundred years, by the end of the seventeenth century, this notion of power had been converted into something like a theory of 'police', which we discussed in detail in Chapter 8. Connections or 'modelling' could be seen between the spheres of self-government,

government of the family, and government of the state, or, to put it another way, between morality, economics and politics. All these forms of government are analogous, and indeed it is widely thought, from the late sixteenth century, that there is something of a developmental path that might best be followed. The wise sovereign first learns self-mastery, then learns to master his immediate surrounds, and is then equipped to rule his territory and subjects. In this way, the concern of 'police' – to govern every aspect of society – was born from this anti-Machiavellian literature. In it power had become a phenomenon internal to the state.

A second important theme in La Perrière, and a second important development in our discussion of historically changing understandings of power, is his statement that 'government is the right disposition of things, arranged so as to lead to a convenient end' (cited in Foucault, 1979: 10). As Foucault analyses this definition, La Perrière's intention is to move us away from the Machiavellian fixation on territory. Foucault glosses what La Perrière means by 'things':

> I don't think it is a question of opposing things to men but rather of showing that government does not bear on the territory but rather on the complex unit constituted by men and things … men in their relations, their links, their imbrication with those other things which are wealth, resources, means of subsistence, the territory with its specific qualities, climate, irrigation, fertility, etc.; men in their relation to that other kind of things which are customs, habits, ways of doing and thinking, etc.; lastly, men in their relation to that other kind of things again which are accidents and misfortunes such as famine, epidemics, death, etc. (Foucault, 1979: 11)

The terrain of power has shifted subtly here. For Machiavelli, there is a circularity to power: power is about ensuring obedience to the sovereign, but power is also guaranteed by the exercise of that very same sovereignty. Power, therefore, has the same means and ends. By contrast, in the anti-Machiavellian literature, government – and hence power – has numerous specific ends, and numerous places of operation. It also focuses on the government of the complex world of men and their relations to life and economic processes.

There is a third important difference between Machiavelli and his disputants that we must dwell on for a moment. The exercise of sovereignty is seen by Machiavelli primarily as the exercise of force; yet for the anti-Machiavellians, the use of force is seen as an indicator of failure and the misplacement of better and more sensible alternatives, which are deployed as a result of the wisdom and patience of the governor. In short, the use of the right to violence, or the use of the right to kill, are not the signs of the good governor; the good governor shows himself rather through his knowledge of the right disposition of things. The governor, then, is wise and patient, and his power flows from this, rather than resting on his use of violence.

Thomas Hobbes and John Locke: the sovereign and power

Hobbes's *Leviathan* (1651) is an important text in the history of power. For Hobbes, the sovereign must have a strong enough power to overcome the potentially dangerous self-interests of the subjects of a territory. 'Bonds of words are too weak to bridle them [the ambitions, desires, etc. of the subjects] ... without some fear of coercive power ... covenants, without the sword, are but words, and of no strength to secure a man at all' (Hobbes, 1651/1991: 117). As we can see, Hobbes re-emphasizes violence (or the potential to use violence) as the basis for sovereign power. Power is a thing that can be possessed, and it is a capacity or potential to get one's own way: human beings struggle to possess power, to use it on other people, and to resist it when it is used against them. It is a possession, however, whose action is 'negative' – it primarily acts as the prohibition and repression of behaviours that are damaging to others' 'interests'. While the state potentially threatens the interests of the citizen, Hobbes none the less sees it as the condition for the happiness of all, and therefore the use of power by or in the name of the state is justified. There is also in Hobbes the idea that while the realm of the state is the place where power is properly used to ensure the common interest, civil life (family, business, personal life) must be kept free.

These are the bare bones of Hobbes's view of power. As Hindess (1996) has argued, there are two crucial elements to Hobbes's theory of power. First, Hobbes lays the ground for an understanding of sovereign power as the most fundamental form of power, a notion from which we have (for better or worse) yet to escape. Second, Hobbes provides us with a cogent characterization of power understood as a capacity. In particular, Hobbes develops the idea of sovereign power as the combined powers of many individuals, and following on from that, develops the linked idea that contests will be won by the side with the greater 'power capacity'.

For Hobbes, the relationship between sovereign power and its subjects only runs in one direction. It is doubly asymmetrical in that not only has the sovereign an enormously superior amount of power, but also the covenant that assures his power binds the citizens to him, while he has no corresponding duty to his subjects (Hindess, 1996: 47–8). Here we can see echoes of the Machiavellian externality and transcendence of sovereign power still at work. John Locke's development of the Hobbesian notion of power remedies this asymmetry by outlining the corresponding responsibilities and obligations of the sovereign to his subjects, or of the powerful to the powerless (see especially Locke's (1689) *Second Treatise on Government*).

Locke's first move is one that questions the analogy made by the anti-Machiavellians between power operating at different levels of society. For Locke, the use of parental power, for example, cannot be understood as analogous to sovereign power. The justification for parental power lies in the fact that children do not have reason, and therefore need to be properly governed, since they cannot do it for themselves. The same justification cannot be used for the sovereign's power over his subjects, since those subjects possess reason. For Locke, a sovereign can only claim legitimate power if the subjects are content that the sovereign's actions are for the benefit of the whole commonwealth. To understand the difference here between Hobbes and Locke, we need to understand that for Hobbes, the people are compelled to obey the sovereign, and have no recourse to remove him, whatever they think of his actions or beliefs; by contrast, for Locke, it is only right and proper that the sovereign be removed if he loses the support of the people.

We can see here in Locke two important themes, more widely discussed in liberal political philosophy, that combine to dilute the absolute power of the sovereign. First of all, the idea of 'reason' as a natural attribute of human beings necessarily brings into question the issue of a sovereign's right to rule, and introduces questions about the rights of the citizen. Second, governments come to be seen as representatives of the people: the latter now are understood as being legitimately able to challenge forms of sovereignty that are tyrannical. The impulse of these twin themes played a crucial part in important developments in world politics, including the establishment of republics in France and in the US, and the 'softening' of the rights of the king through the founding of constitutional monarchies, as in Great Britain.

Let us recap our understanding of power so far. Machiavelli enables us to understand power as a simple capacity, something that is both the means and the objective of sovereign rule. Importantly, power is external and transcendent to a given society. Hobbes develops this notion of power as a capacity, and strengthens our focus on power as sovereign power. To a certain extent, Hobbes allows power to be seen as internal to a society, since sovereign power for him is the result of an accumulation of many subjects' powers. However, earlier than Hobbes, the sixteenth-century anti-Machiavellian writings, which we saw exemplified through La Perriere, expand on this notion of power as a capacity spread throughout society. By the time we get to the late seventeenth century, and the birth of liberal political philosophy, writers such as Locke have taken this notion of power existing within society still further. All human beings that possess reason should have, as of right, the means to refuse any forms of power that are tyrannical or wrong (this is present in an undeveloped form in Hobbes's *Leviathan*: as Hindess (1996: 54) discusses, Hobbes believed that natural law gave the citizen the right to resist a sovereign who threatens their life, but otherwise, the citizen's rights are inconsequential, since they cannot disobey under any other conditions). In this way, Locke continues a trend that makes power internal and immanent to the state, and allows us to see it as embodying much more than just sovereignty.

Marxist conceptions of power

For both Hobbes and Locke, the state is a composition of individuals, and these individuals pre-exist their specific social arrangements. For both these thinkers, in their different ways, the analysis of power, then, is crucially dependent on the analysis of the individual and his/her relation to the state. Marx refused this 'liberal' starting point – as he put it, 'man is not an abstract being squatting outside the world' (Marx, 1871: 131) – maintaining that the relation between individuals was the key to understanding the state, and that, in the modern age, this required an understanding of class relations.

It is common to distinguish two strands to Marx's thought on the relationship between classes and the state (see also our discussion in Chapter 3), and this impacts on our understanding of Marx's use of the notion of power. The first position stems from the early Marx, but appears now and again in his later writings. In this position, there is a relative autonomy between the state, and the variety of bureaucratic institutions attached to it, and the dominant class. In *The Eighteenth Brumaire*, for example, he describes the state as a kind of leviathan, invested with power, even able to resist the ruling class's ability to control it (Marx, 1852).

The second position, and the one that is perhaps more familiar, is especially evident in the later Marx and in writings like *The Communist Manifesto* (Marx and Engels, 1848). In this position (one that Lenin later set out to 'rescue'), the state is visualized as little else than the instrument of class power. The state is a 'superstructure' built on the foundations of economic and social relations, which are, of course, mediated by class. Especially in this second position, which is the model for most radical theories of the state, power is, as for Hobbes, conceptualized as a possession (of the ruling class), which is used for a variety of negative purposes (mainly to frustrate the aspirations of the oppressed classes).

The first position is perhaps the more interesting in terms of our discussion of power, since it immediately promises a complexification of the workings of power. However, in *The Eighteenth Brumaire*, Marx is often eager to assert that political power is a direct result of economic power, and so the interests of the bourgeoisie are translated fairly directly and straightforwardly into political advantage. Power, then, for Marx, stems from economic supremacy: more specifically, it stems from ownership of the means of production. Nash (2000: 5–6) draws our attention to a third model of power in Marx's writings, one outlined in *Capital*, Volume 3 (Marx, 1867). Nash calls this a 'functionalist' model, in which the state (the superstructure) is entirely determined by the economy (the infrastructure). Because economic power is directly translated into all social and political institutions, political power comes to be something of an irrelevance; or, at least, to speak of the relation between economic and political power is to speak tautologously. However, while Marx's theories of power downplay the importance of any other level apart from the economic, it should be noted that it is clear from Marx's work that power is also at work in every social and political institution, since the ruling classes' interests must necessarily be represented there.

Marxism, ideology and power

We can pick up on this last observation of Marx, since it provided the impetus for much of the later Marxist theorizing about power, especially in the 1960s and 1970s. But first we examine Gramsci's consideration of power (see also Chapter 3). Gramsci (1971, 1978), writing from the 1920s onwards, was in prison under Mussolini's fascist regime from 1926 until his death in 1937. Gramsci tried to understand the workings of power and ideology through his notion of cultural hegemony. The problem that faced him was how it is that the working classes will frequently support the various state apparatuses (such as the police) that are designed to repress them. The answer he gave to this question was to be found in the indoctrination of the working classes into the belief systems of the ruling classes by the use of education, media, religion, political parties, and similar bodies. In time, the belief systems of the ruling classes, presented in these forums, took on a semblance of naturalness and inevitability. Gramsci suggested that the operation of power in modern capitalist states could not simply be a matter of the reflection of economic power: a whole series of ideological systems needed to be constructed to ensure the smooth running of civil society, and to alleviate the possibility of social unrest and revolt.

Gramsci's important work certainly makes our notion of power more flexible, since for him, the power of the state was not to be identified with specific institutions, but with a range of multiform activities throughout society sponsored by the ruling classes. In addition, Gramsci directed our attention away from the use of force as the guarantor of power: hegemony, or a state of political stability based on the acceptance of the ruling class's authority to rule, was achieved through the broadcasting and acceptance of ideas and morals. Hegemony required a delicate balancing act, in which the ruling classes, in order to rule by consent rather than by force, had constantly to readjust their strategies, and even make a number of concessions to the lower classes to maintain the equilibrium of society as a whole.

The work of Gramsci highlighted for later Marxists the importance of ideology in any theory of power. We now move on to revisit an important debate within Marxism between Ralph Miliband and Nicos Poulantzas, which we discussed in Chapter 3. As we noted, this took place in the 1970s, and it centred on Gramsci's theories. Miliband (1969) developed a thesis that was a variant of Marx's position in *The Eighteenth Brumaire*, arguing for the relative autonomy of state and ruling class. For Miliband, the state needs to be able to rise above ruling-class squabbles. Miliband also drew attention to what he regarded as an overlooked aspect of the theory of state power – the interpersonal relations between important figures in the ruling classes, the bureaucracies, universities, political parties, and so on. For Miliband, the interests of capital and the state would often coincide because of such links, and the direction of state policy therefore naturally accorded with the interests of the owners of capital. Miliband's notion of power, then, is one in which elites use power in their own interests, but power is firmly placed in the realm of individual agency and social interactions, rather than in social structure.

As we know from our earlier analyses, Poulantzas (1973) criticized this position for its commitment to a 'problematic of the subject'. In line with the fashion for anti-humanist, structuralist thinking in Paris in the 1960s and 1970s, Poulantzas aimed to understand power as an effect of a series of impersonal structures, encompassing economic, political and ideological levels. The state was understood as a system of objective structures on which interpersonal relations have no bearing. Together with Althusser, Poulantzas refined the Marxist notion of ideology, and developed a theory of state power as dependent on two sorts of 'apparatuses': repressive and ideological. The repressive state apparatuses include the military, the police, the judiciary and various other administrative bodies, while the ideological state apparatuses include schools and the education system, organized religion, mass media, trade unions and even the family. While ultimately this system of Poulantzas and Althusser relied heavily on a determining economic base (a criticism Miliband (1972) was quick to make), what is interesting for our purposes is that this emphasis on ideology suggests a much more cunning use of power, and that power is deeply ingrained in everyday life. Indeed, Althusser's assertion that the most important ideological state apparatus today is education is an argument to the effect that the school's most important job is to indoctrinate the young and ensure the smooth continuation of capitalist systems.

These positions view power as operating in a downward direction, from the ruling classes and onto the subjected classes: power is only really understood as domination. Poulantzas supplies an example of a structuralist-Marxist theory of the state, where subjectivity or selfhood is ruled out of the equation except as a kind of receptacle of power. This lineage can be traced back to Marx's rejection of liberal, individualistic notions of state and state power. Miliband, on the other hand, importantly tries to think through a notion of the operation of power that encompasses the problem of agency. This tension between theorizing power as an effect of agency or as an effect of structure is, of course, a well-worn problem in sociology. However, what is most important for our purposes is that Marxist accounts of power, whether attributed to agency, to structure, or to some middle position, tend to emphasize power as the ability of one (person or class) to achieve their goals whatever another (person or class) may wish. Further, in class-based societies, power will operate to ensure the interests of the dominant person or class.

Weber: power, authority and domination

From Hobbes to Marx and Marxism, it might be said that there is not enough of an attempt to differentiate between 'power' and domination'. That is to say, in general, the operation of power is equated generally with forms of domination, either by a sovereign, or by the ruling classes. Weber, however, usefully elaborates the distinction between power and domination.

As Miller (1987: 5–6) summarizes, Weber distinguishes between power (*Macht*) and authority (*Herrschaft*). *Macht* refers to the probability that one actor in a social relationship will be able to carry out his/her will in spite of any resistance that may be encountered. As Weber's famous definition has it, power is 'the chance of a man or of a number of men to realize their own will in a communal action even against the resistance of others who are participating in the action' (Weber, 1948a: 180). *Herrschaft* refers to the probability that a command will be obeyed by those to whom it is addressed (Weber, 1947: 152–4). Miller goes on to suggest that, for Weber, power is a mode of domination that obtains between subjects in an interpersonal process. We should also note that Weber's notion of power has a quantitative character: one person only has power to the extent that another does not. As Talcott Parsons (1960, 1967), who has famously critiqued this idea that power is a fixed quotient, describes it, for Weber, power in a given society is a zero-sum game.

However, there is a second aspect to Weber's work that perhaps advances our thinking about power: that on discipline. Weber defined discipline as the probability that habituation would lead to prompt and automatic obedience to commands. In modern societies, this obedience was less and less based on the charisma of a commander or president, but on a principle of impersonality, a rational obedience based on the 'legal' or 'legitimate' claim to rule that the commander possessed. The model for this form of discipline was military discipline, which gave birth to all discipline. The rational bureaucracies of the modern European states were, for Weber, built on this model (see Gerth and Mills, 1958: 253ff.).

This conception of discipline is linked to Weber's distinction between the three types of legitimate authority: charismatic, traditional and rational-legal (Weber, 1968: 215). Charismatic authority rests on a leader's ability to maintain power through his or her personal qualities; Jesus Christ, Napoleon or Hitler might be good examples of this form of authority. Traditional authority derives from a system in which obedience flows from the fact that things have always been organized this way; the Catholic Church might provide us with a nice example of such authority. Rational–legal authority rests on a principle of impersonality and the perceived rationality of the system of rule, rather than from any charisma or sense of tradition; most modern bureaucracies and corporations work in this way – we might think, for example, of the tax office as an example of such a form of authority. Weber was clear that these forms of authority were 'ideal types', categories to guide our thoughts about authority, rather than a description of actual forms of authority. Weber suggested that most instances of authority in action would comprise mixtures of the three types to varying degrees.

Weber was especially interested in the different ways in which one could conduct one's life (*Lebensführung*) and the impact that bureaucratic forms – the modern, dominant form of rational–legal authority – had upon that mode of life. Given the inescapability of bureaucracy for Weber, and its penetration into many aspects of contemporary life, we can think of Weber's work as being about the constitution of human beings through the operation of power and authority. None the less, in Weber's work a central preoccupation was with the domination of bureaucracy over the individual. How can the individual avoid being overpowered by bureaucracy? How can bureaucratic power be checked? While he was undoubtedly pessimistic about the future of modern society, he yet maintained a faith, as a self-confessed bourgeois liberal, in democracy as a series of practices that might ameliorate the problems of the 'iron cage' of bureaucracy.

However, in terms of power, Weber was clear that a distinctive element of the state was its 'violence'. This use of force guaranteed all the other actions of the state:

> Force is certainly not the normal or only means of the state – nobody says that – but force is a means specific to the state ... the state is a relation of men dominating men ... a relation supported by means of legitimate (that is, considered to be legitimate) violence. (Weber, 1948b: 78)

Again, one sees here a conception of power as a capacity that ultimately works in a negative, repressive manner. *Mutatis mutandis*, Weber's conception of power is not very far removed from that of Hobbes or of Marx. While Weber is not so crude as to tie power simply to sovereignty or to economic interests, none the less it is a fairly straightforward capacity. Further, while Weber explicitly aimed to analyse the relation between power and subjective or intersubjective relations, his conception of power as a form of domination means that power is ultimately a negative category.

Pluralist conceptions of power

Pluralism draws its inspiration from de Tocqueville's (1835) assertion that democracies could only work if the various sections in society were kept in balance; democracy would be threatened by the domination of one faction. While pluralists accept the Weberian zero-sum characterization of the distribution of power throughout society, they do not believe, as the Marxists do, that power is limited to the dominant classes. Because they see each individual as having many different (and often contradictory) interests, they argue that narrow sectional interests (of class, status, party, and so on) are to a certain extent dissipated. The state works as best it can to accommodate these various interests, even though it is unlikely it can do so fully. If pluralist government is successful, it can be described as polyarchy – rule by the multilayered many (Dahl, 1956). Dahl's well-known study (1961) of local politics in New Haven, Connecticut, analysed a number of local political decisions – local education policy, nominations for local political office, and local urban redevelopment – to see whether these decisions were dominated by particular interest groups, or rather whether the outcomes supported his thesis that democracies are polyarchies. The latter prevailed, indicating that the mobilization of power and interests was complex, and that a process of 'interest bargaining' was at work.

Dahl, like many other pluralists, focused on decision-making, but we might think of this as just one of the 'three faces' of power. Bachrach and Baratz (1962) suggest a second face of power – the 'non-decision-making' aspect. Power in this view may be wielded by controlling the agenda for decision-making, and ensuring that certain 'dangerous' decisions cannot be made. Finally, there is a third face to power, as identified by Lukes (1974), which focuses on the extent to which power resides in shaping desires. In this way, power lies in convincing others to accept something they might not without subtle persuasion. Here, Lukes is very close to the notions of ideology and false consciousness that have been so important to Marxist theories of power.

Lukes accepts Bachrach and Baratz's critique of the previously one-dimensional characterization of power. In concentrating only on decision-making, theorists of power had neglected all those tacit knowledges and unexamined biases which constitute the world of 'non-decision-making'. Yet at the same time, Lukes suggests that the 'two faces' approach is little more than a restatement of the previous theory with an acknowledgement of its hidden other. Lukes introduces the concept of 'interests' and turns a two-dimensional theory of power into a three-dimensional one. In this third dimension, an actor (A) attempts to get another actor (B) to accept A's interests at the expense of B's. As Giddens (1979: 90ff) has it, in adding interests to the social structural analysis of power, Lukes is seeking to reunite voluntaristic and structural notions of power (or what Giddens prefers to characterize as the agency–structure problem).

Lukes's 'radical' view of power is characterized by Hindess (1996: 70) as a departure from the quantitative notions we have seen in Hobbes and in Marxist theories. In drawing attention to the control of thoughts and desires, Lukes is suggesting that power is not simply a quantity possessed and expended. In addition, Lukes's account means that we must now consider a number of apparently mundane social interactions as theatres of power (Hindess, 1996: 83). Hindess goes on to suggest that while Lukes's short book only provides a schematic account of this third face of power, similar characterizations of power can be seen in Marcuse's (1972) notion of 'one-dimensional man' – albeit given a psychoanalytic gloss – and Habermas's (1984, 1987b) discussion of a pathologically colonized lifeworld.

Elite theories of power

As we saw in Chapter 3, elite theory is somewhat self-explanatory: society is divided into a number of factions, but elites rule and exercise power through the state. While at first sight there might seem to be similarities to Marxist theories of power, the first elite theorists, Vilfredo Pareto (1858–1941) and Gaetano Mosca (1858–1941), developed elite theory as an argument against Marx, in that they saw the elite's monopoly of power as inevitable and unavoidable, even under socialism. The stability of elites was attributed in part by Pareto (1935) and Mosca (1939) to psychological factors: in particular, the masses are seen as having a psychological need to be governed by elites.

C. Wright Mills provides a different view on elitism to Pareto and Mosca, dropping the mass psychology and the attempts to generalize to all societies. Mills (1956) focuses on the 'power elite' in the US of the 1950s: for Mills, the elite was constituted by a relatively recent accord between three sectors of society – the government, the military and the large private corporations – whose interests had become aligned. In Marxist fashion, Mills suggests that politicians play out politics in a way that benefits the economic power base. The three major arguments of Mills and the other elitist theorists are as follows: first, unlike the pluralists, they do not believe that democracy is effectively in existence – the concentration of power in the hands of elites gives the lie to any talk of society being truly democratic; second, to follow the workings of power, one needs to look at the institutional positions from which it is wielded – power results from an individual's access to these key positions; third, power is understood, once again, as a capacity.

We should also mention that there are clear similarities between Mills's view of the power elite, and the ideas canvassed by Miliband. However, while Miliband argues that the connections between the owners of capital and the state personnel is longstanding and reflect and promote shared interests, for Mills the formation of a power elite is a relatively recent historical event, and one in which shared interests have only gradually been formed. For Mills, the power elite is a much less necessary historical product than it is for Miliband, although, of course, their respective positions may indicate the relative historical 'maturities' of the UK (Miliband) and the US (Mills).

Foucault and power

The perspective developed by Foucault on power is radically different from those perspectives we have discussed so far. In particular, Foucault deals with power as neither capacity nor possession. Foucault's work is a development of the ideas seen in Lukes, as well as in Marcuse and Habermas, in which power is used to shape desires and to produce new forms of self. However, a common theme in theories of power and their relation to the self is that power acts to deny and repress authentic forms of self and self-expression (as we saw in Lukes, actor A's interests triumph over actor B's); by contrast, Foucault's argument is that power is productive of selves, and productive of interests. We have lost our emphasis on the state here: in the Foucaultian tradition, it is common to focus on the way in which power operates above and beyond the state – in effect arguing that there is no realm of civil society easily separable on the one hand from power or on the other hand from state intervention.

Foucault's work on power has, we feel, been misunderstood. In general, political sociologists have picked up on Foucault's notion of power and thought they saw in it something like the notions of power as in the 'Frankfurt School' (Marcuse, Habermas) that we discuss above. In addition, Foucault's own sketchy and (sometimes ill-considered) remarks on resistance have allowed some theorists to press into service a rather Marxist or Weberian notion of power, merely updated with a Foucaultian label. To understand the notion of power in Foucault, one first needs to understand it as a philosophical rather than a political concept. Foucault's early work – up to and including *The Archaeology of Knowledge* (1969) can be understood as *archaeological* in character (see the detailed discussion in Kendall and Wickham, 1999). It is important to note that archaeology is a historical analysis that eschews any discussion of power. Foucault's later work – from *Discipline and Punish* (1975) onwards – can be characterized as *genealogy*, a method that is in essence archaeology, or historical analysis, with the addition of a theory of power.

To the extent that archaeology was a theory of knowledge, it is only with the arrival of the genealogical method that Foucault's much-cited but oft-misunderstood pairing 'power–knowledge' came to the fore. To understand this pairing, we need to make some opening remarks about knowledge. For Foucault, a knowledge is composed of two poles, the sayable and the visible, or, to put it more prosaically, words and things. The relation between these two poles of knowledge is understood by

Foucault to be a discursive relation – by which Foucault means nothing more complicated than to assert that the discursive, or sayable, pole has primacy over and determines the non-discursive, or visible, pole of knowledge. When we imagine a knowledge, then, such as psychiatry, we must understood it as composed of these two poles – its discursive and its non-discursive elements – and be clear that the relation between these two poles within the knowledge has to be understood as one in which 'words' determine 'things'.

Philosophically, this is where Foucault runs into a problem. If words determine things within any knowledge we examine, how can there be any 'play' within the knowledge? How can such a system produce complex iterations, unexpected consequences, the occasional 'fightback' by things? For Foucault, the only way to allow his archaeological system to be more 'realistic' is to introduce the notion of 'power relations', which mediate between the discursive and the non-discursive (between words and things) and stop the latter being utterly consumed and determined by the former.

We can begin to see why it is misplaced to assume that Foucault's work is a mere equation of power and knowledge (Foucault's work is sometimes summarized as if he were saying little more than 'power is knowledge'); power is a relation within knowledge, but itself is not knowledge. Power makes the connections between the two poles of knowledge, yet it must exist outside these poles.

Deleuze (1988: 70) provides a helpful summary of Foucault's treatment of power:

> Power is a relation between forces, or rather every relation between forces is a power relation ... Force is never singular but essentially exists in relation with other forces, such that any force is already a relation, that is to say power: force has no other subject or object than force ... It is an action upon an action, on existing actions, or on those which may arise in the present or in the future; it is a set of actions upon other actions. We can therefore conceive of a necessarily open list of variables expressing a relation between forces or power relation, constituting actions upon actions: to incite, to induce, to seduce, to make easy or difficult, to enlarge or limit, to make more or less probable, and so on.

Power, then, is not repressive, but productive. Power is not a possession, but a description of a series of practices. Foucault does not understand power as an attribute of individuals, but as a characteristic of systems of knowledge (such as psychiatry, criminology, and similar).

As Deleuze suggests, forces have a capacity for resistance, such that power must be exercised in relation to a resistance. For Foucault,

resistance is integral to the exercise of power. Again, lest we characterize this resistance incorrectly in terms of Marxist class antagonism, or
Weberian contestation over subjectivity, we should stress that the best
analogy to use to understand Foucault's work on power and resistance is
taken from physics rather than from conventional political sociology.
Power and resistance are integral to Foucault's systematic theory of
knowledge – they are what make it work and what stop it working – just
as power and resistance light up or dim a bulb in an electrical circuit.

So far, we have argued, with the help of Deleuze, that power is a series
of relations between *forces*; on the other hand, Deleuze claims that for
Foucault, knowledge is a series of relations between *forms*. These forces
and forms engage with each other in a way that Foucault sees as analogous to combat on the battlefield. The two are quite different, however:
knowledge tends to be rigid and inflexible, while power is very flexible
and mobile. Power is also anonymous, in that it is the characteristic of a
system rather than the attribute of an individual. Power certainly does not
have an agenda, and Foucault characterizes it as both mute and blind. We
have to understand power as *mediating* the forms of knowledge yet
avoiding them – power then must be mute and blind since it avoids even
as it connects the sayable and the visible aspects of knowledge).

Subjectivity, or the various forms of self that are possible within
power-knowledge systems, is not for Foucault the locus or the source of
power. Rather, when discussing power as productive, Foucault is drawing our attention to the idea that power produces subjects. The formation of subjects is an element of power's productivity. Foucault writes:
'My objective ... has been to create a history of the different modes by
which, in our culture, human beings are made subjects' (1982: 208).
Foucault is not proposing the subject as producer, but as product.

To return now to some of the more usual concerns of political sociology, we can see that Foucault's notion of power, although it was devised
to deal with a philosophical rather than a political problem, takes us
away from the Hobbesian notion of power as capacity and possession;
it also takes us away from the equation of power with domination as
seen in the Weberian tradition, as well as the notion of power as repression in the Marxist tradition. Towards the end of his life, when his work
focused on the government of self and others, Foucault engaged with
the Weberian notion of domination, to the extent that he sought to distinguish power from domination. As he put it:

We must distinguish the relationships of power as strategic games
between liberties – strategic games that result in the fact that some
people try to determine the conduct of others – and states of domination, which are what we ordinarily call power. (Foucault, 1988: 19)

Here, Foucault distinguishes domination – a situation in which one individual has absolute power over another – from power, a situation in one actor tries to influence the conduct of another. The distinction between these two situations is very important for Foucault, because as he sees it, most of our thinking about power has in fact been thinking about the former. For Foucault, however, such situations of domination are rather rare: usually the object of such procedures has some 'liberties', some possibilities for resistance. When domination occurs, resistance is impossible. Yet as Foucault points out, and as our discussion of liberalism in Chapter 8 makes clear, liberal political strategies are not about the imposition of absolute power upon another who cannot disobey: rather, they aim at the reshaping of desire, and the generation of a subject who can self-regulate and self-govern. Domination is not liberalism's preferred power game.

Bruno Latour: actors and power

The Foucaultian conception of power is one that has become rather popular in the so-called 'new' political sociology. In particular, it has given impetus to a number of new accounts, especially in feminist political sociology, which stress the productivity of power, and generation of forms of self as an important but previously rather unacknowledged aspect of politics, and the importance of power at the micro- as well as the macro-level. Foucault, then, has facilitated the development of a new political sociology that has been able to consider not just the state, but politics at a number of local and mundane levels (although the study of politics outside the state is hardly new in the social sciences). We shall return to these so-called mundane levels shortly.

First, it is worth mentioning that while Foucault attempted to generate a theory of power at the level of subjectivity, especially in his last work on so-called 'techniques of the self' (see Foucault, 1986a), one is still left with a rather nagging feeling that Foucault's early adherence to the anonymous systems of knowledge makes his work on power and the self border on a form of determinism, much as Althusser and Poulantzas explicitly argued that the subject was a result of structures rather than an element in their composition. A paper by Bruno Latour, although rather schematic, allows us to develop the Foucaultian work on power but to understand the problem of the relation between structure and agency.

Latour (1986) follows Foucault to the extent that he refuses the notion of power as a possession. In fact, he suggests that *others* – those who perform the required action – have power when an order is successfully obeyed. Second, he suggests that although we tend to use power as a causal explanation of why someone important got something done, power is perhaps better used as a description of such a state of affairs. He advances these arguments by contrasting the notion of power as diffusion – the usual story – with power as translation – his own preferred description. Diffusion models of power imagine power starting from a 'powerful' source and making its way into the world. Along the way, it will no doubt meet resistances (lack of communication, opposition) that slow it down and weaken it. The initial force of the power may be strong enough to have its way, but it may be that the various resistances are enough to deny it. In such a model, power is a capacity: one can get one's way if one has enough of this mysterious substance that the various resistances one will meet are not enough to put an end to the ambitions of the 'power token' (perhaps an order) that is sent out into the world.

The translation model of power suggests that the movement of power depends upon others not resisting power, but adding to it, spreading it, using it for their own ends. It is others who make power work, by increasing its movement and facilitating its transmission. Power is the consequence of the energy that all these different actors give to the initial impetus. Latour uses the analogy of rugby players who, each in turn, move the ball around; the initial force of the first is worth little if others do not take up the task, and the action of the first is no more important than that of the middle or the last player of the ball. Latour suggests that power is about a chain of actors – not of patients – and that all these actors shape the initial impetus according to any number of projects, aims and ambitions. Power should be understood as made of the 'wills' of all the actors involved, and as a consequence of collective action, not its cause.

What is useful here is that Latour makes it clear that power is very much a result of networks of association between actors, rather than a disembodied and anonymous force. Although his theory is recoverable within Foucault's general schema of power, it adds to it by allowing us to see the ways in which power might be connected to actors as well as to knowledges.

Of course, Latour acknowledges that it may be possible for certain actors to be 'enrolled' – to be faithful to the wishes of those who wish to dominate. As he sees it, the construction of a successful network – being 'powerful' – is about successfully putting together a network. This network will be composed of faithful others, but it will also contain a number of other resources, social as well as material. For example, 'the power of the manager may now be obtained by a long series of telephone calls, record-keeping, walls, clothes and machines' (Latour,

1986: 276). Latour suggests that we are prone to seeing any number of elements – society, capital, power – as the causes, the glues that hold us together. Rather, according to Latour, we are held together by associations or networks.

Underlying Latour's work is a critique of power as it is used in (political) sociology, as a rather mystical cause. For Latour, power is an empty concept (inasmuch as we attribute it as a kind of magical resource to an individual or class) used to avoid doing the real work of explaining how networks and associations are successfully put together. Latour suggests we abandon the concept of power (and he is not afraid to suggest we abandon a whole range of 'magical' explanatory terms, ranging from 'society' to 'capital', on the grounds that they are results rather than causes), and concentrate instead on describing how local 'techniques' are put into action. At this point, Latour's work is integrated with Foucault, who also suggests attention to the local sites where 'relations' are knitted together.

From power to power: analysing sexuality

Foucault and Latour represent a new approach to power in political sociology, an approach which to an extent downgrades power (no longer with a capital 'p'), yet which tries to take it still more seriously by studying carefully its contexts, its forms of association, its reliance on a number of resources (knowledges, institutions, actors, non-human elements), its productivity, and its emergence in local situations. Such readings take us away from power as possession, as capacity, as domination, and as ideology. Yet it is worth stressing that such notions of power owe much to thinkers such as Weber, who was the first to stress the importance of discipline and regularity, those mundane elements of military life that colonized the rest of society, and Lukes, who emphasized that power must be studied in places where desires are shaped and reshaped. We conclude this chapter with a brief look at power in the realm of the politics of sexuality to illustrate the possibilities of the new reading of power.

Foucault's three-volume work on the history of sexuality in the West (Foucault, 1979, 1986a, 1986b) generated a new research paradigm in the field of the history of sexuality, and was the spur to much research in areas such as feminist and queer studies. Foucault directs attention, as in his previous work, to the importance of 'knowledges' for any account of modern society. For Foucault, knowledges such as psychoanalysis and sexology are of crucial importance in the analysis of the government of sexual conduct. As Foucault tells the story, sexual activity became a target of go vernmental intervention, especially in relation to the problematization of 'population'. In the nineteenth century, for example, a number of categories of sexual 'deviance' – the masturbating schoolboy, the hysterical woman, the sexual pervert (especially the homosexual), and the issue of the successful maintenance of the conjugal relation – emerged as problems inasmuch as they were felt to threaten the wellbeing of the population more generally.

In the first volume of *The History of Sexuality*, Foucault argues that these attempts to manage and govern the realm of sexual conduct could not be understood simply as an offshoot of capitalism; nor were they imposed on an unwilling lower class by the dominant orders. In outlining the history of these new forms of problematization, Foucault suggests that human science knowledges were critical in allowing new forms of social intervention to occur, not least since these human sciences provided the evidence and the technical measurement of pathology that justified intervention and guaranteed cure. Foucault also suggests that these governmental interventions did not act upon a pre-existing problem area, but to a certain extent incited and invented the problem. In the field of sexual perversion, for example, Foucault suggests that sexology and psychiatry generated and invented categories of perversion, and new types of personality – most notably the 'homosexual' – came into existence precisely as a result of the government/ knowledge couple.

What can we learn from this new approach about power? First of all, we see that power is no longer understood as operating in a top-down manner. For Foucault, the evidence suggests that the ruling classes experimented on themselves first, and generated new notions of sexual conduct and sexual pathology that only slowly made their way down to the lower classes. In this way, Foucault shows how power does not have to be understood as the imposition of the will of the rulers upon the ruled, which is the guiding principle of Marxist research on power. Second, Foucault shows us that power is not a possession of any class or individual, but is rather an agonism ('working muscle') within a system of knowledge. Power is not something which is held, but something which is put to work; its sphere of operation is within a series of knowledges, including psychiatry, sexology and psychoanalysis. Third, Foucault argues that power is productive rather than repressive. In this sense, he is closer to Parsons (who argued that power was a systemic property that helps societal functionality) than to Weber. The strategies of power generate new forms of social control, new forms of social organization, new problems for government, and new possibilities for all levels of society. Fourth, Foucault suggests that forms of subjectivity are a result of power, rather than pre-existing forms which are repressed and dominated by power relations; clearly, in this argument, Foucault's work is a departure from Marx and Weber.

Conclusion

In this chapter, we have reviewed a number of theories of power in political philosophy and political sociology. In starting with Machiavelli and Hobbes, we saw that power and sovereignty were virtual synonyms. The anti-Machiavellian literature, which we suggested was the forerunner of cameral (legislative and judicial) political ideas, made this notion more complicated, by conceptualizing power as suffused throughout the social body. Locke's contribution to the understanding of power also moved us beyond a notion of an external, transcendent sovereign; for Locke, a mutual relationship between the governor and the governed was one built on reason and rights. We should stress that the new political philosophy began to dovetail with the new sorts of liberal government that we discussed in Chapter 8. These forms of government, built on the notion of the rational, free individual, seek to construct techniques for ensuring efficient government through self-actualization.

After dealing with Locke, we moved to Marx. Although Marx refuses the starting point of the liberal philosophers – the presocial individual – in terms of his theory of power, Marx adds little to the base we have already seen established. For Marx, power is understood as a capacity and possession of the dominant classes, and the state comes to be an instrument of the class-based exercise of power. The subsequent Marxist tradition is especially notable for developing theories of power that tend to connect to notions of ideology. Poulantzas, for example, argues that the way to understand the operation of power is through the ideological devices or state apparatuses that are utilized to ensure the continuation of the interests of capital. Elite notions of power grow from similar sources as Marxism. In the work of probably the most famous elite theorist, C. Wright Mills, one can see close connections between elite theory and Marxism, although Mills stresses the relatively recent historical (and possibly contingent) emergence of a power-elite nexus, unlike Marxists for whom the interests of capital have a much more determining and often structural impact on state policy.

Pluralist theorists of power tend to argue in favour of power as reasonably widespread among different areas of society, and focus on the 'interest broking' between them when political decisions are reached. In taking democracy at face value, pluralists produce a quite optimistic view of the use of power by the state and in public life in general. There are clear links between pluralist theories and Weber's work on power. Weber, of course, engaged with Marxism in suggesting that society is composed of considerably more than just social classes, and drew our attention to the various status and party groups that cut across class lines. For Weber, the uses of power were never understood simply as the domination of the ruling classes. More worrisome was a concern with rational-legal forms of authority, the dominant form in modern society, which threatened to engulf the individual. Because Weber laboured with an understanding of power as a zero-sum game, the acquisition of power by impersonal bureaucracies could only be at the expense of the individual. Similar concerns can be seen in theorists as diverse as Marcuse and Habermas, both of whom show great anxiety about how the power of modern bureaucracies tends to decimate civil society. Weber also made important contributions to our understanding of the spread of military-style discipline throughout society.

In the theories of power reviewed above, repeatedly we see power theorized as capacity, as possession, as a top-down phenomenon, and as an essentially negative phenomenon. Steven Lukes's work on the 'three faces' of power provides a significant advance on these theories. Lukes suggests that power comes in a number of forms, including the ability to set agendas, and the ability to shape desires. Lukes can be regarded as anticipating Foucault on power in liberal societies. We stressed at some length that Foucault's studies on power are perhaps best understood as philosophical rather than political in the first instance; none the less, his emphasis on the productivity of power and its role in the formation rather than the negation of subjectivities provides a watershed in theories of power. Foucault also cuts power loose from dominant social actors, suggesting its omnipresence in social systems pitted by human science knowledges. For Foucault, power is not the prerogative of the rulers, but can be seen in almost any social interaction.

While there are advantages to Foucault's impersonal notion of power, based on a notion of anonymous strategic force relations, we turned to Latour to finesse some of Foucault's work. Latour is extremely critical of notions of power as possessed capacity, and argues that we need to rid ourselves of the notion of power altogether. Rather than use such 'magical' explanations, and rather than mistaking effects for causes, we need to turn our attention to the empirical question of how various actors have other actors do their will. For Latour, the answer to this question lies in the analysis of networks of association, which are composed of other human actors, but also of non-human elements that help guarantee the solidity of the networks.

The theories of power that can be seen in writers like Foucault and Latour have been important in the development of what is sometimes called the 'new political sociology'. To give an example of this new sociology, we looked briefly at Foucault's work on sexuality. In this approach, the role of state power is downgraded: power now tends to be theorized in rather different ways, and it is no longer understood simply as a matter of sovereignty. 'Mundane power' has now become an object of this political sociology. Moreover, power now tends to be studied as a major element in processes of subjectification or person-formation. The 'old political sociology', whether under the impress of liberalism or of Marxism, tends to understand the human individual as a natural phenomenon (whether fundamentally individual or fundamentally social), and power, especially state power, can only be understood as a repression or a deformation of authentic forms of self. In the 'new political sociology', the self has come to be understood as a constructed entity, possessing no essence or authenticity. There is no self to deform or repress, and power is rather understood as constituting and inventing the self. In this way, power *per se* is neither good nor evil; various forms of self emerge in various historical and cultural conjunctures. In concluding, we suggest that it is important to understand that this more fluid notion of self needs to be understood at the same time as we seek to study politics at the more macro-level. We have characterized liberalism and neo-liberalism as reliant, of course, upon particular forms of self; the work of scholars such as Norbert Elias draws our attention to the historical and cultural variability and interconnection of forms of governance and forms of self. If we make use of some of the more recent theories of power we have canvassed in this chapter, we are able to understand better three issues: forms of government, forms of subjectivity, and the interdependence of the two.

Chapter 10

Postscript: The Future of the State

Throughout the previous chapters we have outlined the factors that help explain the development of the modern state – including in countries outside the north-west European region where it may be considered to have originated. In doing so we have elaborated key concepts and descriptions, such as sovereignty and legitimacy, and also the distinction between state and society that has played a large part in theorizing the state, especially in liberalism, and how that line between the two spheres is often hazy, frequently indented and interpenetrated, and has moved according to ideological and political predilection (one way with social democracy and state socialism, and back again with neo-liberalism and policies such as privatization).

For the most part we have been concerned with the liberal democratic state (although we have provided important contrasts with other forms throughout the book), and with its territoriality, nationalism, and inter-state relationships based on respect for borders and the sovereignty within them. This Westphalian model, however, has come under increased challenge in recent years. Globalization, for example, with the growth of worldwide financial integration in finance, currency, capital and other markets, and the virtually instantaneous movement of huge private funds between territories, threatens domestic and popular democratic power. Multilateral and international governance regimes, and the rise of social, cultural and legal issues around human rights and ecology especially, also raise questions about, if not actually the demise of the nation state, then certainly the severe attenuation of its authority. Power appears increasingly found in the practices and institutions of civil and global society that are not easily contained or directed by formal state apparatuses within national territories.

It is worth mentioning that the increased perception of the importance of global level politics and economic management has provided a fillip to a variety of 'alternative politics'. Where once these might have been regarded as trivial, or distractions from the 'real' business of politics, campaigns for rights (human, gay, women's, animal, and so on), and for ecological issues, have come to the fore, especially in the last ten years. Ecological politics has not only emerged as a kind of alternative to 'old-fashioned' sovereign politics, but also as a way of understanding politics that stretch beyond the nation state (pollution, or nuclear disasters such as the Chernobyl disaster, are no respecters of national boundaries). In this way, the sorts of neo-liberal concern with 'going beyond the state' have chimed with a number of alternative politics that do not necessarily have any time for the economic theories of, say, the Chicago School.

Yet our overall approach suggests that the death of the nation state is much exaggerated. Rather than picturing it being assailed from all sides in a battle in which there can be only one victor, we argue that the state is highly implicated in many of the processes that appear to undermine it. We have shown that the representative legitimacy, regulatory powers and the deep pockets of states are resources that continue to impress transnational corporations, although, in turn, states cannot ignore the economic benefits of such organizations for their citizenry in the form of employment and overall prosperity. The consequence is more an alliance (albeit a wary one) than a relationship of mutual antagonism.

There is little doubt, however, that the world has changed and that national state sovereignty is less than it was. It has to be gained and exercised within wider international constraints. But nation states – singly and together – continue to provide both the means for increased worldwide economic globalization and also its regulatory control. And while countries may appear formally equal in the eyes and practices of multinational regimes and associations, clearly they are not. The US, Europe, Japan, and Canada, for example, possess the technical and trade resources to have far better chances of exercising influence than weaker countries. Increasingly, developing nations also face challenges to their sovereign representative powers by the inclusion of global social movements and civil organizations (NGOs) within the consultative practices of the major international governance bodies.

Moreover, we have argued that globalization, too often interpreted in economic terms, is a political phenomenon too. States in recent decades not only fall into military and collective security blocs, but also in their trade and regulatory approaches operate both to spur and to contain the extension of worldwide processes and institutions. Internally, despite the development of the so-called enabling state, and of more inclusive networks and communities of key policy-makers covering both the public and the private sectors that are found in many liberal democracies, states remain ambitious in the scope of their authority. As a result, particularly in perhaps the admittedly exceptional case of Britain, the worry by business and professional bodies is focused more an increasingly interventionist, monitoring and controlling state than on an allegedly powerless one. In eras of democracy, mass media and risk, for every cry for the state to desist there is likely to be at least a matching call for the state to step in and to protect.

It is not clear that the liberal democratic form of state will be triumphant around the world, as some have claimed. Enthusiastic advocates of such propositions, generally writing in the immediate aftermath of the ending of the Cold War and the fall of eastern European communism, have received short shrift in the social sciences, usually on the sound basis that history teaches us to be wary about claims for the triumph of any regime or set of principles. For every principle or approach there is an opposite and, before long, these opposites and their supporters find their voices and build their constituencies. However, alternatives to liberal democracy are not that plentiful, particularly if we leave out the populous case of China where the impact of wider market forces on its political arrangements are not easy to foresee. The issue is less whether constitutionally nation states exhibit liberal democracy than whether their practices – free assembly, an independent mass media, lack of corruption, and so on – live up to liberal democratic ideals. It is only in this sense that it would appear sensible to talk in terms of the worldwide victory of liberal democracy. But there is a strong case for suggesting that the plurality of such forms may better suit the complexity of the modern world than more authoritarian approaches (which generally do not have a good track record of recent success).

In conclusion, many of the key questions for the nation state are likely to focus around its ability to retain popular involvement and democratic authority in an age when global complexity seems to require more technocratic and often law-like interventions for effectiveness and efficiency. State ownership and control are less the chief concerns than the rise of regulation, often perverse and unintended in its consequences, and whether governments will be able to find ways that allow their societies to breathe and to contribute to overall governance, within the frameworks of democratic accountability, in a world where the nation state appears to operate at increasingly length from its populations.

Bibliography

Albrow, M. (1996) *The Global Age* (Cambridge: Polity Press).

Ali, T. (2002) *The Clash of Fundamentalisms: Crusades, Jihads and Modernity* (London: Verso).

Allinson, G. (1997) *Japan's Postwar History* (Ithaca: Cornell University Press).

Almond, G. and Verba, S. (1963) *The Civic Culture* (Princeton: Princeton University Press).

Althusser, L. (1969) *For Marx* (Harmondsworth: Penguin).

Althusser, L. (1970) *Reading Capital* (London: New Left Books).

Amsden, A. (1989) *Asia's Next Giant* (New York: Oxford University Press).

Anderson, B. (1983) *Imagined Communities* (London: Verso).

Anderson, P. (1974) *Lineages of the Absolutist State* (London: New Left Books).

Appadurai, A. (1990) 'Disjuncture and Difference in the Global Cultural Economy', *Theory, Culture and Society*, 7, 295–310.

Axelrod, R. (1984) *The Evolution of Cooperation* (New York: Basic Books).

Axford, B. (1995) *The Global System* (Cambridge: Polity Press).

Bachrach, P. and Baratz, M. (1962) 'Two Faces of Power', *American Political Science Review*, 56, 947–52.

Bagnasco, A. (2001) 'Trust and Social Capital', in Nash, K. and Scott, A. (eds), *The Blackwell Companion to Political Sociology* (Oxford: Blackwell), 230–39.

Baker, G. (2002) 'Problems in the Theorisation of Global Civil Society', *Political Studies*, 50, 5, December, 928–43.

Baumol, W. (2002) *The Free-Market Innovation Machine* (Princeton: Princeton University Press).

Beccaria, C. (1970) *A Discourse on Public Economy and Commerce* (New York: Franklin).

Beck, U. (1992) *Risk Society* (London: Sage).

Beck, U. (1997) *What is Globalization?* (Cambridge: Polity).

Becker, G.C. (1964) *Human Capital* (New York: National Bureau of Economic Research).

Becker, G.C. (1976) *The Economic Approach to Human Behavior* (Chicago: University of Chicago Press).

Beetham, D. (2001) 'Political Legitimacy', in Nash, K. and Scott, A. (eds), *The Blackwell Companion to Political Sociology* (Oxford: Blackwell), 107–16.

Benyon, J. and Dunkerley, D. (eds) (2000) *Globalization: The Reader* (London: Athlone Press).

Berelson, B. (1954) *Voting* (Chicago: University of Chicago Press).

Bessel, R. (2000) 'The Crisis of Modern Democracy, 1919–45', in Potter, D. *et al.* (eds), *Democratization* (Cambridge: Polity/OU Press).

Beveridge, W. (1942) *Social Insurance and Allied Services* (London: HMSO).

Bobbio, N. (1990) *Liberalism and Democracy* (London: Verso).

Botero, G. (1589) *Della ragion di stato* (Venetia: Appresso i Gioliti).

Bourdieu, P. and Passeron, J.-L. (1990) *Reproduction in Education, Society and Culture* (London: Sage).

Bowles, S. and Gintis, H. (1976) *Schooling in Capitalist America: Educational Reform and the Contradictions of Economic Life* (London: Routledge and Kegan Paul).

Braithwaite, J. (2002) *Restorative Justice and Responsive Regulation* (New York: Oxford University Press).

Braithwaite, J. and Drahos, P. (2000) *Global Business Regulation* (Cambridge: Cambridge University Press).

Brown, C. (2001) *Understanding International Relations* (London: Palgrave), Second edition.

Brown, W. (1996) *States of Injury: Power and Freedom in Late Modernity* (Princeton: Princeton University Press).

Budé, G. (1547/1966) *Du l'institution du prince* (Farnborough: Gregg Press).

Bull, H. (1977/1995) *The Anarchical Society* (London: Macmillan).

Burchell, G. (1996) 'Liberal Government and Techniques of the Self', in Barry, A., Osborne, T. and Rose, N. (eds), *Foucault and Political Reason: Liberalism, Neo-Liberalism and Rationalities of Government* (London: UCL Press).

Burnham, J. (1941) *The Managerial Revolution* (Bloomington: Indiana University Press).

Camilleri, J. and Falk, J. (1992) *The End of Sovereignty?* (Cheltenham: Edward Elgar).

Cammack, P. (2000) 'Democracy and Dictatorship in Latin America, 1930–80', in Potter, D. *et al.* (eds), *Democratization* (Cambridge: Polity/Open University Press).

Carr, E.H. (1939) *The Twenty Years of Crisis* (London: Macmillan).

Castells, M. (1996/1998/2000a) *The Information Age,* Vols 1–3 (Oxford: Blackwell).

Castells, M. (2000b) 'Materials for an Explanatory Theory of the Network Society', *British Journal of Sociology*, 51, 1, 5–24.

Castles, S. and Davidson, A. (2000) *Citizenship and Migration* (London: Palgrave).

Castles, S. and Miller, M. (1993) *The Age of Migration* (London: Macmillan).

Cawson, A. and Saunders, P. (1983) 'Corporatism, Competitive Politics, and Class Struggle', in King, R. (ed.), *Capital and Politics* (London: Routledge and Kegan Paul).

Chemnitz, B.P. von (1647) *Dissertatio de ratione status in Imperio nostro Romano-germanico* (Freistadii).

Clark, I. (1999) *Globalization and International Relations Theory* (Oxford: Oxford University Press).

Clarke, M. (2000) *Regulation* (London: Macmillan).

Cohen, B. (2000) 'Money in a Globalized World', in Woods, N. (ed.), *The Political Economy of Globalization* (London: Palgrave).

Cohen, R. and Kennedy, P. (2000) *Global Sociology* (London: Palgrave).

Crouch, C. (2001) 'Markets and States', in Nash, K. and Scott, A. (eds), *The Blackwell Companion to Political Sociology* (Oxford: Blackwell), 240–9.

Dahl, R. (1956) *A Preface to Democratic Theory* (London: University of Chicago Press).

Dahl, R. (1961) *Who Governs?* (New Haven: Yale University Press).

Dahl, R. (1985) *A Preface to an Economic Theory of Democracy* (Cambridge: Polity Press).

Davies, N. (1997) *Europe* (London: Pimlico).

Davies, N. (1999) *The Isles* (London: Macmillan).

De Jong, H. (1996) 'European Capitalism: Between Freedom and Social Justice', in Bratton, W. *et al.* (eds), *International Regulatory Competition and Coordination* (Oxford: Oxford University Press).

Dean, M. (1999) *Governmentality: Power and Rule in Modern Society* (London: Sage).

Dearlove, J. (2000) Review article: 'Globalization and the State', *Politics*, May.

Dearlove, J. and Saunders, P. (2000) *Introduction to British Politics*, 3rd edn (Cambridge: Polity).

Delanty, G. (2000) *Citizenship in a Global Age* (Buckingham: Open University Press).

Deleuze, G. (1988) *Foucault* (Minneapolis: University of Minnesota Press).

Diamond, L. and Platter, M (1995) *Economic Reform and Democracy* (Baltimore: Johns Hopkins University Press).

Dicken, P., Kelly, P.F., Olds, K. and Yeung, H.W.-C. (2001) 'Chains and networks, territories and scales: towards a relational framework for analysing the global economy', *Global Networks*, 1, 2, 89–112.

Dinan, D. (1999) *Ever Closer Union: An Introduction to European Integration* (Basingstoke: Macmillan).

Donzelot, J. (1979) *The Policing of Families* (New York: Pantheon).

Dreyer, J.T. (1993) *China's Political System: Modernization and Tradition* (Basingstoke: Macmillan).

Duncan, G. and Lukes, S. (1963) 'The New Democracy', *Political Studies*, 11, 156–77.

Dunleavy, P. (1991) *Democracy, Bureaucracy and Public Choice* (Brighton: Harvester Wheatsheaf).

Dunleavy, P. and O'Leary, B. (1987) *Theories of the State* (London: Macmillan).

Dunne, T. (1995) 'The Social Construction of International Society', *European Journal of International Relations*, 1, 367–89.

Dunning, J. (2000) 'The New Geography of Foreign Direct Investment', in Woods, N. (ed.), *The Political Economy of Globalization* (London: Macmillan).

Durkheim, E. (1933/1993) *The Division of Labour* (New York: Free Press).

Dutton, M.R. (1992) *Policing and Punishment in China: From Patriarchy to the People* (Cambridge: Cambridge University Press).

Dyson, K. (1980) *The State Tradition in Western Europe* (Oxford: Martin Robertson).

Dyson, K. (ed.) (2002) *European States and the Euro* (Oxford: Oxford University Press).

Economist, The (2001) 'A Survey of Globalization', 29 September.

Edwards, G. (1996) 'National Sovereignty versus Integration', in Richardson, J. (ed.), *European Union* (London: Routledge).

Elias, N. (1978 and 1982) *The History of Manners*, Vols 1 and 2: *State Formation and Civilization* (Oxford: Basil Blackwell).

Elias, N. (1996) *The Germans: Power Struggles and the Development of Habitus in the Nineteenth and Twentieth Centuries* (Cambridge: Polity).

Esping-Andersen, G. (1990) *The Three Worlds of Welfare Capitalism* (Cambridge: Polity).

Etzioni, A. (1993) *The Spirit of Community* (New York: Crown).

Evans, P. (1995) *Embedded Autonomy* (Princeton: Princeton University Press).

Ewald, F. (1991) 'Insurance and Risk', in Burchell, G., Gordon, C. and Miller, P. (eds), *The Foucault Effect: Studies in Governmentality* (Hemel Hempstead: Harvester Wheatsheaf).

Fairbank, J. (1992) *China: A New History* (Cambridge, MA: Harvard University Press).

Feigenbaum, H. *et al.* (1998) *Shrinking the State* (Cambridge: Cambridge University Press).

Financial Times (28 August 2002) 'Government and Regulation'.

Foucault, M. (1969/1972) *The Archaeology of Knowledge* (London: Tavistock).

Foucault, M. (1975/1977) *Discipline and Punish* (London: Penguin).

Foucault, M. (1979) 'Governmentality', *I and C*, 6, 5–21.

Foucault, M. (1979) *The History of Sexuality*, Vol. 1: *An Introduction* (London: Allen Lane).

Foucault, M. (1980) 'Truth and Power', in Gordon, C. (ed.), *Michel Foucault. Power/Knowledge: Selected Interviews and Other Writings 1972–1977* (Brighton: Harvester).

Foucault, M. (1981) 'Omnes et Singulatim: Towards a Criticism of Political Reason', in McMurrin, S. (ed.), *The Tanner Lectures on Human Values*, Vol. 2 (Salt Lake City: University of Utah Press).

Foucault, M. (1982) 'The Subject and Power: an Afterword', in Dreyfus, H. and Rabinow, P., *Michael Foucault: Beyond Structuralism and Hermeneutics* (Chicago: University of Chicago Press).

Foucault, M. (1986a) *The Care of the Self* (London: Pantheon).

Foucault, M. (1986b) *The Use of Pleasures* (London: Pantheon).

Foucault, M. (1988) 'The Ethic of Care of the Self as a Practice of Freedom', Bernauer, J. and Rasmussen, D. (eds), *The Final Foucault* (Boston, MA: MIT Press).

Foucault, M. (1989) 'Naissance de la Biopolitique', *Résumé des cours 1970–82* (Paris: Juilliard).

Frank, A. (1967) *Capitalism and Underdevelopment in Latin America* (New York: Monthly Review Press).

Friedman, M. (1962/82) *Capitalism and Freedom* (London and Chicago: University of Chicago Press).

Friedman, M. and Friedman, R. (1980) *Free to Choose* (New York: Harcourt Brace Jovanovich).

Fukuyama, F. (1989) 'The End of History?', *The National Interest*, 16.

Fukuyama, F. (1992) *The End of History and the Last Man* (New York: Free Press).

Galbraith, J. (1953) *American Capitalism* (Boston: Houghton Mifflin).

Gamble, A. (1981) *Britain in Decline* (London: Macmillan).

Gamble, A. and Kelly, G. (2002) 'Britain and the EMU', in Dyson, K. (ed.), *European States and the Euro* (Oxford: Oxford University Press).

Gamble, A. and Wright, T. (eds) (1999) *The New Social Democracy* (Oxford: Blackwell).

Garrett, G. (1998) *Partisan Politics in the Global Economy* (Cambridge: Cambridge University Press).

Garratt, G. (2000) 'Globalization and National Autonomy', in Woods, N. (ed.), *The Political Economy of Globalization* (London: Palgrave).

Gerth, H. and Mills, C. (1958) *From Max Weber* (London: Routledge and Kegan Paul).

Gibbons, M. (2004) 'Globalization, Innovation, and the Universities', in King, R. (ed.), *The University in the Global Age* (London: Palgrave Macmillan).

Giddens, A. (1979) *Central Problems in Social Theory: Action, Structure and Contradiction in Social Analysis* (London: Macmillan).

Giddens, A. (1985) *The Nation State and Violence* (Cambridge: Polity).

Giddens, A. (1990) *The Consequences of Modernity* (Cambridge: Polity).

Giddens, A. (1994) 'Living in a Post-Traditional Society', in Beck, U. *et al.* (eds), *Reflexive Modernization* (Cambridge: Polity).

Giddens, A. (1998) *The Third Way: The Renewal of Social Democracy* (Cambridge: Polity).

Gill, G. (2000) *The Dynamics of Democratization* (London: Palgrave).

Gilpin, R. (1981) *War and Change in World Politics* (New York: Cambridge University Press).

Gluck, C. (1985) *Japan's Modern Myths* (Princeton: Princeton University Press).

Goçek, F.M. (1987) *East–West Encounter* (Oxford: Oxford University Press).

Goldblatt, D. (2000a) 'Democracy in the Long Nineteenth Century: 1760–1919', in Potter, D. *et al.* (eds), *Democratization* (Cambridge: Polity/OU Press).

Goldblatt, D. (2000b) 'Democracy in Europe: 1939–89', in Potter, D. *et al.* (eds), *Democratization* (Cambridge: Polity/OU Press).

Gordon, C. (1991) 'Governmental Rationality: an Introduction', in Burchell, G., Gordon, C. and Miller, P. (eds), *The Foucault Effect: Studies in Governmentality* (Hemel Hempstead: Harvester Wheatsheaf).

Gramsci, A. (1971) *Selections from the Prison Notebooks* (New York: International Publishers).

Gramsci, A. (1978) *Selections from Political Writings* (London: Lawrence and Wishart).

Green, A. (1990) *Education and State Formation: The Rise of Education Systems in England, France and the USA* (London: Macmillan).

Gummett, P. (ed.) (1996) *Globalization and Public Policy* (Cheltenham: Edward Elgar).

Habermas, J. (1976) *Legitimation Crisis* (London: Heinemann).

Habermas, J. (1984) *The Theory of Communicative Action*, Vol. 1: *Reason and the Rationalization of Society* (Cambridge: Polity Press).

Habermas, J. (1987a) *The Philosophical Discourse of Modernity* (Cambridge, MA: MIT Press).

Habermas, J. (1987b) *The Theory of Communicative Action*, Vol. 2: *The Critique of Functionalist Reason* (Cambridge: Polity Press).

Hacking, I. (1986) *The Taming of Chance* (Cambridge: Cambridge University Press).

Harding, N. (1984) 'Socialism, Society, and the Organic Labour State', in Harding, N. (ed.), *The State in Socialist Society* (London: Macmillan).

Hart, N. (1989) 'Gender and the Rise and Fall of Class Politics', *New Left Review*, 175 (May/June) 19–47.

Harvey, D. (1989) *The Condition of Postmodernity* (Oxford: Blackwell).

Hay, C. and Watson, M. (1999) 'Globalization: "Sceptical" Notes on the 1999 Reith Lectures', *Political Quarterly*, 70, 4, 418–25.

Hay, C. and Marsh, D. (eds) (2000) *Demystifying Globalization* (London: Palgrave).

Hayek, F. (1944) *The Road to Serfdom* (London: Routledge and Kegan Paul).

Hayek, F. (1960) *The Constitution of Liberty* (London: Routledge).

Hayek, F. (1976) *Law, Legislation and Liberty*, Vol. 2: *The Mirage of Social Justice* (London: Routledge and Kegan Paul).

Hayek, F. (1979) *Law, Legislation and Liberty*, Vol. 3: *The Political Order of a Free People* (London: Routledge and Kegan Paul).

Hegel, G. (1821) *Philosophy of Right* (Oxford: Oxford University Press).

Held, D. (ed.) (1991) *Political Theory Today* (Cambridge: Polity).

Held, D. (1996) *Models of Democracy* (Cambridge: Polity Press).

Held, D. (2002) 'Cosmopolitanism: Ideas, Realities and Deficits', in Held, D. and McGrew, A. (eds) *Governing Globalization* (Cambridge: Polity).

Held, D. *et al.* (1999) *Global Transformations* (Cambridge: Polity).

Held, D. *et al.* (eds) (1983) *States and Societies* (New York: New York University Press).

Held, D. and McGrew, A. (eds) (2000) *Governing Globalization* (Cambridge: Polity).

Heywood, A. (2000) *Key Concepts in Politics* (London: Palgrave).

Hindess, B. (1996) *Discourses of Power: from Hobbes to Foucault* (Oxford: Blackwell).

Hindess, B. (1998) 'Neo-Liberalism and the National Economy', in Dean, M. and Hindess, B. (eds), *Governing Australia: Studies in Contemporary Rationalities of Government* (Cambridge: Cambridge University Press).

Hirst, P. (1997) 'The International Origins of National Sovereignty', in Hirst, P. (ed.), *From Statism to Pluralism* (London: UCL Press).

Hirst, P. and Thompson, G. (1996) *Globalization in Question* (Cambridge: Polity).

Hirst, P. and Thompson, G. (1999) *Globalization in Question: the International Economy and the Possibilities of Governance*, 2nd edn (Cambridge: Polity).

Hobbes, T. (1651/1991) *Leviathan* (Cambridge: Cambridge University Press).

Hobbes, T. (1642/1998) *On the Citizen (De Cive)* (Cambridge: Cambridge University Press).

Hobson, J.A. (1902/1968) *Imperialism* (London: Allen Unwin).

Hobson, J.A. (1909) *The Crisis of Liberalism* (London: King and Son).

Hobson, J.A. (1915) *Towards International Government* (London: Allen Unwin).

Hobson, J.A. (1920) *The Morals of Economic Interventionism* (New York: Houghton).

Hobson, J.M. (1997) *The Wealth of Nations* (Cambridge: Cambridge University Press).

Hobson, J.M. (2000) *The State and International Relations* (Cambridge: Cambridge University Press).

Hobson, J.M. and Weiss, L. (1995) *States and Economic Development* (Cambridge: Cambridge University Press).

Hunter, A. and Sexton, J. (1999) *Contemporary China* (London: Macmillan).

Hunter, F. (1953) *Community Power Structure* (North Carolina: Chapel Hill).

Hunter, I. (1994) *Rethinking the School: Subjectivity, Bureaucracy, Criticism* (Sydney: Allen and Unwin).

Hunter, I. (2001) *Rival Enlightenments* (Cambridge: Cambridge University Press).

Huntingdon, S. (1991) *The Third Wave* (Norman: University of Oklahoma Press).

Huntingdon, S. (1993) 'The Clash of Civilizations', *Foreign Affairs*, 72, 22–49.

Huntingdon, S. (1996) *The Clash of Civilizations* (New York: Simon and Schuster).

Imbar, M. (2002) 'Functionalism', in Held, D. and McGrew, A. (2002).

Jessop, B. (2002) *The Future of the Capitalist State* (Cambridge: Polity).

John, P. (1998) *Analysing Public Policy* (London: Continuum).

John, P. (2001) 'Policy Networks', in Nash, K. and Scott, A. (eds), *The Blackwell Companion to Political Sociology* (Oxford: Blackwell), 139–48.

Jones, K. and Williamson, K. (1979) 'The Birth of the Schoolroom', *I&C*.

Justi, J.H.G. von (1768) *Éléments généraux de police*.

Kaldor, M. (2001) *New and Old Wars* (Cambridge: Polity).

Kanter, R.M. (1995) *World Class: Thriving Locally in the Global Economy* (New York: Simon and Schuster).

Keating, M. and Hooghe, L. (1996) 'By-passing the Nation State?', in Richardson, J. (ed.), *European Union* (London: Routledge).

Kendall, G. and Wickham, G. (1999) *Using Foucault's Methods* (London: Sage).

Keohane, R. (1984) *After Hegemony* (Princeton: Princeton University Press).

Keohane, R. (1989) *International Institutions and State Power* (Boulder, CO: Westview Press).

Kerr, C. et al. (1973) *Industrialism and Industrial Man* (London: Penguin).

Keynes, J.M. (1926) *The End of Laissez-Faire* (London: Hogarth).

Knemeyer, F. (1980) 'Polizei', *Economy and Society*, 9, 2, 172–96.

Kornhauser, W. (1960) *The Politics of Mass Society* (Glencoe, IL: Free Press).

Krasner, S. (ed.) (1983) *International Regimes* (Ithaca: Cornell University Press).

Kreiger, J. (1999) *British Politics in the Global Age: Can Social Democracy Survive?* (Cambridge: Polity).

Kurdi, A. (1984) *The Islamic State: a Study Based on the Islamic Holy Constitution* (London: Mansell).

Kymlicka, W. (1990) *Contemporary Political Philosophy: An Introduction* (Oxford: Clarendon).

Lane, D. (1985) *State and Society in the USSR* (London: Blackwell).

Langhorne, R. (2001) *The Coming of Globalization* (London: Palgrave).

La Perrière, G. de (1567) *Miroir Politique* (Paris).

Larner, W. and Le Heron, R. (2002) 'The Spaces and Subjects of a Globalising Economy: a Situated Exploration of Method', *Society and Space*, 20, 6, December, 753–74.

Lasch, S. and Urry, J. (1987) *The End of Organised Capitalism* (Cambridge: Polity).

Latour, B. (1986) 'The Powers of Association', in Law, J. (ed.), *Power, Belief and Action* (London: Routledge), 264–80.

Latour, B. (1993) *We Have Never Been Modern* (Hemel Hempstead: Harvester Wheatsheaf).

Lazarsfeld, P. et al. (1948) *The People's Choice* (New York: Columbia University Press).

Lenin, V. (1916/1933) *Imperialism* (London: Martin Lawrence).

Lenin, V. (1917/1932) *State and Revolution* (New York: International Publishers).

Lenin, V.I. (1902/1967a) 'What is to be done?', in *Selected Works* (New York: International Publishers).

Lenin, V.I. (1904/1967b) 'One Step Forward, Two Steps Backward', in *Selected Works* (New York: International Publishers).

Lenin, V.I. (1905/1967c) 'Two Tactics of Social Democracy in the Democratic Revolution', in *Selected Works* (New York: International Publishers).

Levi, M. (1996) 'Social and Unsocial Capital', *Politics and Society*, 24, 1, 45–55.

Lewis, B. (1982) *The Muslim Discovery of Europe* (New York: Norton).

Lewis, P. (2000) 'Democratization in Eastern Europe', in Potter, D. et al. (eds), *Democratization* (Cambridge: Polity/OU Press).

Lindblom, C. (1977) *Politics and Markets* (New York: Basic Books).

Ling, T. (1998) *The British State since 1945* (Cambridge: Polity).

Linklater, A. (1998) *The Transformation of Political Community* (Cambridge: Polity).

Linz, J. (1990) 'The Perils of Presidentialism', *Journal of Democracy*, 1, Winter.

Linz, J. and Stepan, A. (1996) *Problems of Democratic Transition and Consolidation* (Baltimore: John Hopkins University Press).

Lipset, S. (1960) *Political Man* (London: Heinemann).

Lipset, S. and Rokkan, S. (1967) *Party Systems and Voter Alignments* (New York: Free Press).

Little, W. (2000) 'Democratization in Latin America, 1980–95', in Potter, D. et al. (eds), *Democratization* (Cambridge: Polity/OU Press).

Locke, J. (1689/1988) *Two Treatises of Government* (Cambridge: Cambridge University Press).

Lowndes, V. and Wilson, D. (2001) 'Social Capital and Local Governance', *Political Studies*, 49, 4, 629–47.

Lukes, S. (1974) *Power: A Radical View* (London: Macmillan).

Machiavelli, N. (1513/1988) *The Prince* (Cambridge: Cambridge University Press).

Mainwaring, S. *et al.* (eds) (1992) *Issues in Democratic Consolidation* (South Bend, IN: University of Notre Dame Press).

Majone, G. (1996) 'A European Regulatory State?' in Richardson, J. (ed.), *European Union* (London: Routledge).

Major, J. (2000) *John Major: The Autobiography* (London: HarperCollins).

Mann, M. (1986) *The Sources of Social Power*, Vol. 1 (Cambridge: Cambridge University Press).

Mann, M. (1988) *States, War and Capitalism* (Oxford: Blackwell).

Mann, M. (1993) *The Rise of Classes and Nation States, 1760–1914: The Sources of Social Power*, Vol. 2 (Cambridge: Cambridge University Press).

Mann, M. (1996) 'Ruling Class Strategies and Citizenship', in Bulmer, M. and Rees, A. (eds), *Citizenship Today* (London: UCL Press).

Marcuse, H. (1972) *One Dimensional Man* (London: Abacus).

Marshall, T. (1950) *Citizenship and Social Class* (Cambridge: Cambridge University Press).

Marshall, T.H. (1949/1963) 'Citizenship and Social Class', in his *Sociology at the Crossroads and Other Essays* (London: Heinemann).

Marx, K. (1852/1963) *The Eighteenth Brumaire of Louis Bonaparte* (New York: International Publishers).

Marx, K. (1871/1970) *The Civil War in France* (Peking: Foreign Languages Press).

Marx, K. (1857/1970) *Critique* (Cambridge: Cambridge University Press).

Marx, K. (1867/1981) *Capital: A Critique of Political Economy*, Vol. 3 (Harmondsworth: Penguin).

Marx, K. and Engels, F. (1846/1976) *The German Ideology: Marx and Engels, Collected Works*, Vol. 5 (London: Lawrence and Wishart).

Marx, K. and Engels, F. (1848/1967) *The Communist Manifesto* (Harmondsworth: Penguin).

Mathews, J. (2002) *Dragon Multinational* (Oxford: Oxford University Press).

Mauss, M. (1985) 'A Category of the Human Mind: the Notions of Person; the notion of Self', in Carrithers, M., Collins, S., and Lukes, S. (eds), *The Category of the Person* (Cambridge: Cambridge University Press).

McCargo, D. (2000) *Contemporary Japan* (London: Palgrave).

McGrew, A. (2002) 'Liberal Internationalism: Between Realism and Cosmopolitanism', in Held, D. and McGrew, A. (eds), *Governing Globalization* (Cambridge: Polity).

Michels, R. (1911/1959) *Political Parties* (New York: Dover Publications).

Middlemas, K. (1979) *Politics in Industrial Society* (London: Deutsch).

Miliband, R. (1969) *The State in Capitalist Society* (London: Wiedenfeld and Nicolson).

Miliband, R. (1972) 'Poulantzas and the Capitalist State', *New Left Review*, 82, 83–94.

Miller, H.L. (2000) 'The Late Imperial Chinese State', in Shambaugh, D. (ed.), *The Modern Chinese State* (Cambridge: Cambridge University Press).

Miller, P. (1987) *Domination and Power* (London: Routledge).

Miller, P. (1992) 'Accounting and Objectivity: the Invention of Calculating Selves and Calculable Spaces', *Annals of Scholarship*, 9, 1–2, 61–86.

Mills, C. (1956) *The Power Elite* (New York: Oxford University Press).

Mitrany, D. (1943/1966) *A Working Peace System* (Chicago: Quadrangle Books).

Moise, E. (1994) *Modern China: A History* (New York: Longman).

Montesquieu, C. (1977) *The Spirit of the Laws*, in Richter, M. (1977) *The Political Theory of Montesquieu* (Cambridge: Cambridge University Press).

Moore, B. (1967) *The Social Origins of Dictatorship and Democracy* (London: Allen Lane/The Penguin Press).

Moran, M. (1991) *The Politics of the Financial Services Revolution* (London: Macmillan).

Moran, M. (1999) *Governing the Health Care State* (Manchester: Manchester University Press).

Moran, M. (2002a) Review article: 'Understanding the Regulatory State', *British Journal of Political Science*, 32, 391–413.

Moran, M. (2002b) 'Politics, Banks, and Financial Market Governance in the Euro-Zone', in Dyson, K. (ed.) (2002).

Moran, M. (2003) *The British Regulatory State* (Oxford: Oxford University Press).

Moran, M. and Wood, B. (1996) 'The Globalization of Health Care Policy?', in Gummett, P. (ed.), *Globalization and Public Policy* (Cheltenham: Edward Elgar), 125–42.

Moran, M. and Wright, M. (1991) 'The Interdependence of Markets and States', in Moran, M. and Wright, M. (eds), *The Market and the State* (London: Macmillan).

Morgenthau, H. (1948) *Politics Among Nations* (New York: Alfred Knopf).

Mosca, G. (1939) *The Ruling Class* (New York: McGraw-Hill).

Nash, K. (2000) *Contemporary Political Sociology* (Oxford: Blackwell).

Newton, K. (1999) 'Social Capital and Democracy in Modern Europe', in van Deth, J. *et al.* (eds), *Social Capital and European Democracy* (London: Routledge).

Nozick, R. (1974) *Anarchy, State and Utopia* (Oxford: Blackwell).

O'Brien, R. *et al.* (2000) *Contesting Global Governance* (Cambridge: Cambridge University Press).

O'Donnell, G. (1996) 'Illusions about Consolidation', *Journal of Democracy*, 7, 2, April.

O'Donnell, G. and Schmitter, P. (1986) *Transitions from Authoritarian Rule* (Baltimore: Johns Hopkins University Press).

O'Donnell, G. *et al.* (eds) (1986) *Transitions from Authoritarian Rule*, 4 vols (Baltimore: Johns Hopkins University Press).

O'Malley, P. (1992) 'Risk, Power and Crime Prevention', *Economy and Society*, 21, 2, 252–75.

Oestreich, G. (1982) *Stoicism and the Early Modern State* (Cambridge: Cambridge University Press).

Offe, C. (1984) *Contradictions of the Welfare State* (London: Hutchinson).

Ogus, A. (1992) 'Regulatory Law: Some Lessons from the Past', *Legal Studies*, 12, 1–19.

Ohmae, K. (1992) *The Borderless World* (London: Fontana).

Olson, M. (1965) *The Logic of Collective Action* (Cambridge: Harvard University Press).

Opello, W. and Rosow, S. (1999) *The Nation State and Global Order* (London: Lynne Rienner).

Palazzo, G.A. (1606) *Discorso del governo e dalla ragion vera di stato* (Venice).

Panitch, L. (1980) 'Recent Theorizations of Corporatism', *British Journal of Sociology*, 31, 159–87.

Pareto, V. (1935) *Mind and Society* (London: Jonathan Cape).

Parsons, T. (1960) *Structure and Process in Modern Societies* (Chicago: Free Press).

Parsons, T. (1966) *Societies: An Evolutionary Approach* (New Jersey: Prentice Hall).

Parsons, T. (1967) *Sociological Theory and Modern Society* (New York: Free Press).

Pasquino, P. (1978) 'Theatrum Politicum. The Genealogy of Capital: Police and the State of Prosperity', *Ideology and Consciousness*, 7, 17–32.

Pateman, C. (1970) *Participation and Democratic Theory* (Cambridge: Cambridge University Press).

Paterson, J. and Blomberg, E. (1999) *Decision Making in the EU* (London: Macmillan).

Peukert, D. (1993) 'The Genesis of the "Final Solution" from the Spirit of Science', in Childers, T. and Caplan, J. (eds), *Re-evaluating the Third Reich* (New York: Holmes and Meier).

Pierre, J. and Peters, B. (2000) *Governance, Politics and the State* (London: Macmillan).

Pierson, C. and Castles, F. (2002) 'Australian Antecedents of the Third Way', *Political Studies*, 50, 4, September, 683–702.

Poggi, G. (1978) *The Development of the Modern State* (London: Hutchinson).

Poggi, G. (2001) 'Theories of State Formation', in Nash, K. and Scott, A. (eds), *The Blackwell Companion to Political Sociology* (Oxford: Blackwell) 95–106.

Pollock, S., Bhabha, H.K., Breckenridge, C.A. and Chakrabarty, D. (2000) 'Cosmopolitanisms', *Public Culture*, 12, 3, 577–90.

Porter, M. (1990) *The Competitive Advantage of Nations* (London: Macmillan).

Potter, D. (2000) 'Explaining Democratization', in Potter, D. *et al.* (eds), *Democratization* (Cambridge: Polity/OU Press).

Poulantzas, N. (1973) *Political Power and Social Classes* (London: New Left Books).

Power, M. (1994) *The Audit Society* (London: Demos).

Powers, T. (1994) *Heisenberg's War: The Secret History of the German Bomb* (London: Jonathan Cape).

Prosser, T. and Moran, M. (1994) 'Privatization and Regulatory Change: The Case of Great Britain', in Moran, M. and Prosser, T. (eds), *Privatization and Regulatory Change in Europe* (Buckingham: Open University Press).

Putnam, R. (1993) *Making Democracy Work: Civic Traditions in Modern Italy* (Princeton: Princeton University Press).

Putnam, R. (2000) *Bowling Alone* (New York: Simon and Schuster).

Pyle, K. (1996) *The Making of Modern Japan* (London: Macmillan).

Raeff, M. (1983) *The Well-Ordered Police State: Social and Institutional Change through Law in the Germanies and Russia, 1699–1800* (New Haven: Yale University Press).

Ralston, D.B. (1990) *Importing the European Army: The Introduction of European Military Techniques and Institutions into the Extra-European World* (Chicago: University of Chicago Press).

Randall, V. (2000) 'Why Have the Political Trajectories in India and China Been Different?', in Potter, D. *et al.* (eds), *Democratization* (Cambridge: Polity/OU Press).

Rawls, J. (1972) *A Theory of Justice* (Oxford: Oxford University Press).

Ray, L. (2001) 'Civil Society and the Public Sphere', in Nash, K. and Scott, A. (eds), *The Blackwell Companion to Political Sociology* (Oxford: Blackwell), 219–29.

Ricardo, D. (1817/1951) *On the Principles of Political Economy and Taxation* (Cambridge: Cambridge University Press).

Robertson, R. (1992) *Globalization: Social Theory and Global Culture* (London: Sage).

Robertson, R. (1995) 'Glocalization: Time–Space and Homogeneity–Heterogeneity', in Featherstone, M., Lash, S. and Robertson, R. (eds), *Global Modernities* (London: Sage), 25–44.

Rose, N. (1990) *Governing the Soul: The Shaping of the Private Self* (London: Routledge).

Rose, N. (1993) 'Government, Authority and Expertise in Advanced Liberalism', *Economy and Society*, 22, 3, 283–99.

Rose, N. (1996) 'Governing Advanced Liberal Democracies', in Barry, A., Osborne, T. and Rose, N. (eds), *Foucault and Political Reason: Liberalism, Neo-Liberalism and Rationalities of Government* (London: UCL Press).

Rose, N. (1999) *Powers of Freedom* (Cambridge: Cambridge University Press).

Rousseau, J. (1963) *The Social Contract and Discourses* (London: Dent).

Rueschemeyer, D., Stephens, E. and Stephens, J. (1992) *Capitalist Development and Democracy* (Cambridge: Polity Press).

Rüstow, A. von (1980) *Freedom and Domination: A Historical Critique of Civilization* (Princeton: Princeton University Press).

Rustow, D. (1970) 'Transitions to Democracy', *Comparative Politics*, 3, 337–63.

Schama, S. (2001) *A History of Britain*, Vol. 2 (London: BBC).

Schmitter, P. (1974) 'Still the Century of Corporatism?', *Review of Politics*, 36, 85–131.

Scholte, J. (2000) *Globalization* (London: Palgrave).

Schott, K. (1982) 'The Rise of Keynesian Economics: Britain 1940–64', *Economy and Society*, 11, 3, 292–316.

Schumpeter, J. (1942) *Capitalism, Socialism and Democracy* (London: Allen and Unwin).

Shambaugh, D. (ed.) (2000) *The Modern Chinese State* (Cambridge: Cambridge University Press).

Shaw, M. (2000) *Theory of the Global State* (Cambridge: Cambridge University Press).

Siedentop, L. (2001) *Democracy in Europe* (London: Penguin).

Skinner, Q. (1978) *The Foundations of Modern Political Thought*, 2 vols (Cambridge: Cambridge University Press).

Sklair, L. (2001) *The Transnational Capitalist Class* (Oxford: Blackwell).

Sklair, L. (2002) *Globalization* (Oxford: Oxford University Press).

Skocpol, T. (1979) *States and Revolutions* (Cambridge: Cambridge University Press).

Small, A.W. (1909) *The Cameralists* (Chicago: University of Chicago Press).

Smith, A. (1776/1976) *The Wealth of Nations* (Chicago: University of Chicago Press).

Smith, A. (1992) *Ethnicity and Nationalism* (Leiden: Brill).

Smith, M. (2001) *Transnational Urbanism: Locating Globalization* (Oxford: Blackwell).

Smith, N. (2002) 'The Irish Republic – A 'Showpiece of Globalization?', *Politics*, 22, 3, 125–34.

Sorensen, G. (1998) *Democracy and Democratization* (Boulder, CO: Westview Press).

Soysal, Y. (1994) *Limits of Citizenship: Migrants and Postnational Membership in Europe* (Chicago: University of Chicago Press).

Soysal, Y. (2000) 'Postnational Citizenship: Reconfiguring the Familiar Terrain', in Nash, K. and Scott, A. (eds), *The Blackwell Companion to Political Sociology* (Oxford: Blackwell), 333–41.

Spence, J. (1991) *The Search for Modern China* (New York: Norton).

Stiglitz, J. (2002) *Globalization and its Discontents* (London: Allen Lane/The Penguin Press).

Strange, S. (1996) *The Retreat of the State: The Diffusion of Power in the World Economy* (Cambridge: Cambridge University Press).

Streeck, W. (1982) 'Between Pluralism and Corporatism', *Journal of Public Policy*, 3, 3, 265–84.

Swank, D. (2002) *Global Capital, Political Institutions, and Policy Change in Developed Welfare States* (Cambridge: Cambridge University Press).

Thatcher, M. (1987) 'Interview', *Women's Own*, October, 8–10.

Thatcher, M. (1993) *The Downing Street Years* (London: HarperCollins).

Therbon, G. (1977) 'The Rule of Capital and The Rise of Democracy', *New Left Books*, 103, May–June.

Thompson, J.B. (2001) 'The Media and Politics', in Nash, K. and Scott, A. (eds), *The Blackwell Companion to Political Sociology* (Oxford: Blackwell), 173–82.

Thrift, N. (1996) *Spatial Formations* (London: Sage).

Tibi, B. (1998) *The Challenge of Fundamentalism: Political Islam and the New World Disorder* (Berkeley: University of California Press).

Tilly, C. (1975) *The Formation of National States in Western Europe* (Princeton: Princeton University Press).

Tilly, C. (1990) *Coercion, Capital, and European States* (Cambridge: Blackwell).

Tocqueville, A. de (1835/1946) *Democracy in America* (London: Oxford University Press).

Tomlinson, J. (1981) 'Why Was There Never a Keynesian Revolution in Economic Policy?' *Economy and Society*, 10, 1, 72–87.

Tomlinson, J. (1999) *Globalization and Culture* (Cambridge: Polity).

Tribe, K. (1984) 'Cameralism and the Science of Government', *Journal of Modern History*, 52, 2, 263–84.

Trotsky, L. (1930/1970) *The Permanent Revolution* (New York: Pathfinder Press).

Urry, J. (2000a) *Sociology Beyond Societies: Mobilities for the Twenty-First Century* (London: Routledge).

Urry, J. (2000b) 'Mobile Sociology', *British Journal of Sociology*, 51, 1, 185–203.

Urry, J. (2003) *Global Complexity* (Cambridge: Polity).

Krieken, R. van (2002) 'The Paradox of the "Two Sociologies": Hobbes, Latour and the Constitution of Modern Social Theory', *Journal of Sociology*, 38, 3, 255–73.

Wade, R. (1990) *Governing the Market Economy* (Princeton: Princeton University Press).

Wallerstein, I. (1974/1980/1989) *The Modern World System*, Vols 1, 2 and 3 (London: Academic Press).

Waltz, K. (1959) *Man, The State, and War* (New York: Columbia University Press).

Waltz, K. (1979) *Theory of International Politics* (Reading, MA: Addison-Wesley).

Weber, M. (1947) *The Theory of Social and Economic Organization* (Oxford: Oxford University Press).

Weber, M. (1948a) 'Class, Status and Power', in Gerth, H. and Mills, C. Wright (eds), *From Max Weber: Essays in Sociology* (London: Routledge).

Weber, M. (1948b) 'Politics as a Vocation', in Gerth, H. and Mills, C. Wright (eds), *op.cit.*

Weber, M. (1925/1968) *Economy and Society* (New York: Bedminster Press).

Weber, M. (1930/1985) *The Protestant Ethic and the Spirit of Capitalism* (London: Unwin).

Weir, M. and Skocpol, T. (1985) 'Keynesian Responses to the Great Depression in Sweden, Britain, and the United States', in Evans, P., Rueschmeyer, D., and Skocpol, T., *Bringing the State Back In* (Cambridge: Cambridge University Press).

Weiss, L. (1998) *The Myth of the Powerless State* (Cambridge: Polity).

Wolfe, A. (1977) *The Limits of Legitimacy* (New York: Free Press).

Woods, N. (2000) 'The Political Economy of Globalization', in Woods, N. (ed.), *The Political Economy of Globalization* (London: Palgrave).

Index

MATTERS OF THE MIND

πρὸς τοῖς σκεπτικοῖς,
Beth and John, Gloria and Denis,
Fran and Kevin, Celie and Philippe

Matters of the
Mind

William Lyons

EDINBURGH
University Press

© William Lyons, 2001

Edinburgh University Press Ltd
22 George Square, Edinburgh

Typeset in Sabon
by Pioneer Associates, Perthshire, and
printed and bound in Great Britain by
the University Press, Cambridge

A CIP Record for this book is available from
the British Library

ISBN 0 7486 1439 7 (hardback)
ISBN 0 7486 1440 0 (paperback)

The right of William Lyons
to be identified as author of this work
has been asserted in accordance with
the Copyright, Designs and Patents Act 1988.